MUSIC IN CANADA

Music in Canada

EDITED BY ERNEST MacMILLAN

Published in co-operation with the

Canadian Music Council (Conseil Canadien de Musique)

by the University of Toronto Press

1955

Decorations by Antje Lingner

FOREWORD

by His Excellency, the Right Honourable VINCENT MASSEY, C.H., Governor General of Canada

I am happy to write a foreword to this book. "Music in Canada," under its unassuming title, will perform a very important function; indeed, it will render a two-fold service of great value. In the first place, the volume will give its readers a true and comprehensive account of music in this country from its beginnings. This task has been admirably accomplished. Secondly, in this story of music in Canada, we can find a vivid reflection of a broader theme—the growth of Canadian nationality. At first came the varied threads of musical tradition from other countries; then were these strands slowly woven into a fabric which could be looked on as Canadian. There followed the gradual recognition of the new pattern and a growing determination to preserve it as something which was our own. Thus, the history of Canadian music can help to deepen our understanding of Canada itself.

To all of those who have contributed to this distinguished book, we should be grateful. I hope that the success of "Music in Canada" as a published work will be in keeping with its excellence.

CONTENTS

CONTENTS

THE CONTRIBUTORS

MARCUS ADENEY. Born London (England) 1900; came to Canada at an early age but has travelled widely, studying music in England and continental Europe. A well-known 'cellist, a member of the CBC Symphony Orchestra and of the Solway Quartet; also known as essayist, critic, poet and programme annotator for the Toronto Symphony Orchestra. In 1931 was awarded a valuable prize by the Graphic Press (Ottawa) for a novel dealing with life in Paris, Ont. Teacher of 'cello in music education classes in the Faculty of Music (Toronto) and an editor of the *Canadian Review of Music and Art*.

LOUIS APPLEBAUM. Born Toronto, 1918; studied in Toronto and New York. Has been writing music for the National Film Board since 1941; became its Musical Director in 1942. After a period of three highly successful years (1946–49) in New York and Hollywood, returned to Canada. Now Musical Consultant to the National Film Board and Director of Music, Stratford Shakespearean Festival where he is organizing a Music Festival for the 1955 season. Has written music for several Hollywood films and for more than 100 NFB films. Vice-President, Canadian League of Composers.

MARIUS BARBEAU, B.A., LL.L. (Laval), D. ÈS L., LL.D. (Montreal). Born 1885 at Ste Marie de Beauce, Que. Rhodes Scholar at Oxford 1907–10 (B. SC. and DIPL. ANTH.). As Ethnologist and Folklorist at the National Museum, Ottawa, Dr. Barbeau has made extensive researches into the folk-songs of Canada, particularly those of the French Canadians and North American Indians, and has not only contributed extensively to the literature of the subject but has collected thousands of recordings for the National Museum. Since his retirement from the staff of the Museum, with which he had been connected since 1911, he has continued active in research and writing. Awarded the Lorne Pierce Medal for Literature by the Royal Society of Canada, 1950.

JEAN-MARIE BEAUDET. Born in Thetford Mines, Que. Has been connected with the Canadian Broadcasting Corporation since 1937, serving first as Programme Director, Quebec Region, afterwards as Music Director, French Network and Pacific Regional Representative. Left the Corporation, 1947, to devote his entire time to music and won an international reputation as concert pianist, accompanist, teacher and conductor. After spending a year in France and other European countries, returned to the CBC where he is now Director of Programme Planning and Production.

JOHN BECKWITH, MUS.B.(Toronto). Born 1927 in Victoria, B.C.; studied in Toronto (1945–50) and, under a C.A.H.A. Scholarship, in Paris (1950–52). Now a Lecturer at the Royal Conservatory (Faculty of Music) and as CBC Staff Writer provides programme notes for many musical broadcasts. Secretary of the Canadian League of Composers and has himself composed extensively.

LESLIE BELL, M.A.(Toronto), MUS.DOC.(Montreal). Born 1906 in Toronto. In addition to his taking Arts degrees in English Literature and History, he studied music from an early age, playing the piano and various other instruments, especially the clarinet. Gained experience in band and symphonic music, directing various bands and orchestras. Director of Music at the College of Education (1939–48) and Assistant Professor in the Faculty of Music, University of Toronto. Known as a lecturer and newspaper columnist but still more so as Director of the Leslie Bell Singers (see chapter on Choral Music). Has published many choral arrangements and original partsongs which are in extensive use in schools and radio, in Canada and in the United States.

RICHARD W. COOKE. Born Leeds (Yorkshire) in 1903 and came to Manitoba in 1910. Both as a boy soprano and as a member of Winnipeg Male Voice Choir, he has had much experience in choral singing; he was also a church choirmaster for sixteen years. Secretary, Men's Musical Club of Winnipeg; a member of the Advisory Council, Winnipeg Symphony Orchestra; Secretary, Manitoba Musical Competition Festival; Secretary, Federation of Canadian Music Festivals, since its inception.

GEORGE ROY FENWICK, MUS.BAC.(Toronto), MUS.DOC.(Montreal), L.MUS. (Toronto). Born in Hamilton, Ont., he has had much experience in choral direction in various churches and as Conductor of the Elgar Choir, Hamilton (1935–36). His main interest, however, has been school music: was Director of Music, Hamilton Public Schools, 1922–35, and since 1935 Provincial Director of Music in the Ontario Department of Education. Well known as commentator on school broadcasts and as a festival adjudicator, he has also edited a number of song-books and music text-books.

HELMUT KALLMANN, MUS.BAC. (Toronto). Born in Berlin, 1922; following a short period in London, came to Canada in 1940 and to Toronto in 1943. After graduation from the Faculty of Music in 1949, joined the CBC where he is now a Music Librarian. His *Catalogue of Canadian Composers*, published by the CBC in 1952, is a valuable source of information about Canadian music.

R. S. LAMBERT, M.A.(Oxon.). Before coming to Canada was Editor of the *Listener* (BBC). Author of a number of biographies and of three Canadian children's books, one of which (*Franklin of the Arctic*) won the Governor-General's Medal in 1949. Supervisor of School Broadcasts for the CBC, having been appointed in 1943, and also Secretary of the National Advisory Council on School Broadcasting.

SIR ERNEST MACMILLAN, B.A.(Toronto), D.MUS.(Oxon., Laval); LL.D. (U.B.C., Queen's, Toronto); LITT.D.(McMaster); F.R.C.M., Hon. R.A.M., F.R.C.O. Born Mimico, Ont., 1893. Conductor of the Toronto Symphony Orchestra (since 1931) and of the Toronto Mendelssohn Choir (since 1942); 1926–42, Principal of the Toronto (now Royal) Conservatory of Music; 1927–52, Dean of the Faculty of Music, University of Toronto. Chairman of the Canadian Music Council; President of the Composers, Authors and Publishers Association of Canada, Limited. Knighted, 1935, by His Majesty the late King George V "for services to music in Canada."

REV. JULES MARTEL, O.M.I., B.A., B.J.C. Born Acton Vale, Que., 1905; ordained, 1929; Director, since 1939, of the School of Music and Elocution, University of Ottawa; Président, Comité Interdiocésain de Musique sacrée de la Province de Québec; Fondateur et Directeur, Le Chœur Palestrina.

ETTORE MAZZOLENI, B.A., B.MUS.(Oxon.), MUS.D.(Rochester). Born in Switzerland and educated in England; has been resident in Canada for more than twenty-five years. Principal of the School of Music, Royal Conservatory of Toronto, he has become known as a progressive leader in music education and, in his capacity as Conductor of the Conservatory Orchestra, has introduced many new works by Canadian composers and has launched on a professional career many young Canadian artists. For some years Associate Conductor of the Toronto Symphony Orchestra, he has from time to time made guest appearances with other orchestras—notably the CBC Symphony. Also well known as lecturer and essayist.

CHARLES PEAKER, MUS.DOC. (Toronto), F.R.C.O. Born in Derby (England). Adjudicator, lecturer and recital organist; at present Organist and Choirmaster, St. Paul's (Anglican) Church, Toronto. Has given recitals throughout Canada and the United States as well as in England (Westminster Abbey and over the BBC); for fifteen years past has given series of diversified and well-attended Advent and Lenten recitals in St. Paul's Church. Conductor of the Hart House Glee Club (University of Toronto) for fifteen years and also for some time Conductor of the Coliseum Choir (2,000 voices) at the Canadian National Exhibition. Lecturer at the University of Toronto in choral technique.

WILFRID PELLETIER, C.M.G., MUS.DOC.(Montreal). Born in Montreal in 1896 and receiving the greater part of his musical education in Paris, Dr. Pelletier has for many years been a regular conductor at the Metropolitan Opera House, New York. Has constantly maintained a close connection with the musical life of Canada and particularly with that of his native province, having been the first Musical Director of Les Concerts Symphoniques de Montréal. Now Director of the Conservatoire de Musique et d'Art Dramatique de la Province de Québec. Director of youth concerts for the New

York Philharmonic Society and Les Concerts Symphoniques de Montréal; Musical Director of L'Orchestre Symphonique de Québec.

COLIN SABISTON. Member of Editorial Board, *Globe and Mail* (Toronto). He has specialized in articles dealing with economics and questions of applied aesthetics. Member of the American Society for Aesthetics. His wife, PEARL McCARTHY, M.A. (Toronto), B.LITT. (Oxon.) is art critic for the *Globe and Mail.* Since returning to Toronto in 1929 after graduate studies at Oxford, she has written extensively on the arts in Canada, including music.

GEOFFREY WADDINGTON. Born Leicester (England) in 1904 and came to Canada in 1907. Has been identified with radio since its earliest days, first as Musical Director, Station CKNC (1926–33), then as Director of Music, Canadian Radio Commission (1933–36); Musical Adviser to the CBC, 1947–51, and since 1952 its Musical Director. Many of the works of Canadian composers have been given first performances under his conductorship.

ARNOLD WALTER, JUR.UTR.DR. (Prague). Born in Austria; after graduating from the University of Prague, attended the University of Berlin, where for some time he acted as critic and writer on musical subjects. Went in 1933 to Spain, where he spent three years in the study of mediaeval music and South European folk-lore. Came to Canada in 1937 as head of the music department in Upper Canada College. Appointed in 1945 the Director of the newly formed Senior School of the Royal Conservatory of Music, and in 1952 the Director of the Faculty of Music. President of the International Society of Music Education sponsored by UNESCO and a Director of the Canadian Music Council. Internationally known as a lecturer; a composer whose works have been heard in Canada, the United States and Europe.

MUSIC IN CANADA

INTRODUCTION

Ernest MacMillan

O Canada, terre de nos aïeux. . . .

"Land of our forefathers." So sings the French-Canadian, and with conviction, for his ancestors have been here for well over three hundred years. In English-speaking Canada we sing "our home and native land"[1]: a significant difference perhaps, for our ancestors, in so far as they were Canadian at all, came much later to these shores. Except in the Maritime Provinces and the trading-posts of the Hudson's Bay Company, English-speaking settlements date back no further than the American Revolution; many are much more recent.

Nurtured through colonial infancy and adolescence by a wise and tolerant, though occasionally autocratic mother, Canada has grown up to become a lusty, energetic young nation. While still cherishing a warm affection and respect for her parent, she has cut her leading-strings and asserted her independence. Economically she has greatly prospered: though barely past the fifteen million mark in population, she is third in international trade among the nations of the world. To many a European, harassed by the ravages of two disastrous wars and having perhaps lost home, possessions and hope, Canada must appear a veritable El Dorado. Thousands continue to make their way here, meeting with varying degrees of success or failure as determined by luck, individual talents, adaptability and assistance offered by others. Stroll through almost any of our larger cities and you may overhear a bewildering variety of languages; it would take an exceptional linguist to identify—let alone understand—them all.

It is during this period of expansion that the seeds of a national culture are coming to fruition. Our musical past is outlined in these pages. It is perhaps not very impressive, especially with respect to English-speaking Canada: nineteenth-century England was hardly an ideal source of musical inspiration except in certain restricted fields. Nowadays, when musical life in the Motherland presents so much brighter and more varied a picture, it exercises relatively less influence on Canada. Here many differing traditions, styles and methods press their

---

[1]In the customarily used English version of our unofficial but universally sung "National Anthem." It is hardly necessary to add that the official National Anthem is *God Save the Queen*. Frequently both are sung or played at public functions.

3

claims on our attention. Our musical resources are great and increasing: are we putting them to the best use?

Sudden access of wealth is dangerous to a young nation as to a young man. The *nouveau riche*, congratulating himself like Little Jack Horner on his cleverness in extracting a plum from the pie, is liable to forget the responsibilities entailed by wealth and to squander a large part of his fortune on trivialities. Canada is, it must be confessed, not guiltless in this respect, yet, having passed the pioneer stage, when the satisfaction of physical needs overshadowed every other consideration, she is turning in increasing measure to those things of the spirit that have so greatly enriched the life of older nations.

A perusal of this book should convince the most sceptical that Canada teems with musical activities. Practically all of them were originally, and most of them still are, purely local or at most provincial in scope. It is desirable that many remain so, for nothing could be duller than a uniform pattern. Yet it is also desirable that we develop more institutions of nation-wide influence, if only to give strong leadership and assistance to worthy local effort. Throughout this book the reader will note what is being done in this respect by the Canadian Broadcasting Corporation, by far the most influential organization affecting the musical field. A chapter is devoted to a detailed account of its musical achievements; they are mentioned here to indicate how much a single national and publicly controlled body can do for Canadian music under wise direction and efficient management. Another public body, the National Film Board, has also done much in its own field to foster and utilize musical talent. Our leading schools of music too are public institutions, being under the control of universities. No private institution in Canada (where the substantial endowments of certain American schools are lacking) can offer equal advantages to its students.

Radio, television, films, music education—all these are recognized as matters of public concern. But much remains to be done in other fields. We have no nationally supported opera, ballet or orchestra; though a few such organizations enjoy moderate subsidies from municipalities and, still more rarely, from provincial governments, the greatest measure of support comes from private sources. We have no national library of music and very few extensive music libraries of any kind.[2] Nor have we periodicals dealing with musical life on a national scale. Our leading dailies, though often covering a large area in cir-

2It is reassuring to learn that the new National Library of Canada, now in process of formation, will include an extensive music section.

culation, cannot in the nature of things exercise the nation-wide influence of a *Times* or a *Manchester Guardian*. Their musical columns, though sometimes containing astute and well-written criticism, deal for the most part with local events and only occasionally with matters of more permanent and general interest. The concert field in Canada is largely dominated by New York agencies whose ability to offer internationally famous artists naturally enables them to do for the less known far more than can any Canadian agency. Vast geographical distances render it exceedingly difficult for the small agent to operate beyond a local or provincial area, whereas the resources of great American agencies enable them to send representatives and distribute promotional literature everywhere. The result is that the young Canadian performer finds it hard to break into the concert field, especially outside his immediate locality. A limited number of Canadian artists, by putting their business affairs in the hands of New York agents, are able to ensure appearances in the United States as well as in their own country, but the exchange between the two countries—even apart from "great names"—is very ill balanced. One private organization, Les Jeunesses Musicales, has of recent years succeeded, through its international affiliations, in effecting exchanges between Canadian and foreign artists on a more equitable basis, but its activities are at the moment largely confined to French-speaking Canada. One might remark in passing that this enterprising body has recently undertaken the publication of a *Journal musical canadien* which promises to fill a long-felt need for French-speaking readers; it is greatly to be hoped that before long a similarly comprehensive periodical will appear in English.

These and other facts indicate a need for the kind of co-ordination only to be achieved by a publicly controlled and nationally operating body on the lines of the Arts Council of Great Britain or of the Ministry of Fine Arts found in many a European country. The *Report* (published in 1951) of the Royal Commission on the Arts, Letters and Sciences, of which the present Governor-General of Canada, the Right Honourable Vincent Massey, was Chairman, strongly recommended the establishment of a Council of Fine Arts (to be called the Canada Council) which would be of paramount importance in developing and co-ordinating the musical, as well as the other artistic resources of our country. As yet this portion of the *Report* has not been implemented but we are encouraged, as we go to press, to have the assurance of the Prime Minister that it is being given earnest consideration.

In the meantime foreign countries and individual foreign musicians, whose numerous inquiries indicate a great interest in our musical life, are amazed to find that no official body exists to supply such information. Proposals for the exchange of artists and students fall through because, apart from the efforts of Les Jeunesses Musicales, there is in Canada no machinery for their realization. Our leading orchestras and other performing bodies have to decline invitations to make extensive tours outside of Canada, especially in the United States, because no Canadian orchestra can command the full-time services of its members and few members of chamber groups can afford to be long away from home. Composers are rarely able to find a publisher who will, in view of the restricted domestic market, undertake publication of extended works—still less the expense of pushing their sale abroad. Even the expense of copying and duplicating scores and parts by photographic processes falls as often as not on the composer himself.

In his interesting biography of Calixa Lavallée (composer of *O Canada*), Dr. Eugène Lapierre describes how in the early 1880's that colourful and energetic musician approached the Premier of Quebec, de Boucherville, with a scheme for the public support of a School of Fine Arts. The time was unpropitious and, although Lavallée pleaded most eloquently, the Minister's succinct reply was that "Il n'avait pas d'argent pour ça." Shortly afterwards Lavellée took up permanent residence in the United States—only one among many gifted native musicians lost to Canada. In the intervening years approaches have been made to governmental bodies on behalf of many musical ventures but the reply, usually more suavely phrased, has in most cases been to the same effect. The Province of Quebec has in the interim shown itself much more liberal minded than in the days of de Boucherville, but Canada as a whole, though now wealthy and prosperous, seems but rarely able to find public funds "for that." Nor have private endowments and gifts, in spite of the generosity of a few individuals and foundations, materially altered the situation. Legacies to musical organizations are exceedingly rare and, in view of heavy succession duties and other taxes, are likely to remain so. Public-spirited men and women who undertake annually to raise "sustaining funds" for orchestras, opera associations and similar bodies find their task none too easy, and in consequence some of our prominent musical organizations lead a hand-to-mouth existence.

One must not paint too dark a picture. The past twenty or twenty-five years have shown a growing practical recognition of the claims of music. The need of scholarship and bursary funds for music students is now increasingly felt and in some of our schools such funds have grown to considerable proportions. This is significant, for during the first forty years of its existence the Toronto (now Royal) Conservatory of Music received no gifts whatever for scholarship purposes. More and more widely is it being recognized that fine symphony orchestras, operatic companies and schools of music are public institutions like art galleries and museums and that they cannot be expected to operate effectively on a commercial basis. Increased expenditures have been matched by increased donations and such organizations may face the future with a fair degree of confidence.

Yet, as we have seen, countless problems remain and it is with a view to coping with a few of the most pressing that the Canadian Music Council has been formed. With very slim financial resources it faces a formidable task. The Council originated in 1944, when briefs on the Fine Arts were presented by a number of organizations to the House of Commons' Committee on Post-War Reconstruction. These briefs, though divergent in viewpoint and matters of detail, were at one in stressing the need for government action. Literature, Painting, Architecture and the other arts were represented by bodies already in existence—some of them large and influential—but for music no organization of nation-wide scope could be found. The hastily assembled "Music Committee" which presented the solitary brief on music grew subsequently into the present Council. It has tried to cope as best it can with the situation, confining its activities for some years to urgent routine work, while cherishing the hope that the new Canada Council would be established and either assume the functions of the existing Council or provide it with adequate subsidies. However, in the absence of government action, it is now attempting to meet some of the most pressing needs.

The first function of the Canadian Music Council is, in the nature of things, informative: hence the present book. Coupled with this is the project of establishing a good musical journal; little progress in this direction has, it must be confessed, been made as yet but it is hoped that ways and means will be found at no very distant date. Through the co-operation of a number of Canadian music publishers who have provided copies of works by Canadian composers, a start has been made towards assembling a library of published Canadian music. This obviously cannot be regarded as truly representative, for most of the more important and extended works from Canadian pens are still in manuscript and no machinery exists for their control and distribution. Presumably the new National Library, still in its infancy, will eventually handle and distribute works of all types by our composers, including the Council's present collection.

The Council has been constituted a National Committee representing Canada on the International Music Council of UNESCO; thus it acts as a liaison with similar bodies in the outside world. Lack of funds, however, prevents its paying the expenses of delegates to international conferences; Canada must either be unrepresented or depend on the chance of finding a suitable person whose private arrangements allow of his being on the scene at the right time. We have up to now been fortunate in finding such representatives but these matters should not be left to chance.

Recent donations from the Canadian Music Publishers Association and a number of the firms they represent, together with more substantial contributions from the Composers, Authors and Publishers Association of Canada, Limited (CAPAC) and B M I Canada Limited, have enabled the Council to carry on and, to some extent, expand its work. Practically all of that work is still done on a voluntary basis; special tribute must be paid to the unselfish labours of the Secretary, Mr. John Cozens, and to those who have assisted in compiling this book—in all cases without remuneration.

The assembling and classifying of information for this account of music in Canada has been a formidable task for all concerned, particularly as, in a majority of cases, it was being done for the first time. None of our collaborators would, I fancy, claim to have covered all aspects of their subject; many names and facts have—inadvertently or from lack of space—been omitted; whole phases of our musical life have had to be postponed for later treatment. The original scheme of this volume, for example, included a chapter on Canadian bands and band music; for various reasons which need not be detailed here, this had to be regretfully abandoned. Yet it must be recognized that the thousand or more bands in Canada reach and influence a very wide audience indeed. Television too has been merely touched upon; its growth over a short period has been prodigious but it is still a little early to assess its ultimate effect on our musical life. Nor do these by any means exhaust the list of omissions. One might write a chapter on the history and present state of instrument making in Canada; another on the special problems of the Canadian music publisher; one on the relationship of unions to instrumentalists and singers; one on the operations of the Canadian Copyright Act as it affects the musician;

one on the numerous music clubs and societies of Canada. Some of these topics are touched upon briefly in various sections of the book, but a really adequate survey would call for much more space than we have at our disposal. However it is hoped that this first effort to give a lucid and reasonably complete picture of music in Canada will meet the present needs of the many who take an interest in the subject.

We began by pointing out the local and provincial nature of so many Canadian musical activities. Perhaps, however, in some of the ensuing chapters the reader may discern the emergence of a national pattern. At any rate an attempt has been made to avoid any suggestion of sectionalism and to deal with each subject as far as possible from a national point of view. This is by no means easy: Canada is a sub-continent and it is difficult for anyone to get the perspective of a sub-continent. *The Unknown Country* is the title given to his book on Canada by Bruce Hutchison; he himself knows this land as do few others. But though few Canadians can know Canada as a Frenchman can know France or a Scot Scotland, we cherish an affectionate loyalty and pride for those parts that we do know. To the Maritimer, the rugged and often foggy coasts of the Atlantic and the Gulf of St. Lawrence have become part of himself; the French Canadian loves the Fleuve Saint-Laurent as the German does the Rhine; the meadows, lakes and forests of Ontario, the wide horizons of the prairies and foothills stir the hearts of their people; the British Columbian feasts his eyes and warms his heart on the magnificent scenery of the Rockies and the Pacific coast. No part of Canada indeed fails to awaken a response from those who know it. As the years pass, however, we are gradually learning to apprehend the nature and significance of the entire vast panorama; newcomers feel the spirit that is so rapidly growing among us. Whether or not it is "terre de nos aïeux," Canada is for all "our home and land"—native or adopted.

In music, whatever our origins, we speak one language and share the expression of thoughts and feelings common to all mankind. In the world of commerce and politics, divergent interests may make for division; in the world of the Arts, the universality of human nature makes for union—the true Brotherhood of Man. Music, the most social of the arts, possesses supremely that unifying power which, given due support, will play a unique part in fostering and preserving the spirit of devotion that welds together a great nation.

HISTORICAL BACKGROUND

Helmut Kallmann

Underneath the surface of Today lies Yesterday and what we call the Past—the only thing which never can decay.

Eugene Lee Hamilton, *Roman Baths*

On Sunday, October 3, 1535, Jacques Cartier, the French discoverer of Canada, paid a visit to the Indian village of Hochelaga, a palisade settlement of some 3,000 Iroquois near the site of present-day Montreal. He and his men received a most hearty welcome. Overawed by the strange attire and manner of the visitors, the Indians presented their sick for healing. Thereupon Cartier recited from the Gospel of St. John and rings, knives and other presents were given to the Indians. "The Captain next ordered the trumpets and other musical instruments to be sounded, whereat the Indians were much delighted; we then took leave of them and withdrew."[1] Thus the recorded musical history of Canada begins at the climax of the first ceremonial meeting between European and Indian in Canada.

In the centuries since, music in Canada has passed through many phases of pioneering and achievement, from the plain-chant and folk-song of New France to the symphony orchestras and choirs of today. Later in developing than literature and painting, composition became an integral part of our cultural life only towards the middle of the twentieth century. Thus Canadian musical history deals chiefly not with a sequence of great composers and their changing styles, but with the transplantation of European traditions, their re-building and modification under the influence of a new environment. Indian and Eskimo music has had little influence on our musical life, except in a few works of twentieth-century composers, but the European heritage has been kept alive by waves of immigrants, who have always made up a large proportion of our music teachers, performers and composers. Often disappointed by the sparseness of musical culture in Canada, they have been surprised and delighted by the wealth of natural

[1]H. P. Biggar (ed.), *The Voyages of Jacques Cartier* (Ottawa: Public Archives of Canada, 1924), p. 166.

talent. Musical pioneers would, immediately on arrival, gather other musical people around them and by teaching, organizing and performing, begin to recreate the musical atmosphere of their homelands. The folk-songs of the early immigrants, the music of the concert hall and most musicians themselves were imported from abroad.

Under pioneer conditions, local characteristics were slow to assert themselves. For many years it was difficult to print music and musical textbooks, to give advanced instruction to talented students and to provide a professional outlet for talent. But gradually, a genuinely Canadian element began to make its appearance in changes of folk-song texts, and in the interchange of folk-dances between people of varied national origins. The upsurge of creative expression, especially since World War I, the improvement in standards of performance, and the growth of educational autonomy—all these point towards the establishment of national traditions.

Permanent French settlements date from the early seventeenth century—the time of Samuel de Champlain's explorations. Port Royal, the short-lived colony in what is now Nova Scotia, is famous for its "Ordre de Bon Temps," an attempt to banish loneliness by entertainment. Marc Lescarbot, a young lawyer from Paris, wrote a masque, *The Theatre of Neptune*, which called for incidental music and was performed on barges "upon the waves of the harbour." The first historian of Canada, Lescarbot took an interest in music and noted down in 1612 Indian music which he heard outside the wigwam of the Micmac chief Membertou. Through Lescarbot we learn that Baron de Poutrincourt, the commander of Port Royal, composed some of the music regularly used in divine service.

Early historical incidents like these have a charm of their own, even though they may have little significance as typical examples of musical conditions in their time. The French missionaries later found music very helpful in their efforts to befriend and convert the Indians. A report by Father Louys André (1631–1715) tells us how in 1670 he set out from Sault Ste Marie on an assignment to an island in Lake Huron. After his arrival he conceived the plan of composing some spiritual canticles. "No sooner," he writes, "had I begun to have these sung in the Chapel, accompanied by a sweet-toned flute . . . than they all came in crowds, both adults and children; so that, to avoid confusion, I let only the girls enter the Chapel, while the others remained without, and thus we sang in two choruses, those without responding to those within."[2] Father André's account illustrates the Indians' great musical aptitude and the fascination that the music of the Church held for them. The use of instruments to attract the natives was as characteristic as the composition or adaptation of liturgical tunes, the words of which were often translated into native dialects. In 1676, Father Jean Enjalran exclaimed: "The nuns of France do not sing more agreeably than some savage women here; and, as a class, all the savages have much aptitude and inclination for singing the hymns of the Church, which have been rendered into their language."[3] It is quite credible that the missionaries were selected in France for Canadian duty with consideration of their musical talents. Certainly music played an important part in their successes, limited though they were. The chants taught to the Indians by missionaries 300 years ago have made a permanent impression on the music of certain Indian tribes of eastern Canada.

Almost from the time of its foundation in 1608, music flourished in Quebec, the centre of missionary and trading activity. The priests' daily reports to their superiors in France, the famous *Jesuit Relations*, enable us to trace musical life in great detail: how in 1635, when the French population of Canada was less than one hundred, Father Le-Jeune (1591–1664) began to instruct French and Indian boys in the elements of Gregorian chant and musical notation; how Ursuline Sisters began to teach music to girls a few years later; how every musical boy, clergyman and "gentleman" was asked to sing or play during divine service; and how the number of flutes and viols increased. We even know the names of some of the Christmas carols sung. Quebec had 800 French inhabitants when Mgr Laval returned from Paris in September, 1663, with a fine organ, which was heard for the first time in the following year. Perhaps it was not the first organ in Quebec, but even so, it antedates the first known organ in the United States by about thirty years. In Montreal, which was founded in 1642, an organ was installed at the beginning of the eighteenth century.

Church music was the first European music introduced to Canada because the first settlers were priests and explorers, rarely farmers. This situation was soon to change when Jean Talon, an energetic In-

---

[2]*Jesuit Relations and Allied Documents, 1610–1791*, ed. R. G. Thwaites (Cleveland, 1896–1901), LV, 147.
[3]*Ibid.*, LX, 145.

tendant of New France, brought to Canada a great number of farmers and fishermen from northwestern France. The French-Canadian population increased from 2,500 in 1663 to 6,700 in 1675. After this time, population grew by natural increase rather than immigration.

These immigrants brought to Canada one of our most valuable possessions: the folk-songs of French Canada. It has been estimated that of the seven to ten thousand songs that have been collected in the Province of Quebec in recent decades, no less than nine-tenths are derived from the songs brought to Canada before 1673. The very mention of folk-song in Canada sounds odd to many who think of Canada chiefly in terms of its great industrial development. The fact remains that Canada has been not only a great preserver, but also, to a limited extent, a producer of folk-song.

Folk-song is discussed in a separate chapter of this book. We cannot, however, draw a complete picture of music in early Canada without stressing the enormous importance of singing and dancing in the lives of the *habitant* and *coureur de bois,* and later, of the *voyageur* and the settler of Nova Scotia, Newfoundland and New Brunswick. Song was the faithful companion of work in the fields, or at the spinning-wheel during long winter evenings, and of travel through endless stretches of bush and lakes. Song preserved the memory of the ancestral home; it enlivened social gatherings and added cheer to dreaded days of cold, want and solitude. The French-Canadians in particular were passionately fond of singing, dancing and fiddling. The music of no other class of people has been given so many glowing reports as that of the *voyageurs,* the men whose canoes were the sole means of transportation between the settled regions along the St. Lawrence River and the western and northern wilds. The glorious period of *voyageur* song was the first half of the nineteenth century. With the coming of the railway and steamship, the *voyageur* disappeared and with him many of his typically Canadian songs. Of the numerous eye-witness accounts, we shall quote one, written by John Mactaggart in 1829:

They are good at composing easy, extemporaneous songs, somewhat smutty, but never intolerant. Many of their *canoe-songs* are exquisite; more particularly the *air* they give them. . . . We must be in a canoe with a dozen hearty paddlers, the lake pure, the weather fine, and the rapids past, before their influence can be powerfully felt. Music and song I have revelled in all my days, and must own, that the *chanson de voyageur* has delighted me above all others, excepting those of Scotland.[4]

[4]John Mactaggart, *Three Years in Canada* (London, 1829), I, 254–5.

Until the middle of the nineteenth century, folk-song was the predominant music in all parts of Canada. Then began the importation of printed concert and popular music, with the result that the gulf between the music of the city and that of the country was widened. Although Ernest Gagnon's collection (1865) made the world familiar with a hundred odd Canadian folk-songs, it was not until early in the twentieth century that scholars like Barbeau, Massicotte and Creighton opened our eyes to the vastness of our treasure.

The struggle for control of Canada between England and France, begun in the early seventeenth century, ended in 1760 when the British became masters of all of Canada that had been explored up to that time: the country east of the Great Lakes and a few outposts in the West and North.

To the two existing forms of music—folk-music and Roman Catholic liturgical music—the British made a new and important addition through the medium of the regimental band. The drum and fife bands of earlier days were small affairs compared to the large wind bands stationed in garrison towns such as Halifax, Quebec, Montreal and Niagara. For a whole century, from the British conquest until Confederation, regimental bands were the backbone of instrumental music in Canada. In addition to performing at military functions, they became a true communal force, reaching a wide and warmly appreciative public. Almost daily a band could be heard: at a gathering of high society, at a garden party, on a public square, or, more rarely, between the acts of a theatrical performance. A Montreal directory for 1819 admits that "Montreal is not at present over-burthened with amusements," but states: "By the indulgence of the Colonel of the regiment stationed here, the company assembled are in summer time frequently amused in the evening by the music of an excellent band."

Sometimes bands were interchanged between various parts of the Empire, and thus Canadians had an opportunity to hear some of the finest British bands. (Many of these have been brought to Canada as a special attraction of the Canadian National Exhibition, held annually in Toronto since 1879.) The personnel in earlier years included a number of musicians of non-British origin, especially German bandmasters. Many of the musicians, upon retirement or discharge, stayed in Canada as performers, teachers, instrument makers or music dealers.

One of the oldest purely Canadian bands was organized by a German bandmaster, Jean-Chrysostome Brauneis (1785–1832). Founded in 1831 in Quebec, it was disbanded after the death of the conductor the following years. A native Canadian, Charles Sauvageau (1809–1846), revived it in 1836 under the proud title "Musique Canadienne," and its history in these turbulent and rebellious years was closely linked with French-Canadian struggles for a greater share in Canadian government. This band was made up of three clarinets, piccolo, serpent, bassoon, trumpet, three horns, trombone and percussion.

Throughout the later nineteenth century, beginning in the 1830's, brass bands were formed in many towns of Upper Canada. Some were established on a family or neighbourhood basis, others were attached to the local fire brigade or volunteer militia. Some played just for their own amusement, whereas semi-professional "name" bands offered their services to taverns, weddings, lake steamers and the like.

The first local band in Upper Canada to achieve fame belonged not to a city, but to a little village south of Lake Simcoe. The residents of Hope (now Sharon), the "Children of Peace," were a splinter group of the Quakers, in reaction to whose severity they evolved a colourful and quaint cult. The Temple at Sharon is a standing reminder. Following the initiative of their leader, David Willson, a self-made theologian, music became a prominent feature of their community. About 1820 a choir and a brass band were formed. Their first organ, of 1820, is supposed to have been the earliest built in Upper Canada. It had 133 pipes and 2 barrels of ten sacred tunes each.

After Confederation many Canadian military bands were established, often with musicians from the departing British bands as instructors. The first notable Canadian bandmaster was Joseph Vézina of Quebec (1849–1924), the founder and leader of several bands and a prolific composer for this medium. In any Canadian town one could now find a bandstand and on summer evenings concerts would be given regularly—a custom which is just a memory in many of our cities today.

Perhaps the most significant stimulus provided by the British regimental bands and their officer-patrons was the encouragement of the performance of secular art music. We have no records of concerts before the British conquest and the few scattered instances in the late eighteenth and early nineteenth centuries do not permit us to consider them a regular institution. Nevertheless, in Halifax and Quebec, concert music flourished in modest fashion and such works as a symphony by Leopold Kotzeluch and a concertante by Ignaz Pleyel were performed before 1800. Coffee houses, taverns and other improvised concert halls were the scenes of these performances.

The dates of several early concerts in Halifax have been traced by Miss Phyllis R. Blakeley of the Nova Scotia Public Archives in a number of articles in the *Dalhousie Review* (1951). In Quebec, a series of subscription concerts was held on Monday evenings for 24 weeks during the season 1790–91. A detailed balance sheet mentions 104 subscribers and 7 paid performers. Probably there were unpaid performers as well, for we know of other concerts in which regimental musicians were supported by amateurs from among the officers and local "gentlemen" who certainly would play without remuneration. Although we lack records of the programmes, there is a second violin part of Mozart's String Quintet in C major in a collection of music in Quebec, with the inscription "Quebec Subscription Concert 1793." How the work must have baffled the citizens with its modernism and complexity!

In 1841 responsible government united Lower and Upper Canada and with Confederation in 1867 the Dominion of Canada was born. Coinciding with these steps of political maturing, and with the development of trade and industry, the characteristic features of urban musical life made their appearance: concert societies, music teachers, instrument builders, visits from world-famous artists, and, a few decades later, conservatories and musical periodicals.

After Confederation music expanded not merely in complexity but also geographically when the completion of the transcontinental railway in 1886 helped to open up the West of Canada. Villages and towns sprang up overnight. It is interesting that in spite of all the pioneer work that had to be done and the many hardships undergone, there was very rapid musical development in the western provinces. Some sort of organized music appeared within a very few years after the foundation of each town. In 1870 Fort Garry had a population of only 240, but five or six years later Winnipeg, newly established on the same site, had an organ, a city band and a Glee Club. We could give many similar examples. One of the most notable developments of more recent years in the West has been the competitive music festival, described elsewhere in this volume.

In studying the nineteenth-century period one wonders alternately at the apathy and hostility shown to good music and at artistic achievements quite amazing for their time. The key to this seeming contradiction is found in the conflict, sometimes open and bitter, that went on between two tendencies. With the exception of a few religious sects who considered the fiddle an instrument of the devil and condemned song as wicked, the country folk indulged in an abundance of enthusiastic music-making, and the musicians and music-lovers of the towns would get together to play or sing and to organize musical societies and concerts with a missionary zeal that is a monument to the pioneer spirit. On the other hand, nineteenth-century North America is not unjustly thought of as predominantly utilitarian and commercial with little appreciation for arts. Music was considered chiefly an "accomplishment" of young ladies who played the piano and delighted their suitors with waltzes, polkas and assorted salon pieces. The selections always had to be "pretty" and serious practising was shunned. An artistic career, like any other not aiming at the acquisition of wealth and social position, was regarded with suspicion. The musician was apt to be identified with the Bohemian and the morally loose. When Emma Lajeunesse, later famous as Mme Albani, left Canada to study abroad, an attempt to raise funds resulted in failure. In the singer's words:

The French-Canadians . . . had the old-world traditional misgiving of a public career, and especially that dislike for any one belonging to them to go on the stage itself, a feeling which was then very much still alive in Canada, although the idea was already beginning to die out in other countries. Consequently all help, as they then honestly thought in my best interests, was withheld from me in that quarter.[5]

Hostility towards music was sometimes based on religious grounds; many congregations bitterly opposed the introduction of instruments in their churches. More unfortunate still was the attitude of those most able by virtue of wealth or position to patronize the arts. The critic who in 1868 complained about the "very indifferent taste evinced for *good music* by the higher social and better educated classes of this city"[6] has often been re-echoed. It is this type of attitude that has created the impression of Canada as a somewhat unmusical country, an impression which ignores the intensely musical atmosphere of pre-industrial Canada and the many achievements of early musical societies in the industrial age.

It is wrong, however, to explain the lack of interest in art entirely

[5]Emma Albani, *Forty Years of Song* (London, 1911), p. 173.
[6]*Evening Telegraph*, Feb. 5, 1868, on a "Grand Concert of the Montreal Amateur Musical Union." Seen in the F. H. Torrington scrapbooks, on file in the Toronto Public Library.

in terms of attitudes. Attitudes were often created by living conditions. The tremendous tasks of clearing the land, building homes and securing the necessities of life were good reasons for neglecting higher forms of recreation and accomplishment. Besides, the lack of facilities for musical training and of opportunities to hear good music was common alike to native Canadians and to many of the poorer immigrants from Europe.

Against this background musicians and music-lovers worked to raise the level of taste and accomplishment by teaching, performing, importing sheet music and many other activities. The pioneer musician had to be versatile and enterprising. Even if trained as a violinist, he had to be prepared to do anything from playing a church organ to tuning pianos. His reward was not glamour and fame, but the quiet glory of waking to the beauty of music people who had never before heard an orchestra or a chorus.

All pioneer work culminated in the musical societies, instrumental or, more often, choral groups. To trace in detail the varying fortunes—enthusiastic beginnings, shipwrecks, reorganizations and so on—of every philharmonic society from Halifax to Victoria would require a volume in itself. Yet even though musical life ran along independent local and provincial lines, musical conditions were strikingly parallel everywhere. Suffice it to give the dates of some of the earliest societies and to trace the achievements of a few of the most famous ones.

Probably the earliest of all was the Philharmonic Society of Halifax, which presented an oratorio at St. Paul's Church in 1769 but does not appear to have been a permanent organization. Several singing societies were formed in Halifax after 1800; among them an Amateur Glee Club, organized in 1837, was noteworthy as an early musical organization of working men. Lunenburg, N.S., had a Harmonic Society for the cultivation of sacred music in 1828 and a society by that name was founded in Quebec in 1820. We must remember, however, that the Quebec subscription series of the early 1790's were arranged by a musical society in all but name. The Montreal Philharmonic Society of 1848 was probably preceded by a Société de Musique of 1837. In Toronto a Choral Society was formed in 1845, and the first large musical event in Hamilton was the Philharmonic Society's performance of the *Creation* in 1858, with a chorus of 90 and an orchestra of 25. Over two thousand miles to the west, in Victoria, the oldest town on the Pacific coast, we find in 1859 a Philharmonic Society and a few years later a German *Singverein*.

It is significant that even in French-Canadian cities some of the early musical organizations had English names; Anglo-Canadians have always been natural organizers. Yet dependence of musical life on organized activity has been a weakness as well as a strength. Musical societies often achieved spectacular successes, but once they collapsed, all musical activity collapsed with them. Among the French-Canadians music is far more taken for granted: for music-making in the home, a healthy voice, a violin or a piano in the living room are all that is required.

Before continuing our description of musical societies in nineteenth-century Canada, mention must be made of an important stimulus to musical enterprise: the first visits of world-famous artists. The invention of the steamship and the railway made these visits easier but the chief factor was the vicinity of the United States with a larger population. Those who performed before Canadian audiences between 1850 and 1880 included Jenny Lind, Henri Vieuxtemps, Ole Bull, Sigismund Thalberg, Hans von Bülow, Louis Gottschalk and others. The Germanians, a German-American orchestra, celebrated some of their first triumphs in Montreal and Toronto in their tour of 1850. Their repertoire was an excellent one. Later in the nineteenth and early twentieth centuries many American orchestras paid visits to Canada, often to support a Canadian choir. It is significant that the first musicians of world fame to impress Canadians were performers, not composers. The public was addicted to that star-worship which puts all the emphasis on virtuosity. This also led often to unjust neglect of the native artist.

Nevertheless the excellence of visiting artists gave a great impetus to local musical leaders and the true pioneer age in Canadian music began about the time of Confederation. Organizations, at first unstable, hindered by intrigues, change of personnel or a fickle public, became much stronger and many flourished for decades. Choirs of two or three hundred voices, drawing many of their singers from church choirs, became very popular. It was far more difficult to train and keep together orchestras. As a rule, therefore, orchestras were assembled for each individual concert from among regimental musicians and other professional and amateur performers. Some players might be borrowed from neighbouring towns, but even so, certain instruments would often be lacking and the balance would be unsatisfactory.

The type of concert depended largely on the forces available. For some concerts, almost anybody willing to stand on a podium and face

an audience might be invited to participate. There would be a colourful succession of amateurs and professionals, singers and instrumentalists, whose selections would be held together by a few orchestral
numbers. This type of concert can still be heard at some church or
small-town concerts. The programmes were often a hodge-podge of
operatic fantasias, national songs, and showy instrumental pieces.
Many concerts, however, as early as the 1850's and increasingly in
later years, did contain a large amount of serious music: overtures,
symphonic movements or entire symphonies, oratorio and operatic
selections by Handel, Haydn, Mozart, Beethoven, Weber and Mendelssohn. Radical composers, from Berlioz to Debussy, were rarely
heard. Altogether, concert life could be compared to that of provincial
towns in England and France.

In the twenty-two years of its existence, the Montreal Philharmonic
Society (1877–99) gave close to ninety concerts, devoted chiefly to
oratorios, masses, and other large-scale choral works. Many of the
soloists were guest artists from the United States or Europe. The conductor during most of the Society's existence was a native Montrealer,
Guillaume Couture (1851–1915); his memory is still alive in that city.
He graduated from the Paris Conservatoire with high honours and
was considered a musician of profound craftsmanship and discipline.
As examples of the Philharmonic's enterprise, we mention performances of Mendelssohn's *Elijah* (1884), Mozart's *Requiem* (1888), Beethoven's Ninth Symphony (1897) and concert performances in the
1890's of *The Flying Dutchman* and *Tannhäuser*.

In Anglo-Canada, the centre of population and culture had begun
to shift from the Maritimes to Ontario. The Toronto Philharmonic
Society (1846–57, intermittently; 1872–94) was in many ways similar
to its sister group in Montreal, but never ventured into opera. Its programmes included many Canadian first performances, such as the
Mendelssohn oratorios. The climax of the Society's history came with
the great festival of 1886, so typical of the time, a concentrated effort
that involved over a thousand singers and a large orchestra. From
1873 on, the conductor of the Philharmonic Society was Frederick Herbert Torrington (1837–1917), a musician of English birth who had
come to Canada as a young man and was one of the first to play Bach
fugues on a Canadian church organ. Torrington continued to play a
notable part in the musical life of Toronto until well after the turn of
the century.

Two types of musical performance usually remained outside the philharmonic societies' sphere of activity: opera and chamber music. Apart from a single instance of opera in the eighteenth century, operatic performances began about the middle of the nineteenth century. The Quebec performance of Rousseau's *Le Devin du Village* in 1846 by the Société des Amateurs Canadiens under Napoleon Aubin, the Swiss consul, marked a new era. By 1870 most Canadian cities had been visited by operatic troupes from the United States and Europe. From then until World War I, operas were heard more frequently in Canada than they are now (apart from broadcasts). To be sure, performances with Canadian talent were rare. The first act of *Lucrezia Borgia* had been presented with piano accompaniment in Toronto in 1853, but Ontario directed its efforts towards oratorio rather than opera. Quebec was an opera-loving province, and concert or stage performances with local talent of *Si j'étais roi, La Dame Blanche* and other operas date back to the 1860's. Opera classes established in Halifax in the 1890's led to successful performances of *Martha, Faust* and *Der Freischütz*. It is astonishing that some of Wagner's operas were introduced to Canada before those of Mozart. Even *Parsifal* was performed by a visiting company in 1905.

The light musical stage, from minstrel shows to Gilbert and Sullivan, was amply represented by travelling and amateur groups all over Canada. *The Mikado*, for instance, was performed in Halifax only two years after its world *première*.

The lines between orchestral and chamber music are hard to draw. As a rule, chamber ensembles were miniature orchestras, playing orchestral music in arrangements rather than original chamber music. Performances of original chamber music were often restricted to single movements from string quartets or trios.

Quebec City was the oldest centre of chamber music, partly owing to the foundations laid by Frederic Henri Glackemeyer (1751–1836), one of those all-round musicians who had been a regimental bandmaster. He not only taught several instruments, but collected a library of orchestral and chamber music which, expanded by later additions, is now in the possession of Laval University. Notable pioneer work in chamber music was accomplished about the 1820's by the Hon. Jonathan Sewell, Chief Justice of Lower Canada, who led an amateur quartet, and at a later date by Arthur Lavigne (1845–1925) who was for years the soul of almost all musical enterprises in Quebec.

In other cities, chamber music led a more precarious existence, depending on what musicians were available at a given time. A pioneer of chamber music in Montreal deserves special mention: the violinist Frantz Jehin-Prume (1839–99), probably the first virtuoso of international recognition to settle in Canada. He was the earliest of the many Belgian musicians who have made their homes in Montreal.

The reader may well ask who, if any, were the composers writing music in the days when Paul Kane and Cornelius Krieghoff, Thomas Haliburton and Louis Fréchette won early laurels for Canadian painting and literature. In devoting ample space to nineteenth-century concert life, we merely reflect the fact that the performer was considered far more important than the composer. To be exact, we should speak not of composers but rather of musicians who earned their living as teachers, performers or in the service of the church, and who composed in their leisure hours. The environment certainly did not stimulate composition. A wealth of printed masterworks from Europe was available. Guest artists and immigrant musicians did not take the trouble to find out the local composer. Audiences, relying on foreign judgment in all musical matters, were too timid to appraise the composer independently and thus to encourage him. Chances of performance and publication were small. Musical intercourse between the different provinces of Canada was almost non-existent and the composer had little hope of gaining more than local reputation.

Composition then was limited to the everyday functions of teaching, dancing or marching, and nearly all composers wrote music for the service of their church. Larger compositions were restricted to patriotic events: for instance, the cantatas written for the visit of Prince Edward in 1860 and for Confederation in 1867.

The oldest preserved composition in Canada is by Abbé Charles-Amador Martin (1648–1711), a native Canadian who in the 1670's wrote the liturgical *Prose de la Sainte Famille*, considered by Ernest Gagnon to be of "incontestable beauty" and "remarkable correctness." The existence of an operatic composer in eighteenth-century Montreal is something of a freak in our musical history. Joseph Quesnel (1749–1809) was a French ship's officer, who settled in Canada in 1779 and found leisure to write poetry and plays, composing his own music for the latter. The vocal parts for two are still preserved and it would be possible to reconstruct the entire scores. At least one of the plays, *Colas et Colinette*, was performed in Montreal in 1790 and in Quebec in 1808. The music belongs to the "comédie mêlée d'ariettes" genre cultivated by Grétry and other French composers of the period.

For more than half a century no composer of equal ambition appeared in Canada. Patriotic songs and marches were the chief output, celebrating Wolfe's victory at Quebec or expressing French-Canadian political sentiment and the desire for national unity. Sabatier's *Le Drapeau du Carillon*, Lavigueur's *La Huronne* and Labelle's *O Canada, mon pays, mes amours* became very popular about the middle of the century. One of the earliest patriotic works to be published in Upper Canada was James P. Clarke's *The Lays of the Maple Leaf* (1852).

With Confederation the need for a national hymn became felt. Many national songs were written (and still are), but only two won wide and lasting favour: *The Maple Leaf Forever* (1867) by the Toronto school principal Alexander Muir and restricted in its appeal to Anglo-Canadians, and Calixa Lavallée's *O Canada* which was first performed on June 24, 1880. Today we remember Lavallée (1842–91) chiefly for this single composition. We forget that it was not *O Canada* that made him famous. The reverse is true: it was due to his great reputation as composer, conductor and pianist that Lavallée was asked to write a national song. The story of his short life has been told by Eugène Lapierre in a book which has had several French editions and which is long overdue in an English translation. It was a life full of adventure and struggle, disappointment at home and reward abroad. Few other musicians have been so consciously Canadian; few have sacrificed so much for their country. Yet Lavallée did not succeed in inducing the authorities to help establish a national opera and a national conservatory, which he considered our greatest needs. Throughout his life he had spent various periods in the United States, as accompanist and opera conductor, and there he finally went into exile in the very year when the famous song was born. His greatest reward was his election as President of the Music Teachers National Association (U.S.) in 1886.

As a composer Lavallée showed talent early. Even in 1873, before completing his studies in Paris, he was hailed as "Canada's national musician." His works include almost every type of music: light operas, symphonies, chamber compositions, music for band and piano, and songs. Most of the larger works were written outside Canada. The *Bridal Rose Overture* is still performed occasionally, and the piano piece *Papillons* had no less than ten different publishers. From the few surviving works one may conclude that Lavallée was little influenced by the radicals of his time. Rather, his strength lay in facility of invention and melodic fluency. The greatest tribute to Lavallée was paid by Augustus Vogt, himself one of Canada's foremost musicians. Vogt, who as a music student had met Lavallée in Boston in the 1880's, is quoted as saying: ". . . he impressed me as a man of extraordinary ability—not merely as a clever executant of the piano, and not merely as an adroit deviser of pretty melodies and sensuous harmonies, but as a genuinely creative artist, a pure musical genius."[7]

Besides Lavallée, a number of French-Canadian musicians of his generation took a serious interest in composition. Born between 1844 and 1864 were Romain-Octave Pelletier, Joseph Vézina, Guillaume Couture, Alexis Contant and Achille Fortier. With the exception of Vézina's band music, the output of these composers consists chiefly of church music. Apart from a few operettas, masses and oratorios, the bulk of their work is in short forms. Among Anglo-Canadians, William Reed and Wesley Octavius Forsyth were the first with impressive lists of compositions.

Many other composers were immigrants. A great number of British musicians, brought up in the tradition of cathedral music, wielded an enormous influence as organists and choirmasters as well as teachers and conductors. Some of those who settled in various parts of Canada between 1880 and World War I are Charles A. E. Harriss, Albert Ham, William Hewlett, Herbert Sanders, Alfred Whitehead and Healey Willan. On the other hand, a few Canadians sought their fortunes abroad. Best known among these are Clarence Lucas, Nathaniel Dett, Gena Branscombe, Geoffrey O'Hara and, at a later date, Colin McPhee.

Most of the native composers named studied abroad, usually in Paris or Leipzig. It was there that the majority of their larger works were written. But on returning to Canada, many a good talent was condemned to stagnation. There was little impetus to write serious works and less hope of material reward. Above all there was no broad public with cultural interests, so essential for the artist's encouragement. A few large works were performed in Montreal, the oratorios *Cain* (1905) by Contant and *Jean le Précurseur* (posthumously, 1923) by Couture, and *Torquil* (1900), an opera by Harriss. The scores of the two last works appeared in print. On the other hand, there is no evidence of symphonies or concertos by resident composers having been performed in Canada before World War I.

To judge the style of these composers is difficult. Hardly anything written before World War I survives in performance. Those composers who managed to establish contacts with publishers abroad had

[7]J. D. Logan, "Canadian Creative Composers," *Canadian Magazine*, September, 1913.

a good many of their works printed but unfortunately Canadian libraries contain little of this music. It would be a noble task for the new National Library to collect original or photostat copies of all surviving compositions.

In general the style of both native and immigrant composers reflected French or English influences (the latter under the spell of German romanticism), as the case might be. There was little relationship between composition and the folk-song of Canada and few composers used folk-song material. We must remember, however, that those French Canadian songs which remained popular even in the cities, were strung together in medleys or "rapsodies canadiennes." Not only Canadian composers, for example Vézina (*Mosaïque*, 1880), but also Europeans like Paul Gilson and Sir Alexander Mackenzie wrote such works.

The nineteenth century then could hardly have been expected to produce a distinct school of Canadian composers. The quantity of music written about the turn of the century is impressive and sometimes the craftsmanship demands sincere admiration, but music which does not firmly root in its human and geographical environment is often derivative and sterile.

With the increase of performance and composition came a need for musical education, for music printing, for instrument building and for the exchange of news through music journals.

From the days of Father LeJeune in Quebec until the early nineteenth century, educational facilities remained primitive. Instruments were scarce, music had to be taken down by hand from the teacher's copy and, above all, good teachers were rare.

In the 1840's music appeared on the curricula of several "higher ladies' academies" and boys' colleges. In 1856 the first musical doctorate was conferred on James P. Clarke by the University of Toronto. It was several decades, however, before regular examinations for degrees in music were held by Trinity College, Toronto, and other universities. By the outbreak of World War I, about 50 doctorates in music had been granted by Canadian universities. Universities had no faculties of music; instruction was given through affiliated conservatories and the universities supervised the examinations. Many of the Trinity degrees were taken in Great Britain by candidates who had never been in Canada, and in due time a minor scandal arose when British musicians objected to this practice.

Most music teaching was private and of very uneven quality. The unwary layman found it difficult to distinguish the quack, often operating under an adopted foreign-sounding name, from the genuine musician. Among the conservatories, too, it was hard to single out the authentic music school from the two or three teacher establishment, inflated by a grandiose name. The genuine educational institutions which still exist include the Quebec Académie de Musique (founded 1868), an examination and award board, the Toronto (now Royal) Conservatory (1886), the Halifax (now Maritime) Conservatory (1887) and the McGill Conservatorium (1904) in Montreal.

In elementary and secondary schools systematic music instruction was rare and too often depended on the presence of a qualified teacher and a sympathetic school board.

The first printed music in Canada was for church use. In 1800 and the following two years, three bulky volumes appeared in Quebec, entitled Le Graduel [Processionel, Vespéral] Romain. They contained Roman Catholic liturgical music in four-line Gregorian notation. From then on, textbooks of musical rudiments and collections of hymns and sacred songs appeared from time to time. The bulk of printed music, however, was imported from Boston, London or Paris.

Some of the earliest printed compositions appeared as appendices to literary journals, for instance in the Literary Garland (1839) or Le Ménestrel (1844). A little later separate sheet music made its appearance as a number of music dealers took to publishing, notably A. & S. Nordheimer with headquarters in Toronto and A. J. Boucher in Montreal. Other publishing firms were founded later in the century. The Canadian market was small and copies of early Canadian sheet music are extremely rare today.

Concert reviews became frequent in newspapers and journals about 1850 and the earliest periodical entirely devoted to the cause of music, L'Artiste, was issued in 1860. It was a premature effort, for only two numbers appeared. The first Canadian music magazine in the English language was the Toronto Music Journal of 1887 and 1888. During the following twenty years at least ten magazines, entirely or partly devoted to music, were founded. The cost of publishing them and the competition from American journals must have been considerably less than now, when there is not a single musical periodical of national coverage in Canada. To be sure, some of these old journals ceased publication very quickly, but at least two of them flourished for long periods, Le Passe-Temps (1895–1950) and Musical Canada (1906–33).

Instrument building developed into a lively industry. Perhaps the cost and danger of shipping big instruments across the ocean, as well as the abundance of wood in Canada, contributed to the establishment of piano and organ factories.

The pioneer work of the second half of the nineteenth century culminated in a genuine flourishing of music in the opening years of the twentieth. Orchestras, formerly organized primarily as adjuncts to choral societies, now assumed a large degree of independence. Professional, semi-professional and amateur orchestras were founded in most of the large cities. In solo appearances the amateur gave way to the professional, and many world-famous artists appeared in the cities every season. On the other hand, an astonishing number of amateurs participated in choral singing. Every town from coast to coast had choirs of all possible sizes, for church or concert music, singing *a cappella* or with accompaniment. Toronto claimed to be "the choral capital of North America." This prestige was based on at least five large choral organizations that flourished in the early years of the century: the National Chorus (Albert Ham), the Oratorio Society (Edward Broome), the Schubert Choir (H. M. Fletcher), the Orpheus Society (Dalton Baker) and the Mendelssohn Choir (Augustus Vogt). The latter was founded, oddly enough, in the very year, 1894, when a thirty-year old group by the same name in Montreal, with an excellent reputation, was disbanded. It is the only one of the choirs just mentioned which survives in Toronto. Some account of the Mendelssohn and other Canadian choirs will be given elsewhere in this volume.

If Anglo-Canada was a land of choral music, French Canada excelled in opera. A large musical venture there, crowning decades of pioneer work, was the Montreal Opera Company under Albert Clerk-Jeannotte, which presented opera in various Canadian cities and in Rochester, N.Y., from 1910 to 1913. It relied heavily on foreign talent. The first season (13 operas in 73 performances) ended without financial loss in spite of an expenditure of $80,000. Eventually, however, the lack of an adequate hall or theatre in Montreal rendered the company's continuation financially impossible.

All in all, Canada had definitely become music-conscious. A British musician, J. Mackenzie-Rogan, wrote after his tour of 1903: "I had no idea until then of the fine taste for music prevailing in the Dominion. I remember it all even now with glowing pride and pleasure. . . ."[8] Canadians themselves also took stock of achievement. This is reflected

[8] J. Mackenzie-Rogan, *Fifty Years of Army Music* (London, 1926), p. 152.

in the numerous surveys of musical life—modest forerunners of the present volume—which appeared in reference books. An attempt to write our musical history by J. D. Logan, like several after his, was not carried through, but B. K. Sandwell edited a large volume, entirely devoted to the record of music in Montreal from 1895 to 1907. In the field of composition, this consciousness of achievement was evident in the first recital entirely devoted to Canadian music, given in Montreal in 1903.

When war broke out in 1914, choirs and orchestras were seriously depleted and many musical enterprises collapsed. The Toronto Symphony Orchestra, for instance, which had given fine service for almost ten years under Frank Welsman, was disbanded in 1918 and Toronto lacked an orchestra until 1923. The post-war period was one of fundamental changes. Later chapters of this volume will trace some of its history in detail. Here we shall merely indicate some of the new trends.

The most obvious changes resulted from technological advance. Beginning with the 1930's mass communication through phonograph record, radio and, later, television caused a great shift of emphasis in our musical habits. Radio carried music for the first time to distant regions where the appearance of outstanding concert artists was out of the question. For a time at least, amateur participation in musical organizations and music-making at home declined. On the other hand, records and radio introduced to Canadians standards of performance hitherto known to only a limited number—standards which spurred our own musicians to greater efforts. The shift in popularity from vocal to instrumental music also may be partly accounted for by these technological changes. In any case, it is characteristic that the Canadian group with the widest international fame in this period was an instrumental ensemble, the Hart House Quartet of Toronto, which made numerous North American and two European tours.

The former centres of musical life, the bands, churches and choirs, lost much of their relative importance. The new musical leaders are orchestra conductors, composers, radio producers, concert agents, union officials, people who have less contact with the amateur than had the old leaders.

Hand in hand with professional specialization went the secularization of music. The organist-choirmaster has become less and less the undisputed leader of music in his community. Formerly the musical experience of many Canadians originated in the church service; now it roots largely in the secular music of the radio. From an economic point of view as well, radio and instrumental work offers greater inducements than do the churches, although salaries in church positions are often substantial enough. Among our younger composers, relatively few are church musicians.

The most important recent trend, however, can be found in the fact that musical life in all its aspects is more definitely Canadian than formerly. In the second quarter of the century the sense of Canadian identity and the awareness of a national heritage have immeasurably grown. With its nationwide network, the Canadian Broadcasting Corporation in particular has helped to break down the regional and provincial barriers and has given our composers and artists a wider hearing. Creative activity has also increased enormously.[9]

Independence in the educational field has grown considerably. Following World War I, musical faculties were established in the Universities of Toronto (1918), McGill (1920) and Laval (1922). Music has also been introduced in many other universities; several conservatories now give more advanced instruction. A complete musical education can now be obtained in Canada and a new type of musician, more intimately concerned with Canadian affairs, is the product. This does not mean that Canadian students do not or should not go abroad to widen their musical horizon. On the contrary, opportunities for study abroad have been widened by the Quebec government's Prix d'Europe, instituted in 1911, by Canadian government scholarships and other awards.

Another important development has been the re-discovery of folk-song in Canada, of which we have already spoken. Through the medium of folk-song festivals and through song-books, Canadians have been made aware of the variety and wealth of their heritage. Composers have arranged and harmonized folk-songs, or used folk material in extended compositions. However, up to now such material has not become the basis of any school of composition, and musical nationalism remains an isolated phenomenon found chiefly in the work of a few French-Canadian composers. Nevertheless our living composers are no longer people who merely happen to live in Canada, they are consciously Canadians.

---

[9]EDITOR'S NOTE. As an illustration of how composition in Canada has increased, I might mention that in 1927, immediately after my appointment as Principal of the Toronto Conservatory of Music, I tried to arrange concerts of music by our student composers. After two such concerts were given, there was not enough material to continue this series! Today no such difficulty would be encountered.

The colonial phase in our musical history has passed; French and English influences have lost their monopolies. Musicians of many different national origins contribute to cultural life, and the impact of our Canadian environment asserts itself more strongly.

This brief sketch may suggest that more pride in the musical achievements of their own past would be fitting for Canadians. That our musicians are preoccupied with the future at the expense of the past is in itself a healthy sign. But too often Canadians speak of their musical history in terms of thirty or forty years as though their ancestors in Canada a century or two ago were completely ignorant in all higher aspects of the art. Too often they mistakenly claim some particular musical event as the "first" in Canada, when in fact a similar event took place at a long-forgotten time. We should bear in mind such facts as that music was composed in Canada before Bach and Handel were born; that Johann Christian Bach and Mozart were performed in Canada when they were musical news in Europe; that no Canadian singer has yet outshone Mme Albani's nineteenth-century fame; that in the season of 1890–91 there were 91 performances of 4 grand and 20 light operas in Toronto; and that there have been generations of fine musicians, whose knowledge of counterpoint and harmony was in no way inferior to that of our living composers.

Our musical shortcomings are often excused by the plea that Canada is a young country. This is a doubtful explanation even if youth were a shortcoming. For our musical history is relatively old and rich, not of world importance, but abounding in events and personalities, many of whom would make fine subjects for writers of historical fiction and biography. The real shortcoming is, perhaps, that in spite of such a long musical record, so many achievements failed to establish traditions and were allowed to collapse and be forgotten. New starts have had to be made too often.

Many musical organizations stand and fall with the personality of their leader. But a more important reason why musical enterprises so often had to begin afresh is insufficient patronage and endowment. Many musical projects are initiated in the hope that, once their value is proven, financial support will be forthcoming from one source or another and thus secure the future of the particular orchestra, choir, club or journal. However, sufficient support has rarely been given, and many fine groups, after carrying on for years with enthusiasm and hope, have had to be disbanded. Music in Canada has never enjoyed aristocratic sponsorship, and the state, with the exception of the Province of Quebec, and private wealth have taken up this sponsorship inadequately. Thus musical organizations often have had to be established on a purely commercial basis, which in many cases was patently impossible. Economics are, of course, but one side of the problem; public apathy towards art is only too common in Canada.

It would be wrong to regard Canada's musical history as proceeding directly from primitive beginnings to higher and higher levels of achievement, following each other like the steps of a ladder. Such simple "growth" has indeed taken place in organizational and technological aspects of music. But progress has been anything but even and uninterrupted in creative work, in standards of performance and in appreciation of fine music. It must be admitted, however, that in all these aspects recent years have produced the highest level yet achieved.

It would be wiser to view our musical history as a path through a changing scenery: summits of achievement in particular phases of music were often followed by decline. Wars, depressions and other outside influences have obstructed progress. The development of music in Canada has been determined by individual and collective efforts and failures; it has been given new direction by technological and social forces, bringing both new advantages (e.g., radio) and new obstacles (e.g., the high cost of publishing); it has been modified by changes in taste and leisure-time habits. Through all these variations it has had a basic theme: how people with differing traditions have helped to build the musical life of their new homeland. Today Canadian orchestras, choirs and music schools compare with the best anywhere and for the first time there is a firm link between the different generations of composers. These are indications that the basic weakness in our musical history, a lack of permanence and continuity, is disappearing with the establishment of sound and lasting traditions.

FOLK-SONG

Marius Barbeau

Let us humbly admit it: the folk, the old country folk are the makers of our language and our masters in poetry. These born poets do not seek the full rhyme as in modern verse; they are satisfied with the simple assonance. Their line is not wrought for the eyes of the reader; it is studded with elisions beyond the pale of grammar.

These songs are a whole world by itself, and an enchanted world for all. We find them north and south, east and west. The king's oldest son, the bold captain, the noble lord, the trifling miller, the poor soldier, the handsome prisoner, and Cathos, Marion, Madelon, the three wise maidens or the three girls in love— they all go by threes—pour out their heartaches to the nightingale, messenger of love, over the crystal fountain.

Translated from Anatole France's *La vie littéraire*, I

Canadian folk-songs, like those of other lands similarly endowed, cannot be grasped fully unless you go out on your own to seek and discover them. For they belong to the past and the unknown. Long sheltered by isolation and nurtured by perennial traditions, they now have been silenced by the impact of our machine age. Should you be prompted by a *penchant* for adventure, then follow me, but first sweep routine out of your mind and shed all superiority complexes. With a receptive soul, enter sensitively upon a borderland of strange voices and self-expression, where modern progress is lagging and the folk are still free and fondly reminiscent. They are apt if led on to revert to half-forsaken patterns of their younger days. You will hear from an aging generation mostly analphabetic odd Canadian dialects of French, English, Irish, German and Gaelic (not to mention the "New Nationalities"), and native languages such as those of the Indians, from the reserves of the northeastern woodlands to those of the Great Lakes, the prairies, the Rockies, the North Pacific coast, and the boundless wastes of the Arctic. To be a Canadian scholar looking for folk and Indian songs is certainly to plumb an unfathomed patrimony of tunes, rhythms, scales and modes, vocal production, words, and inherent mental and spiritual processes. This truly New World is still largely unsurveyed and unpublished, if not undiscovered.

If you wish to venture alone, it is not too late, though five minutes to twelve—as an American ethnologist once put it; when the clock strikes twelve, it will be all over. It may be easier to follow me around and to share some of my experiences as a collector and student. For more than forty years, I have been a pioneer in this field. I have recorded Huron-Iroquois chants by the hundreds, French-Canadian songs by the thousands, English-Canadian by the score, and North-western Indian songs up to nearly one thousand. My old singers have long since passed away, and only a few survivors are still versed in the old lore.

Such huge expanses cannot easily be covered through the mere medium of paper and print, even with the help of illustrations. Were you visiting the National Museum of Canada or the Music Division of the Library of Congress at Washington, you might be shown numerous shelves containing wax records dating back to 1911, taken on the now-antiquated Standard Edison phonograph, and more recently, on disks and magnetic tapes. You might peruse index cards of numbered items with accessory data, manuscripts of texts, translations, and musical transcriptions; plus printed books and pamphlets. But all these would seem rather musty to one who like you is looking for first-hand impressions. So let us try to be life-like! As everything in nature is haphazard, we may begin at the end or in the middle, and end up at the beginning. It does not really matter when you go exploring into the unknown.

In 1924, Ernest MacMillan—not as yet knighted—belonged to a musical world quite apart from my own museum background. Yet he became interested in my first full book of French-Canadian folk-songs,[1] and reviewed it favourably. An understanding friend, I felt, had been gained in him. Soon after, I dropped in to see him at the Toronto Conservatory of Music of which he afterwards became the head. He sat at the piano, and we began to hum some of the tunes in that book while he improvised an accompaniment on the keyboard, which struck me as being beautiful. I craved for more of this type of musical lining for folk-tunes. The melodies of the early colonists and the Indians have always appealed to me as prime materials for a musical expression in a language that is first of all our own!

An opportunity for channelling pioneering efforts in this direction occurred three years later when (the now late) J. M. Gibbon asked

[1]*Folk Songs of French Canada*, by Marius Barbeau with English translations by Edward Sapir (Yale University Press, 1925).

me to organize with him, under the joint ægis of the National Museum and the Canadian Pacific Railway, a Festival of Folk Songs and Handicrafts at the Château Frontenac, Quebec, in May, 1927. The success of this first festival, consisting of six concerts and a concourse of *habitant* and lumberjack singers, dancers, weavers and carvers—even cooks in the Château kitchen—was such that it called for a second festival, in the spring of 1928. Some of the guests from New York, Boston, Toronto and elsewhere were partial to the folk singers, Bédard and de Repentigny in particular; others were thrilled by the Ouellet family of five fiddlers from Kamouraska, consisting of the father and four sons. A discriminating few were moved by the nostalgic *complaintes*, like plain-chant, of François Saint-Laurent and Joseph Ouellet, two cod fishermen of remote Gaspé. A conductor of the Metropolitan Opera followed the quartet of the Bytown Troubadours as they walked about the halls, interpreting *voyageur* and lumberjack songs arranged for four voices by the Ottawa musician, "Père" Gauthier. But I had been acquainted with these "raw" elements in their own surroundings and they were no novelties to me. What entranced me was the interpretation on the concert platform of sets of songs I had transcribed from the phonograph, the most lyrical and lovely I could choose, by Ernest MacMillan at the piano to Campbell McInnes' singing; Alfred Laliberté's elaborate but admirably performed accompaniments of *pastourelles* and *chansons à répons* to the singing of two or three of his disciples; or again Healey Willan's powerful, at times fugue-like, developments, executed under his direction by a small orchestra, in the performance by a group of singers of de Montigny's "Ordre de Bon Temps." This sketch was based on an ancient manuscript going back to the days of Samuel de Champlain at Port Royal.

To some observers at the time it seemed that Canada's own music was born and would soon be coming into its own. Perhaps we were too optimistic. Yet definite progress has been achieved since, in spite of a climate in North America averse to originality and fundamentals.

INDIAN SONGS OF THE NORTH PACIFIC COAST

Once the first festival was over, I went back to my summer fieldwork on the Nass River close to the Alaskan border. There, and in other parts of the Rockies and the North Pacific coast, I had in previous years recorded on the phonograph many Indian songs. This experience had opened for me a world of unexplored Mongolian-like culture.

Chants, dirges, mountain love songs, visions of mystic spirits, had deeply impressed me by their beauty and significance. Embodied in unfamiliar musical idioms, rhythms and patterns, they were marked by drum beats and accentuated by intricate guttural languages. I had not yet tried my hand, as I intended to do, at transcribing them on paper. Some songs sounded most intricate and challenging; they passed my comprehension. But I was itching under this challenge. What was the use of storing up so many native songs if all you could do was to listen passively to them and wear out delicate wax records of which no duplicates were available?

To secure the collaboration of an experienced musician seemed the answer to this question. MacMillan's quick-silver appreciation of French-Canadian tunes marked him for a preference. I invited him to join me on the Nass River, in July, 1928. He appeared on the scene one sunny day in that month. In the clearings were bushes of blue huckleberries and of lustrous salmonberries against a background of tall hemlocks and red cedars, on a rocky tidal shore covered with sea-weeds and lichens. Beyond this could be seen a west-coast panorama of Indian and Japanese boats drifting their nets for salmon on the Portland Canal near the Arrandale Cannery. A deserted government cabin was my headquarters, set in a wild tapestry of verdure and the red berries of the mountain-ash, where the ravens cawed and cooed. The next cabin had been the gaol; it now remained without "birds" or locks. The government customs office had been vacated recently, and bootleggers were now making hay while the sun shone. But I, a later occupant, was concerned only with ethnology, totem poles, language and songs. This was the rich home of salmon, halibut, "oolachen" (candle fish), of eagles, ravens, cranes and sea-gulls. Farther up the Nass River dwelt the grizzly bear, the moose; on the mountains, the mountain goat and sheep. Kincolith (Place-of-Scalps) stood at the foot of a high cliff, opposite the bay, and up the river lived the Niskæ tribes. Once not so long ago they had been a proud and warlike people who traced their migrant ancestry to the Bering Sea and Siberia. Their songs sounded Siberian and Mongolian-like, and their round skin-and-hoop drums were like those of North Asiatic shamans.

Before MacMillan arrived, I had already recorded several scores of native songs, marking with a red cross the most interesting and puzzling; on those I wanted him to work, and this would be my chance to penetrate into what seemed a forbidding sanctum of native voice and music. As in a Hindu temple, we must enter humbly and barefoot!

There on a table stood the Edison phonograph, with ear-tubes, a
record ready to serve, music sheets and pencil. A tune was put on, and
he listened, very interested. "Now, will you write it down?" He did
and it seemed easy enough, for some exotic chants are not difficult.
But I was saving a more enigmatic record for the next. It was *Haguhl-
æn*, "Why don't you mind your own affairs?" a challenge composed
and sung by the old chief Gitiks, who was known as the "last pagan"
of the Nass. This challenge had something new for us. Its drum beats
were 3/4, while the tune maintained itself in a syncopated 2/4; the
seemingly Phrygian scale was of the pentatonic type, which is typically
Indian.

Another day, we and two guests from Rochester, N.Y., went out in
a motor boat up the Nass, to the abandoned village of Angyadæ.
Totem poles, some of them decaying and moss-covered, stood in the
thick brush. We set foot on shore, cutting and beating down the sap-

lings and the foliage, in order to take photos and motion pictures of the Grizzly Bear, the Beaver, and the Eagle on the poles. The pungent smell of fireweed, nettles, and wild crab-apples assailed us while the mosquitoes nearly ate us alive. After we had hastily fallen back, we went on to a village where two old Indians—Gitiks and Weerhæ, head chiefs respectively of the Eagle and the Wolf clans—responded to our invitation and sang a few of their native songs. One of these we found hard to apprehend because of its strange cross-rhythm; the tune itself was easy enough. "Wait! I have already recorded it on the phonograph. You will tackle it at leisure to-morrow!"

MacMillan did, but for the first time he shook his head at something that eluded his grasp, and I was amused, although, had he been completely baffled, I would have been greatly disappointed. "Please try it again!" I left him alone spinning the cylinder and beating the floor with his foot while, humming the tune, he repeated again and again: "One, two, three, four, five . . . nine. . . . It can't be done!" At long last, he burst out, "Ah! I've got it!" The drum beats were 6/4 against a 9/8, both coinciding perfectly in a dirge belonging to the Wolf tribe, *Lip-kakæt* (I am heartbroken).

The next day, chief Weerhæ came along and gave us the same song. It was gradually becoming feasible to us. Along with the chief, we clapped our hands and sang 9/8 to the provoking drum rhythm of 6/4. A little girl of six who stood close to her grandfather meanwhile swayed her head, balanced the rhythm on her hands, and gracefully with utmost ease sang a flute-like obligato. What struck us as strange

was only natural and facile to a people inured by tradition from childhood up to different musical standards!

Many other songs of the northern Rockies which I recorded over the
years are now silently awaiting musical transcription on the shelves of
the National Museum; they may be deteriorating because of a fungus
which at times affects wax records. I wrote down nearly a hundred of
them, and MacMillan left me about a dozen in manuscript. These have
been embodied since in a substantial monograph, with musical scores
beautifully drawn, with texts and translations accompanied by due ex-
planations, with musical analyses by Mme Béclard d'Harcourt of Paris.
This important manuscript, ignored in Canada, was finally brought
out—about 800 copies—by the American Ethnological Society in the
United States, and there are probably no more than a dozen copies in
the whole of Canada. Of what use then can be Indian music with all
its resources to aspiring Canadian composers and interpreters who look
for fresh materials to work upon, if it is not possible to present it in
accessible form?

The grandiose strangeness of northern British Columbia and Alaska,
with their high dented mountain peaks, glaciers, canyons, and throb-
bing wild life in forest and rivers, might be oppressive if it remained
silent. But this land of natural wonders finds a voice in native songs.
They conjure up tribal recollections of the Asiatic-like people who
have searched and roamed all over its expanses and recesses. They express the soul of bold and restless races and arouse emotions seated
deep in the lives of the singers. And what is of concern to us, their
musical language is endowed with enough universality in tone and
texture to appeal to our poets, musicians and historians. Our composers, if they knew these songs, might well be stirred into recasting
them in broader moulds and patterns of their own. And in the free use
of them, one might truly say that the sky is the limit.

These songs are almost endlessly varied and movingly human.
Hunters sang implorations over slain bears and mountain goats to
appease their spirits. This religious expression is comparable to our
plain-chant. Medicine men clamoured incantations and loudly beat
their drums. Warriors intoned hymns of victory or chanted their grief
at the thought of fallen brothers. Peace was sealed to the tune of
Haida *Kawagyenees*. The chiefs in the feast house boasted of their
prestige, invested new owners with hereditary names, and presented
their grandchildren, while the guests acknowledged their assent in
song. Privately owned lullabies and dirges greeted new-born children
and sped the departed over the threshold of death. Lyric songs were

the solace of many lonely and love-lorn souls, whether in the wooded valleys or in the mountain solitudes. Women gathering wild berries were fond of singing, as were the men who trod the paths of their trap lines. The singing of the Indians reached out for greater things and wider spaces. It was the expression of transient emotion in terms of power and permanence. Hence its diversity and importance even for us who have conquered them and taken over their country. We should not allow any of their cultural wealth to be lost.

The custom of those Northwestern tribes of singing to words rather than to meaningless syllables, as North American tribes usually do, offers wide vistas of historical and literary interest. The songs also open the door to a rich Mongolian mythology. The mountain-songs of the once nomadic tribes of the Déné in the Northwest are swaying and ethereal. The voices of the singers, especially the women, are beautifully lofty and lyrical. Indeed expressiveness of the voice is a feature of native singing on both sides of the Pacific Ocean. Like the songs of Mongolia and Siberia, which they resemble, these songs are glowing with colour. They often climb to a high pitch and vibrate with longing and passion; then they descend from the heights like cascades of sweet and remote sound. The sea-coast songs, on the other hand, are not so musical and appealing. Their compass is narrower. They are usually sombre and brooding. The voices of the singers, no less colourful, are chesty and throaty, sometimes harsh. On the coast, the function of singing is largely restricted to rites and ceremonies. The majority of the songs are the exclusive property of definite clans and families. Like totems or coats-of-arms they are heirlooms, and almost never changed hands in the past.

Just as the songs of the coast differed from those of the mountainous interior, so did the respective drums. The coast drums were made of a thin slab of red cedar bent into a large square box, which was suspended from the roof of the house by a cord that fanned out at the bottom like the fingers of a hand. The drum of the interior, like that of the palæo-Siberian tribes, consisted of the dressed skin of a moose, beaver or caribou, stretched on a slender wooden frame, round and perfectly even, and was held in the singer's left hand and beaten with a drumstick. The sound of the coast drum was muffled and cavernous; it seemed to rise from the lower world. That of the interior was clear, tuneful, vibrant; it came from the heights, from the sky.

A few examples, disembodied of texture though they may be in mere black and white, will give a faint idea of their life-like quality. One of the so-called mountain love songs—*Temrsta angyalaw* (I am a chief)—is the challenge of a chief who boasts of his victories over women. Its tune is like the breeze in the clear air. The words are strong: "You shall not be my successful rival, for I have always been bold since my youth. I am a chief, you cannot excel me. I will blaze the trail and you will follow like a slave in my path." Yet it sounds more like an appeal or the cooing of an adolescent pining for love in the foliage. It was first sung by a Bear Lake Indian of a Wolf clan, named Otter, who composed it about sixty years ago. It was meant to relieve his feelings, after his wife had deserted him. Yearning in the tune prevailed over his futile taunts.

Another lyric song, of a different kind, is *Haythwil nuway* (Near death am I). It goes on to say: "What has befallen me! The people have cast me aside. I walk about among the tall trees. Where can I find a thing to gladden my heart? If you speak to me now your voice will soothe my heart." Its tune, unaccompanied by the drum, is "primitive" and strange. It is of the chromatic type, but is at variance with our musical habits because of its whole-tone scale with gaps; its range is wide—an octave and a fourth. A Gitksan song, from up the Skeena River, it was sung by Watserh, "Mad Otter," who said that it had been a favourite of the old people in the interior.

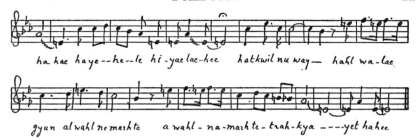

Among the finest songs of this musical people—for the natives are in the habit of singing by tradition from birth—are the lullabies and the dirges. The lullabies are graceful and lovely, showing the deep affection of parents for children, the pride of the chiefs in their heirs, and their hopes for a bright future. They are the private property of the families that use them; in so far as they refer to family history and privileges they are like the coats of arms or totems familiar on the carved poles of the Northwest Coast.

Nadudu (Dear little boy!), given here, belongs to a clan of Eagles on the Nass and speaks of the hunting grounds of Hyanmas, on the Portland Canal. This Eagle clan still remembers its migrations down the coast from the north. Originally it had come from Asia over the Bering Strait, like the other tribes of the far Northwest. The words of the song in the refrain are: "Dear boy [*nadu*], dear boy, dear little boy." The child then is supposed to speak to his mother, while she rocks him to sleep in her arms: "Sit up at night, my sister! Sit up at night with me, to make me grow, till I become a man. I will go to the large creeks of my forefathers, to Hyanmas, where I will catch the spring salmon. Then I will fish at Echo-cliffs, and I will gather the backbones of salmon—only the backbones!—for Thunder Woman, my sister!" Thunder Woman is a term applied to an old woman unable to work any longer; and she is fed on fish spines.

The scale in *Nadudu* is of the pentatonic type, with an intriguing augmented fourth. In Mme d'Harcourt's opinion, it oscillates between two scale forms, the one major in feeling, the other minor, with the rise and fall involved in this shifting.

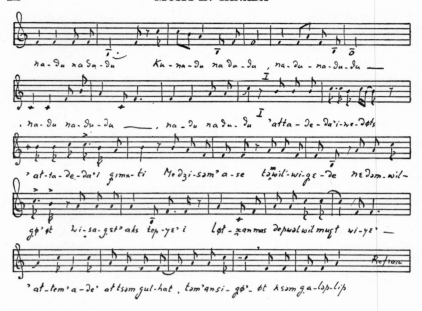

na-ᵭu na ᵭu-ᵭu   Ku-na-ᵭu na ᵭa-ᵭu , na-ᵭu-na-ᵭu-ᵭu ＿

. na-ᵭu na-ᵭu-ᵭu ＿ , na-ᵭu na ᵭu-ᵭu 'atta-ᵭe-ᵭa'i-�-ᵭots

' at-ta-ᵭe-ᵭa'i gimn-ti Meᵭᴣi-sɔm' a-se tᵊwil-wi-gɛ-ᵭe neᵭɔm-wil-

gᵩ'ᵩt wi-sa-gɛt'aks tep-yɛ' i   lᵩt-ᴣanmas ᵭepwalwilmuʃt wi-yɛ' ＿

' at-tem'a-ᵭe' attsɔm gul-hat , tɔm'ansi-gᵩ'-ᵩt ksɔm ga-lɔp-liʃ

The dirges are more poignant than anything I have yet heard anywhere. Some of them are weird in the extreme. For once in the lives of
stoic Indians, they cast restraint to the winds, and give vent to pathos
and grief. No one could resist the sense of utter tragedy that fills the
air as soon as the drum beats its deep note and a voice redolent with
pain cries out the first sounds of the traditional dirge. The gates to the
nether world are opened and the people bow their heads in the
presence of Fate. Professional criers (like those of ancient Greece)
rend the air with their lament, tear their hair and sprinkle ashes over
their heads. When Ernest MacMillan and I were spending some time
together on the lower Nass, close to the Portland Canal, a tragedy un-
expectedly brought grief to the natives stationed at a cannery where
we camped: several Indians died of poisoning after eating decayed
salmon roe. Dirges broke out early one morning, and throughout the
days that followed we could hear women moaning in the woods
around us. Even their weeping was song-like, though very uncon-
ventional.

For impressiveness nothing approached the song of Skateen, the
Wolf head chief of a Nass River tribe. The lament of the mourners

rose plaintively and fell in descending curves, like the wind in a storm.
It was the voice of nature crying out. In modernity it went beyond the
moderns. The intervals sounded strange, at times rather like quarter
tones. I heard MacMillan say, when he was transcribing it from the
phonograph: "These things can't be written down on our stave, they
simply can't." But they could to a modest extent, our stave being a
rack upon which to pin down sounds and rhythms whatever they are,
at least approximately. And here is his transcription as it looks. The
syllables *Hano* are meaningless. The only words of the song are: "He
used to be the head chief!" Mme d'Harcourt comments that this song
is a magnificent, yet primitive, chant, with a groping, tragic grandeur,
which is very close to a pure natural lament, and cannot be analysed
according to our usual musical standards.

The songs of other nations in the Rockies are often quite different
from those of the Skeena and Nass River tribes. Only one example,
The Blue Jay, can be given here. It belongs to the Salish tribes of the
Rockies closer to the American border. It was recorded in 1912 from a
Thompson River chief, along with a number of other Salish songs that
closely resemble the chants of palæo-Siberian tribes, among them the
Chukchee and the Koriaks. Its vocal utterance is at times bird-like
(like the blue jay's warbling).

SONGS OF THE WHITE MAN

French-Canadian songs and those of other white races in Canada are utterly different from those of the original Canadians—the Indians. Their appeal for us is that they are better known, being part of the heritage of all Europeans. Their scales, modes and rhythms, although none too familiar at the present day, have a ring of pertinence that will be of help here, in their token presentation.

After the French had established their early settlements (from 1608 on) on the St. Lawrence, Detroit, Ohio, Missouri, and Red rivers, and in Louisiana, the colonists had frequent opportunities to rub elbows with the Redskins. This happened still more frequently when the *voyageurs* and *coureurs de bois* engaged in the fur trade. Their journeys extended as far as the western prairies, and some of them adopted the Indian way of life. The missionaries from the first endeavoured to implant Christianity among their neophytes and taught them hymns and Gregorian chants. The Ursulines and other nuns in Quebec, Three Rivers, Montreal, and New Orleans educated native girls in their convents, and made of them French *demoiselles*. The Indians and the French were friendly to one another, and cultural exchanges between them were common. The French borrowed the snowshoe, the toboggan, the birchbark canoe and many other useful devices. The Indians imitated whatever appealed to their fancy or aroused their admiration in costume, embroidery with moose hair, porcupine quill or bead work, and adopted metal utensils and trinkets. Canticles, like *Jesus ahatonhia* in Huron (already well known in print), were composed by the missionaries for the missions and were chanted in the chapels. Native and French songs should have mingled and produced a blend that might intrigue our curiosity. Yet this did not happen, save that the Huron way of singing "sagamité dances" at Lorette, as recorded in 1911, was somewhat assimilated to the French scales and tonality. French folk-tales were readily transfused into the lore of the Northeastern woodlands. Otherwise, the prehistoric traditions, on one side, were left unimpaired almost to the present day, and, on the other, the French-Canadian repertoire contains no trace of skin drum and dance rhythms and pentatonic tunes.

What songs the *voyageurs* and canoemen used in the early days of exploration and fur trade in the Far West had long seemed a problem. The usual assumption was that they differed from those current among the home folk along the St. Lawrence. The Ermatinger Collection presented in 1954 in the *Journal of American Folklore*[2] brings a clear answer to this question. A set of eleven typical paddling songs, collected about 125 years ago by Edward Ermatinger, a Swiss servant of the Hudson's Bay Company, at York Factory on the Red River and on the Columbia River, was recently discovered in manuscript form in Oregon. "Their tunes are rhythmical, and the solos, as in most work songs, alternate with a chorus ("refrain") which prolongs the action. . . . these songs belong . . . to the common stock of traditional folk songs brought over by the colonists from France at the beginning—

[2]No. 264, April-June, 1954, pp. 147–61.

mostly from 1640 to 1680. Even their deviations from the original pattern resulted from their vitality. Alive and variable, they constantly yielded a trifle to the mannerisms of individual singers and the utilities they served either in the settlements or in their peregrinations. Canoemen, more than others, were apt to fashion refrains that reflected new surroundings," such as rapids and portages, paddle and canoe.

The *voyageur* songs of the West were the first to attract the attention of European explorers, traders, and chroniclers; many references to them are found in print, all of them expressing surprise and praise. For instance, de la Rochefoucault, a French nobleman visiting Upper Canada in the early nineteenth century, wrote:

We were led by Canadians who, as is their wont, never ceased singing for a moment. Their songs are gay. . . . They are only interrupted by the laughter they bring forth. In all the canoe journeys undertaken by Canadians, songs follow the paddle, beginning as soon as it is picked up and ending when it is dropped. One has the pleasant illusion of being in provincial France.[3]

Among the best-known songs of the repertoire of French America, are *A Saint-Malo, A la claire fontaine, Le Rossignol y chante, M'en revenant de la jolie Rochelle, Ah! si mon moine voulait danser, Les Roses blanches.* Of *Trois Beaux Canards* alone, over 100 versions so far have been recorded, and 92 of them have been published in condensed form, with over 30 entirely different tunes, in the *Archives de Folklore.*[4]

The first Canadians to collect folk-songs in earnest and to publish them were F. A. H. Larue and Ernest Gagnon, of Quebec, in the early 1860's.[5] Gagnon's substantial *Chansons populaires du Canada,* in several editions since 1865, contains about one hundred songs. This collection produced the impression that with it the repertoire of French-Canadian folk-songs was exhausted. It was only in 1915, fifty years later, that I felt prompted to probe the possibilities of a further

[3]*Ibid.,* p. 148. Other descriptions were given by Duflos de Mofras for the Columbia River (in 1844); Thomas Moore, the Irish poet, for the upper St. Lawrence (1803); Mrs. Simcoe (*Diary,* 1792–6); Mrs. Anna Jameson (1836); Baird in his *Recollections of Wisconsin* (1859); Frank B. Mayer (Diary, 1851); R. M. Ballantyne, in his *Hudson's Bay* (1848); John Mactaggart, in his *Three Years in Canada* (1829); Gabriel Franchère, in his *Relation* . . . (1810); John McGill, a bourgeois of the fur trade and the Beaver Club, Montreal; John J. Bigsby, in *The Shoe and Canoe* (1850); J. G. Kohl, in *Kitchi-Gami* (about 1850); and a number of others. All these are quoted in *Journal of American Folklore,* no. 264, 1954.

[4]No. 2, 1947 (Université Laval, Québec).

[5]Cf. *Journal of American Folklore,* no. 264, 1954, p. 167.

collection. The results have since proved overwhelming—500 items for a single summer in 1916 in Charlevoix and Chicoutimi counties of Quebec. The heritage of French-Canadian folk-songs and legends, after many more years of research, now seems inexhaustible. Over 7,000 tunes and 13,000 texts have been rescued from oblivion since in all parts of the old French territories. These records were made at first on the phonograph and in manuscript, later on magnetic tapes. They are now preserved at the National Museum of Canada in Ottawa and in the Archives de Folklore at Université Laval, Québec. The harvest still goes on, in the face of rapidly declining resources. "Progress" in our country is as destructive as it is abroad, in this and other fields of oral tradition.

In a space so short, it is impossible to give enough illustrations of the outstanding traits of French-Canadian folk-music. The reader must make use of the publications already available in order to realize their variety and merit. A few examples here may, however, serve to emphasize some of their least-known features. These and others, in a rich assortment, should furnish musicians and composers with materials for inspiration in a refreshed musical language.

To use the words of Mme Marguerite Béclard d'Harcourt again:[6] "The treasure saved for us is a splendid restoration [restitution merveilleuse] for which we no longer had any reason to hope. . . . These songs fill us with joy because of their expressive beauty, their ornate flexibility, their rhythmic and modal variety. They make us realize the musical empoverishment that France has undergone since it gave birth to this amazing New World expansion." Gabriel Marcel, a French commentator, added: "One feels that this music which originated in our land long ago, has been saved all the while as if under a protective blanket of snow." And Mme d'Harcourt concludes: "The French Canadian rhythms make us sensible of the flexibility of our ancient chants. Fortunately, they have not been brought under the rigid rule of the barred measure, and the tunes have gone on swaying to the free inspiration of the *muse populaire*. This does not mean that they cannot be written like our modern music, . . . but they accept fantasies, syncopations [enjambements], displaced and unexpected accents which show us once more that rhythm and measure must not be mistaken for the same thing. . . ." In France, says Mme d'Harcourt, the notation of folk-songs in our time often has been falsified, and "the tunes have abdicated all independence, to accept the new mould

[6]Marius Barbeau, *Romancero du Canada* (Montréal: Editions Beauchemin, 1937), pp. 10–11.

forced upon them. But the voice which comes to us from French Canada has preserved all its youth and freshness. This is what makes it now so precious to us."

The following examples of melodies (without the full texts) will speak for themselves, and illustrate the modes, the modulations, the syncopated rhythms or *enjambements* and displaced accents, and the barred or measured tunes.

The melody of *Les Trois Roses empoisonnées* was the object of the following analysis in my *Romancero* (pp. 107–11): "No better example of an intricate profile [ligne fleurie] can be found. The form and structure of this tune are mediaeval and we seem to hear the accompaniment [déchant] in fifths and fourths under the melody, like an embryo of vocal counterpoint which was to reach such perfection in the sixteenth century, among the masters of the Renaissance. One must possess a well-trained voice to execute with elegance its curvilines, and its integral preservation is due to the vocal skill of the Canadian folksingers. . . ." Its mode is G, with the G tonic.

One of the loveliest melodies of the whole lyrical repertoire, *Jolie Batelière*, oscillates nonchalantly between the two divisions of the 2/4 and 6/8 rhythms and its syncopations are brought out in repeated accents on the regular beat. Its mode is Dorian (in D) and secondary emphases are on A and C.

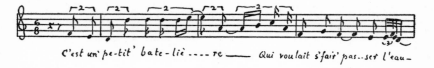

The lively rhythm of *La Liptitou* (see *Romancero*, pp. 237–8) is free and syncopated and quite suitable for dance steps. Key of D major.

FOLK-SONG TODAY

The blight that has descended upon the sheltered expanses of French folklore in recent decades has also visited all the rest of Canada from the Atlantic to the Pacific and the Arctic. A few communities still retain the vital integrity of their folk traditions because of geographic isolation; these are still to be found in many English folk-songs imbued with Irish traditionalism; in Gaelic songs of Cape Breton; in English songs less conservatively preserved and often with a Scottish flavour, in Nova Scotia; in Cayuga and Seneca (Iroquois) songs of the Grand River reserve of Ontario and the reserves of western New York state. This is also true of the Kwakiutl of the North Pacific coast, and some of the Eskimo to the far north, the prairie tribes of Saskatchewan and Alberta and among the nomadic Dénés of the far Northwest. Some of the new Canadians of western Canada—Ukrainians, Doukhobors and others, as represented by their elders—still cling to a fast disappearing heritage of eastern Europe; a number of their songs have been recorded by Mrs. Laura Boulton under the auspices of the National Film Board of Canada. Archaic Yiddish folk songs of real quality have been recovered in recent years by Mrs. Ruth Rubin[7] in Montreal. She wishes to extend her research to Quebec and Toronto, where there is a considerable Jewish population from various parts of eastern Europe.

A notable outpost of folk-song is Newfoundland, which recently has been explored on behalf of the National Museum of Canada, first by Margaret Sargent (now Mrs. MacTaggart), and then twice by Kenneth Peacock. Other folklorists, chiefly Maud Karpeles,[8] and Elisabeth B. Greenleaf and Grace Y. Mansfield,[9] discovered this field, while the other Maritime Provinces have been probed extensively by W. Roy Mackenzie,[10] Helen Creighton,[11] whose research is being continued for the National Museum, and Louise Manny, of Newcastle, Miramichi, New Brunswick, who has amassed a large number of folksongs and tales for the private collection of Lord Beaverbrook.

The recent discoveries of Kenneth Peacock cannot be described in better terms than his own, as expressed in six CBC broadcasts on

---

[7]*Journal of American Folklore*, no. 257, July-Sept., 1952.

[8]*Folk Songs from Newfoundland*, 2 vols. (1934).

[9]*Ballads and Sea Songs of Newfoundland* (Cambridge, Mass., 1933).

[10]*The Quest of the Ballad* (Princeton, N.J., 1919), and *Ballads and Sea Songs of Nova Scotia* (Cambridge, Mass., 1928).

[11]*Songs and Ballads from Nova Scotia* (Toronto: J. M. Dent and Sons, 1932); *Traditional Songs from Nova Scotia*, collected by Helen Creighton and Doreen H. Senior (Toronto: Ryerson, 1950); and other publications.

"Folk Songs from Newfoundland," in the winter of 1954. From these only a sample or two can be given here by way of illustration.

. . . from the countless impressions of the island I remember and half-remember, three stand out clearly from all the rest—a dogged spirit of independence, an unreserved hospitality, and the sea. . . .

Wherever people are situated in isolated groups facing common hardships and dangers it seems inevitable that they should develop and preserve specialized customs, songs, stories, superstitions, and so on—in short, a unique tradition. Such is the case in Newfoundland. North, south, east, and west, the island abounds in stories and songs about the sea, the lumber camps, and the ancestral life in Britain and Ireland. It is a veritable treasure-house of medieval legends, Elizabethan ballads, and local stories and songs. . . .

As you might suspect, the older songs of English and Irish vintage are more numerous in [the] comparatively remote settlements where there has been little contact with our urban culture, and where the old customs and religious orthodoxies still persist. Elsewhere, the locally composed song holds sway. . . .

. . . although the fiddle has lost its former popularity, you can be sure someone will bring along an accordion or guitar to furnish music for dancing. The player often sings alone, banging out the rhythm loudly with his foot. Since the kitchen is the focal point of social life, table and chairs are moved to one side or thrown out altogether, and the dancing begins.

. . . there is . . . a large body of . . . older songs, many of which were popular in the Old Country two or three hundred years ago—songs which have been passed on through many generations of Newfoundlanders. Some can even be traced back to medieval times. . . . While travelling in some of the remoter areas in northeastern Newfoundland, I felt I was entering a completely different world, a world held in suspension since Elizabethan times. . . .

. . . With the exception of a Gaelic community in the Codroy Valley and one or two French settlements . . ., almost all the Old World songs come from Britain and Ireland. Although the English songs are quite numerous, it is the Irish tradition which colours the style of singing and the composition of local songs. . . . As a matter of fact, most of the English songs I collected were sung by people of Irish descent living in Roman Catholic communities where the old customs and values are continually fostered. . . .

[In performance] complicated melodic turns and squiggles are often used to emphasize key words in the text. And when the singer comes to one of his favourite passages in the song, he may depart from the basic form altogether and swing into an improvised cadenza of his own.

It was in . . . four outposts [Fogo Island, Joe Batt's Arm, Barred Island, Tilting] I came across [this] unusual style of singing. . . .

The tradition of composing songs about local events is still kept up in some parts of Newfoundland, and each year brings a new crop of ballads about life in the outports on the sealing expeditions, or in the lumbercamps. Often a group of men sharing a common experience will spend an hilarious evening composing a song about it, each of them contributing a verse or two. Or perhaps if one of the men is exceptionally gifted and is widely known for his previous songs, the job of composing will be entirely handed over to him. In Barred Islands I met a man whose reputation for composing songs has spread all over the northeast coast. Everyone told me to be sure and drop in on Chris Cobb who could sing for three days without repeating himself. I didn't have a chance to put him to the test, but when he produced several school notebooks filled with hundreds of songs his daughter had copied for him, I was inclined to think the legend was a little conservative. He writes about every conceivable facet of outport life including a personal experience of his own when he was cast adrift on an ice floe for several days. One of my favourites described the election of a famous old-time politician Sir William Coaker, the man who started the local fishermen's union. It's the first song Chris Cobb ever composed. . . .

Michael Aylmard, of King's Cove, Newfoundland, sang for Kenneth Peacock in 1952 *My Gallant Brigantine*, described by the collector as "Pure Dorian, with a fairly wide range (from C to high G), and swinging phrases of great breadth."

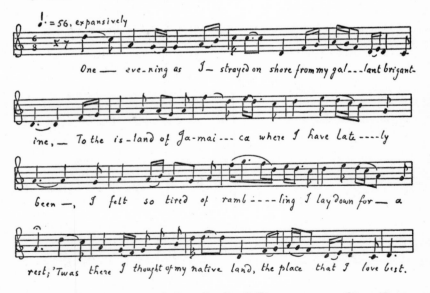

Margaret Sargent recorded a Gaelic fulling song on Cape Breton Island, from Lilias Towers, in 1950. It is sung when fulling the homespun. This is done by a group assembled around a long table, on which the wet and soaped cloth is kneaded by many hands swinging to the rhythm of this work song. It has been transcribed by Kenneth Peacock. Its mode is Aeolian.

The Maid on the Shore has been adapted from W. Roy Mackenzie's collection in *Ballads and Sea Songs from Nova Scotia*. It is in the Mixolydian (G) mode.

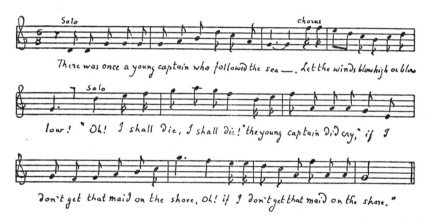

There was once a young captain who followed the sea ___. Let the winds blow high or blow low! "Oh! I shall die, I shall die!" the young captain did cry, "if I don't get that maid on the shore, Oh! if I don't get that maid on the shore."

Lastly I give *A Rose in the Garden,* an Irish love song in the Dorian (D) mode, which I recorded and transcribed from Linda Kearns, of Low, Gatineau River, Quebec, about 1920.

Oh! come, sit- down close to me, my dear, While I sing you a mer-ry song! 'Tis now for- us well - o- ver a year Since together you and I have

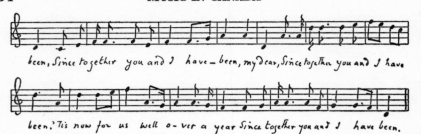

been, Since together you and I have — been, my dear, Since together you and I have

been.' Tis now for us well o-ver a year Since together you and I have been.

Much might be said of folk-songs of other origins found in Canada, but the writer hopes he has shown how immensely rich is the field.

COMPOSITION

Jean-Marie Beaudet

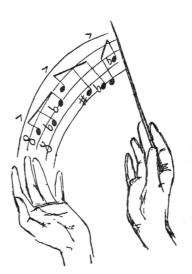

It is usual to begin the criticism of a modern composer by speculating about his ultimate position in history. When this custom has become obsolete, musical criticism will have some chance of uttering a few sensible remarks. The present age will be like every other age in the history of the fine arts, in that a small fraction of one per cent. of what is now most talked about will be not only talked about but enjoyed a hundred or two hundred years hence. Of this I am quite sure, but I am not going to be such a fool as to say which works of the present day will belong to that percentage. Posterity has done nothing for me that should oblige me to bother about its judgement.

Donald Francis Tovey, *Essays in Musical Analysis,* **IV**

Although in this country musical composition has lagged far behind performance, a surprising amount of music has been written here by Canadians, born and adopted. Three hundred and fifty-six names are listed in Helmut Kallman's *Catalogue of Canadian Composers;*[1] of these composers about two-thirds are native-born. It is significant that about two-thirds are still living, although some thirty are no longer resident in Canada. A few French names date back to the eighteenth and even the seventeenth centuries but the vast majority of Canadian works are contemporaneous—or nearly so.

Evidently our traditions were neither old enough nor deep enough to be considered as the foundation of truly characteristic and distinctive Canadian music, especially as so much of our musical development has taken place on local and provincial lines. In order to be national an art must reflect the way of thinking, the social conditions, the aspirations of a people. Even the many excellent arrangements of our folk-music—French, English, Scottish, Irish and so on—cannot be said to constitute a Canadian style. It may never prove possible to develop such a thing. Whether it is even desirable to do so is a moot question; perhaps a people so diverse in origin and traditions, living in a country so vast and varied in geographical features, may by-pass the national phase through which most European nations have passed.

[1]Published in 1952 by the Canadian Broadcasting Corporation.

As is to be expected, in the majority of Canadian works one can trace European influences. Many of our teachers are of European origin and education. Some of our composers have acquired much of their training in Europe; many of our students still go abroad to complete their studies. Of recent years a large number of internationally famous composers have taken up residence in the United States and young Canadians have taken advantage of their presence to work with them. Hindemith, Milhaud, Stravinsky, Bartok, Schoenberg and others have played their part in the education of Canadian students. Nor are such influences to be in any way deprecated for, at the origin of all arts, there has been a period of imitation and each generation carries forward the accomplishment of the last. The wise and conscientious teacher does not impose his own style and personality on a pupil: rather does he guide him and open up new horizons to his imagination. Time and hard work are often the most important factors in the long process of reaching full maturity.

But the opening up of new horizons does not depend upon the teacher alone. Thirty years ago even the most talented student was rarely encouraged to stray far beyond the field represented by his own instrument and his knowledge even of the literature of that instrument was in many cases woefully meagre. The average student heard far too little music—sometimes almost none in fields other than his own. Nowadays the concert season in our larger centres affords rich opportunities to those who will take advantage of them. Still more helpful has been the influence of the radio and the gramophone record, which enable the student—or for that matter any music-lover—to hear far more music of past and present than was possible in any previous generation. And in listening to mechanically reproduced music, the hearer is more acutely conscious of the personality of the composer and less hypnotized by that of a glamorous performer than in the concert hall.

Another factor making for the recent creative activity in Canada has been our growing consciousness of nationhood. Even though we have not developed any recognizably national musical idiom, we feel all about us a growing realization that a nation without art is no nation at all. It may be that, at the present stage, we are too self-conscious about our need of culture—a typically adolescent attitude. There are those among us who welcome a new work, not on account of its innate merits, but because it is the work of a Canadian. Some of our composers are themselves aware of this. "It is not desirable," says one of them, Jean Vallerand, "that the public should acclaim every stammering effort simply because it has been written by a Canadian; the Canadian composer must fall in line, accepting comparison and competition with all the composers of the past two or three centuries. We ask neither of the Canadian composer nor of the French or Czech composer that he have as much genius as Monteverdi, Bach or Mozart; but we demand that he teach us things which we would not know of ourselves, for it is the chief function of a work of art to reveal Man to Man."[2]

It cannot however be said that as a rule the Canadian composer suffers from excessive acclaim and recognition: rather the contrary. He finds it difficult to get his more important works published, for publishers, being business men rather than philanthropists, are generally reluctant to publish works for which they do not forsee a reasonable financial return. A glance at Mr. Kallmann's catalogue, already mentioned, will reveal that nearly all the published works are songs, short piano or violin pieces, choral numbers suitable for use in churches or competition festivals and, of course, works in the so-called "popular" vein. The vast majority of serious and extended works remain in manuscript. However even these are often made available through various types of photographic reproduction. Often such reproductions are made at the expense of a composer who can ill afford such a luxury but sometimes he can find an organization or individual who will assume it for him. The CBC, or example, has been very helpful in this respect, especially with works commissioned by the Corporation.

Royalties on published music amount on the whole to less than they did formerly, when people depended on live performances and accordingly bought copies for themselves. However the composers whose music is performed can usually derive some revenue from performing fees through the Composers, Authors and Publishers Association of Canada (CAPAC), affiliate of ASCAP, PRS and similar societies in other countries. Broadcast Music Incorporated (B M I) also compensates its members and in some cases undertakes publication of their works. These bodies have, on occasion, made valuable contributions by sponsorship of complete orchestral programmes of Canadian works; the New York concert organized by B M I in October, 1953, and that arranged by CAPAC in Toronto some years earlier are notable instances. A most enterprising symposium of Canadian music, covering several days and presenting a wide variety of styles, was held in Van-

[2]From an article in *Le Journal musical canadien*, June, 1954.

couver about five years ago under the sponsorship of the British Columbia Arts Council. The Forest Hill Community group in Toronto for some time commissioned two works annually to be presented on its programmes. Other organizations have played their part but perhaps the most notable endeavour of recent years has been that of a group of the composers themselves. The Canadian League of Composers, the membership of which is largely of the younger generation representing the more "advanced" schools, gives a series of programmes annually in Toronto and Montreal of works selected by a special committee; these range from fully orchestral works to chamber music for small groups and solo numbers. In this project the League has received financial support from private individuals and, in some cases, the cooperation of the CBC. Les Jeunesses Musicales have also assisted materially in presenting Canadian works from time to time. Our leading orchestras and other concert-giving bodies frequently include Canadian numbers on their programmes, sometimes, it must be confessed, in the face of public apathy, for the majority of concert-goers in Canada do not seem to take kindly to novelties.

All in all, the outlook for Canadian music is brighter now than at any previous time. True, the composer of serious music is not yet able to make his living through composition alone but he continues his creative activity and the volume of his output is very considerable. Let us now attempt to review some of the more notable features of contemporary Canadian works; some mention of the composers of the past will be found in the historical chapter of this book.

For the purpose of a classification—though to some people the result may appear arbitrary—it does not seem unfair to divide Canadian composers into three categories: those whose styles are derived respectively from French, British and other traditions. The last group might be subdivided in two: neo-Canadians who follow traditional methods derived from various European countries and those composers, native or adopted, who employ a newer technique such as Schoenberg's twelve-tone or Stravinsky's neo-classicism. The merits of individual composers have in my opinion nothing to do with this grouping, nor would I wish to classify them according to merit. My only concern is to find out whether the state of our music production is healthy or anaemic.

Claude Champagne and Georges-Emile Tanguay are possibly the outstanding names in French-Canadian music, if not on account of the volume of their works, certainly because of their influence on the younger generation—even though some of their disciples are now flying on their own wings and have evaded "the enchanting atmosphere of tranquillity and contentment" which Dr. Arnold Walter finds characteristic of French-Canadian music. Tanguay's writing is serene and discreet. His music tends to be lyrical and reveals subtle harmonies rather than rhythmic or dissonant experiments. In too few and too short works he shows himself a pure musician. Champagne is one of the few composers who has made discriminating and intelligent use of French-Canadian folk-song. The rhythmic and moral characteristics of folk-song have been the source of inspiration of many of his compositions, especially in his *Symphonie gaspésienne* and the *Images du Canada français* for chorus and orchestra. His style has the clarity and logic of the best French tradition and his orchestration is always very colourful.

I could not ignore the names of the late Guillaume Couture, J.-J. Gagnier, Alexis Contant and Léo-Pol Morin. Guillaume Couture with his oratorio *Jean le Précurseur* was himself a "précurseur" and Léo-Pol Morin, under the pen-name of James Callihou, as one of the most ardent propagandists of contemporary music about the 1920's certainly aroused interest and curiosity in the musical idiom then considered modern.

Hector Gratton and Gabriel Cusson are also members of the more conservative wing of the French-Canadian composers.

The younger generation, however, has departed somewhat from the older French tradition. Pierre Mercure, Jean Papineau-Couture, Clermont Pépin, Jean Vallerand, Maurice Blackburn, François Morel, Roger Matton, Rosette Renshaw and others all follow the more intricate and hazardous paths of modernism, be it Bartok's, Stravinsky's, Messiaen's or Hindemith's. If to many people their music sometimes sounds too experimental, one must not forget that the law of the pendulum will probably correct what may at first sight appear extravagant.

I would also be remiss if, to what I consider an already impressive list, I did not add the names of Michel Perrault, Maurice Dela and Victor Bouchard who bring a delicate, peaceful and more consonant voice to the French-Canadian concert.

The English tradition is certainly predominant in Canada outside of Quebec. Healey Willan is the dean of English-Canadian musicians; born in England, he has made Canada his home since 1913. His musical influence has been tremendous. He, like Champagne in Montreal, has been the guiding light of many a young composer. Walter Mac-Nutt, Godfrey Ridout, Eldon Rathburn, Robert Fleming and Harry Freedman, to name only these, have benefited from his vast knowledge and experience.

Dr. Willan has written some two hundred works ranging from symphonies to poetic arrangements of folk-songs and including three operas as well as a very large amount of church and organ music. His music has sound architectural construction, and his lyricism, if more dramatic at times than Tanguay's, is always predominant. The harmonies, though traditional, are always rich and colourful. He is in complete possession of his *métier*.

Another leading figure as a composer as well as a performer is Sir Ernest MacMillan, Conductor of the Toronto Symphony Orchestra since 1931 and of the Mendelssohn Choir since 1942. Sir Ernest has been at the forefront of the musical life of Canada, but his many activities have of late years left him little time for composition. Besides a number of choral, orchestral and chamber works, he has made many settings of French-Canadian and Indian folk-songs.

A number of our leading composers, in addition to some already mentioned, have occupied positions in Canadian universities where they have exercised a steady influence on students of the younger generation. One thinks of Graham George, at Queen's University, Kingston and of Murray Adaskin at Saskatoon; both of these have contributed considerably themselves to the list of Canadian works. The late Leo Smith of Toronto is remembered for his many songs and chamber works. Alfred Whitehead, recently retired from the directorship of music at Mount Allison University, has produced much extensively used church and organ music as well as folk-song arrangements. Thomas Crawford, formerly a member of the faculty of the Royal Conservatory, has made many contributions in the organ, orchestral and other fields. The choral music of W. H. Anderson of Winnipeg is also greatly in demand for use in churches and at competitive festivals; Arthur Egerton, too, has written a number of fine choral and organ works. Indeed one might expand the list to large proportions.

It would be unfair to pass over a number of Canadian-born composers who are no longer resident in Canada but have gained notable reputations in other lands: for example, Gena Branscombe, Minuetta Borek, Dorothy Cadzow, Colin McPhee and Geoffrey O'Hara—writers of entirely different types, who are now living in the United States—

or Robert Farnon who as a composer of light music has won wide acclaim in England. We must regret the return to England of the Australian-born Arthur Benjamin, a number of whose notable works were written during the period of his residence in Vancouver and who during that time exercised an important influence on some of our younger composers.

A significant group of composers is engaged chiefly in writing background music for films and for radio drama. For many years the direction of music for the National Film Board (of which an account will be given elsewhere in this volume) was in the hands of Louis Applebaum, who now divides his time between this and similar activities in the United States. The Film Board has at present three composers on its regular staff—Maurice Blackburn, Robert Fleming and Eldon Rathburn—and frequently engages other composers for special work. Lucio Agostini, who writes extensively for films, is perhaps the best known among writers of dramatic background music for radio; another name familiar in this connection is that of Morris Surdin. All these show great resource, ingenuity and skill in adapting themselves to the exacting demands of these special techniques. Having to write frequently for small instrumental groups, composers of background music have often relied on striking rhythm, dissonant effects, linear though amelodic themes and even on abstractions. These composers have not, of course, confined themselves to background music but have contributed, sometimes extensively, to the concert repertoire.

The "independent" group—which might include some of the young French-Canadians already mentioned—has been experimenting with various techniques. It would be neither easy nor profitable to label these composers with the name of this or that school; a number base their methods on more than one type of modern music and some seem still to be finding their feet. A great deal of their music is enjoyable to those whose ears are attuned to contemporary music of other countries; its ultimate value will be decided by posterity. One cannot, however, say that the greater part of it appeals to the majority of present-day audiences.

Perhaps the most consistent followers of Schoenberg's twelve-tone technique are John Weinzweig and Barbara Pentland. As the president of the League of Composers and a professor in the Faculty of Music at the University of Toronto, Weinzweig exercises a strong influence on many of the younger writers, such as Harry Somers, Harry Freedman, Andrew Twa and others. In Montreal, Alexander Brott has a wide following and much of his music has won acclaim abroad. Among women writers, Violet Archer and Jean Coulthard have produced a number of noteworthy works. The music of John Beckwith often shows a delicate fancy and feeling for colour, and that of Neil Chotem, who is also an excellent pianist, has a strongly individual flavour. Above all, the work of these younger men abounds in vitality and augurs well for the future.

Among our neo-Canadians I would mention particularly Dr. Arnold Walter, Director of the Faculty of Music at Toronto, Walter Kaufmann, Conductor of the Winnipeg Symphony Orchestra, the brilliant organist Quentin Maclean, the Esthonian Udo Kasemets and the Czech Oscar Morawetz. The first four received their training in Europe, Mr. Morawetz partly in Canada. Moderately conservative though by no means reactionary, their music might well re-establish a balance with that of the more extreme modernists.

Most of the composers mentioned above, whatever their idiom, have written in the elaborate forms of music. Their works include symphonies, symphonic poems, overtures, suite for large and small orchestras, concertos, operas, oratorios. Many have written chamber music works for varied instrumental combinations as well as solo numbers for different instruments.

However, there are two fields of activity which play an important part in our musical life although less known to the general public: sacred music for chorus, organ or vocal solo and teaching manuals. Few realize how many Canadian composers have devoted at least part of their energies to sacred music. A list would include W. H. Anderson, Violet Archer, Gerald Bales, Maurice Blackburn, Gena Branscombe, Marius Cayouette, Alexis Contant, Guillaume Couture, Maurice Dela, Marvin Duchow, Arthur Egerton, Robert Fleming, Henri Gagnon, Graham George, Frederick Karam, Ada Twohy Kent, Claude Lavoie, Clarence Lucas, Quentin Maclean, Ernest MacMillan, Frederick Silvester, Georges-Emile Tanguay, Alfred Whitehead and Healey Willan. (The reader is also referred to the chapters on church music.) A precious contribution to the teaching repertoire has been made by composers Boris Berlin, Frank Blachford, Ada Twohy Kent, Healey Willan, Clarence Lucas, Ernest MacMillan and Walter MacNutt.

We have now come to the end of our survey. It is by no means complete, and much more could be said about Canadian music. Its state of health is most reassuring. A few years ago it would not have been possible to organize the concert of Canadian music given in New York in 1953 under Leopold Stokowski, the yearly concerts of the Canadian League of Composers, the Vancouver Symposium, and numerous other regular broadcasts of Canadian works by the CBC.

Our music may not yet have found its own distinctive language but it is certainly making rapid progress in that direction. We should not stop at this point and be satisfied to look behind. Canadian music has grown out of its infancy and cannot be considered any more as the poor relation of any other musical tradition. We must combine our energy and enthusiasm so that it may reach its maturity.

ORCHESTRAS

Wilfrid Pelletier

All music is what awakes from you when you are
reminded by the instruments,
It is not the violins and the cornets, it is not the oboe
nor the beating drums, nor the score of the baritone
singer singing his sweet romanza, nor that of the
men's chorus, nor that of the women's chorus,
It is nearer and farther than they.

Walt Whitman, *A Song for Occupations*

In this changing world, anyone attempting to write an account of orchestral playing in Canada must content himself with merely stating the facts: any other kind of approach may, within a short period of time, prove to be pure conjecture. For instance, in the *Report* of the Royal Commission on National Development in the Arts, Letters and Sciences, 1949–1951, the following statement appears on page 185: "In Canada, however, in addition to the normal indifference or hostility of audiences to new music and in addition to the consequent reluctance of orchestras and of performers to present music with very limited popular appeal, the composer of serious music is confronted with certain peculiar disabilities and hazards." This statement is already in 1954 open to challenge. In 1953 an orchestral programme of works by Canadian composers was given in Carnegie Hall, New York, the Conductor being Leopold Stokowski. A repeat performance of this programme in Montreal resulted in a sell-out, and was most enthusiastically received by the audience. A recent study of programming by various orchestras throughout Canada shows that the music of Canadian composers is being presented successfully and increasingly to Canadian audiences. At least one orchestra reports that one Canadian work is performed on each programme; there is reason to hope this will become the practice with more of our major orchestras. Today a symphony orchestra, in eastern Canada at least, cannot afford to ignore the Canadian artist or the Canadian composer.

The symphony orchestra in Canada is barely fifty years old, the oldest, that of Quebec, having been organized in 1902. Today at least thirty orchestral groups are in operation. Such a record is most encouraging. A steady advance has been made in the development of symphonic orchestras throughout a half-century marked by two world wars, a major depression and a period of intense, accelerated technological progress in sound reproduction.

Many factors have been involved in the growth of Canadian symphony orchestras. In the early years of its development, this young nation had little time or money to devote to formal, organized music. In fact, most of the musicians of that period played for their own enjoyment of the music rather than as a group identified with a community and with a special cultural mission. Recently, the son of the founder of the Quebec Symphony, Joseph Vézina, told me that the musicians of that orchestra—the first to be organized in Canada—gathered together weekly for the purpose of being able to play music together to their hearts' content.

Later on, serious problems arose. Assembling a sufficient number of trained musicians to form a group, establishing a means of developing and encouraging young musical talent, ensuring sufficient financial returns to support such a group within the community—all these present difficulties which have confronted, retarded and in some cases discouraged to the point of abandonment symphony orchestras in Canada. But they are not peculiarly Canadian problems. They have through the centuries attended the formation of many cultural movements in all parts of the world. Financing—perhaps the most critical one—has rarely been solved without the assistance of subsidies from public funds, local or national, or from individuals and groups. Some Canadian orchestras have benefited directly from provincial and municipal grants and indirectly from special concessions with regard to amusement tax. In Quebec the provincial government has played a major role in the cultural advancement of the Canadian artist through the Provincial Secretary's department and "L'Aide à la Jeunesse," which have subsidized and encouraged conservatories of music, orchestras, composers, instrumentalists, singers, writers, painters and sculptors, among others. Further public assistance, however, is greatly to be desired.

More peculiar to Canada is the handicap presented by the lack of adequate concert halls in all but a very few Canadian cities. Most Canadian orchestras give their concerts in school halls, picture theatres and other buildings where a small seating capacity may restrict box-office revenue or where acoustic qualities may leave much to be desired. In some communities concerts are given in large sports arenas whose capacity allows of low admission prices but whose acoustic properties have not been considered in their design. Although many Canadian schools are provided with excellent and sometimes large halls, it is rare to find one with a platform capable of accommodating seventy or eighty players. Great distances and comparatively small populations act as a further restriction to touring, especially in western Canada.

Rapidly changing conditions, the tremendous industrial growth of recent years, immigration, the expansion of our larger cities to suburban areas—all these have had their effect, both for good and ill, on our orchestras. But the most powerful factors have been the sound-movie and the radio, both of which have progressed rapidly and almost simultaneously since the late 1920's. Radio especially has played a definite and interesting role in this country's musical development. The radio station (usually in a metropolitan area) attracts qualified musicians away from the smaller communities, and symphony orchestras in those outlying areas suffer badly as a result. On the other hand, the radio not only affords the musician the opportunity of playing regularly—often in an ensemble—but also increases his means of livelihood. Above all, the radio and the gramophone record have created a widespread audience with a responsive ear for symphonic music. They have unquestionably been responsible for the rapid expansion of musical appreciation on a broader scale—more rapid than could have been accomplished through any other medium. The Canadian Broadcasting Corporation, with its well-planned programmes, has done more to create this awakening in Canada than any other single organization. Television holds much of the same potential, if intelligently used and properly directed.

As has been said, the oldest Canadian orchestra, according to official records, is L'Orchestre Symphonique de Québec, founded in 1902 and chartered the following year. In 1906 the Toronto Conservatory Symphony (which two years later became the Toronto Symphony) came into being. This was followed by the Edmonton Symphony in 1920, the Toronto Symphony (revived after some five years of inactivity) in 1923, the Regina Symphony in 1927 and the Vancouver Symphony in 1933. Montreal has had a somewhat chequered orchestral career. The original Montreal Symphony Orchestra, established in 1930, continued to function with Douglas Clarke as Conductor until 1941; in the meantime Les Concerts Symphoniques de Montréal were established in 1934 and have operated continuously since that time.

In 1954 the organization adopted the name of Montreal Symphony Orchestra. The year 1934 also witnessed the birth in Toronto of the summer Promenade Symphony Orchestra which was later to adopt the name of Toronto Philharmonic. From 1940 to 1946 five major orchestras were founded: the Montreal Women's Symphony, the Ottawa Philharmonic and the Victoria, Windsor and Winnipeg Symphonies, besides three amateur groups, in Kitchener, Sherbrooke and Three Rivers. Between 1948 and 1954, more than ten new orchestras have come into existence; three are professional—the Edmonton Symphony, the Halifax Symphonette and the York Concert Society (all beginning in 1952); two semi-professional—the Hamilton Philharmonic and the Edmonton Pops (1949); and four amateur—the St. Catharines Civic Orchestra, the London Chamber Orchestra, the Fredericton Civic Orchestra and the Victoria Little Symphony. Thus we see that, whereas in the thirty-five years from 1902 to 1937 ten orchestras were formed, the short span of the war years alone witnessed the formation of nine and the post-war years of at least as many more.

All of the provinces, except Prince Edward Island and Newfoundland, have at least one active orchestral group functioning. Ontario and Quebec have the largest concentration: Ontario with four professional, two semi-professional and four amateur orchestras, and Quebec with one professional, three semi-professional and one amateur group.

Reported budgets for the various orchestras range from about $6,000 to $300,000. In some cases orchestras are partially subsidized by municipal grants (e.g., in Montreal, Quebec, Toronto, Hamilton, Halifax, Winnipeg and Vancouver) or by the province (Nova Scotia and Quebec). The remainder of the budget is in most cases raised through public subscriptions or special donations.

The amount of orchestral music presented by the CBC is very large and the quality of the playing is often excellent. In addition to regular broadcasts of "live" concerts by the Toronto, Montreal, Vancouver and Winnipeg orchestras, and occasional broadcasts of others, the Corporation has organized its own orchestras of varying size in the leading cities; these are usually composed in part of members of the regular symphonic orchestras in their respective localities and give enterprising programmes, both under members of the staff and under guest conductors. Unlike the Australian Broadcasting Commission, and to some extent the British Broadcasting Corporation, the CBC does not undertake to give public concerts but, apart from a few exceptional cases, broadcasts programmes from its own studios usually without an audience. Since 1952 the CBC Orchestra has given regular weekly programmes from Toronto; the Little Symphony of Montreal has functioned over a longer period. Further evidence of the effect of broadcasting is seen in the increasing popularity of the chamber orchestra—so admirably adapted to broadcasting—and this has its effect also in the concert field. A number of the orchestras listed below number thirty players or less.

The following alphabetical listing of currently active orchestras,[1] (other than those devoted exclusively to broadcasting) has been compiled from information recently solicited and obtained from the orchestral groups themselves. The status of these orchestras is based on current activity, applicable to the season 1954–55. It is difficult to establish a completely fair standard of classification for all orchestras with regard to their rating—professional, semi-professional or amateur. Conditions vary in different localities. Some orchestras employ only full-time union men; others are made up of union men who may, however, be only part-time musicians. Others are composed chiefly of amateurs with a few professionals, and still others operate with varying numbers of all three types plus some qualified students. Because of this situation, only those groups which can be strictly classified as amateur have been so indicated in the listing.

CALGARY SYMPHONY ORCHESTRA (partly amateur)

Conductor: Clayton Hare

Organized in 1929, and reorganized in 1949, the Calgary Symphony presents four subscription and four children's concerts during its regular season, in the Grand Theatre (seating capacity 1,500). It has also appeared in neighbouring towns. Its business affairs are handled by a Board of Directors.

EDMONTON SYMPHONY ORCHESTRA

Conductor: Lee Hepner

The first Edmonton Symphony Orchestra was founded in 1920, and for ten years presented a winter concert season until sound films and the depression forced it out of existence. This group was followed by the Edmonton Philharmonic which performed from 1945 to 1950. Both of these orchestras were organized by interested musicians, and

[1]Since the writing of this chapter, the Hart House Chamber Orchestra has been founded in Toronto, under the conductorship of Boyd Neel. This orchestra will play a prominent part in the Stratford Festival of 1955.

their policies and affairs were administered by an executive chosen by and from the orchestra. The present Edmonton Symphony was founded in 1952 by Lee Hepner. It is subsidized by the Edmonton Symphony Society, which was organized at the same time and which assumes complete financial responsibility. The orchestra, consisting of sixty-five musicians, has a twenty-week season of five subscription concerts plus four for students. During the summer a series of "Pop" concerts are presented bi-monthly. The performances are given at the Capitol Theatre (capacity 1,250) and average attendance last year was over 1,000 per concert. One programme a year is broadcast in a tape recording over CBC. Orchestral works by Canadian composers are presented from time to time but, on the whole, music from the standard repertoire dominates the programmes.

EDMUNDSTON (N.B.) SYMPHONY ORCHESTRA (amateur)

Conductor: Georges Guerrette

Organized in 1946, the Edmundston Symphony numbers forty-two musicians and presents a winter season of four "Pop" concerts at the Edmundston Centre (capacity 800) plus two concerts on tour in New Brunswick and Maine. Total attendance for last season was approximately 2,000, including the tour concerts. The orchestra receives a small grant from the City of Edmundston and a donation from a local industrial firm; the remainder of the budget is financed through concert receipts. The orchestra has no paid musicians.

FREDERICTON CIVIC ORCHESTRA (amateur)

Conductor: Janis Kalnins

Founded in the spring of 1952, the Fredericton Civic Orchestra has an active membership of forty-eight musicians. Last year it presented one subscription and one youth concert at the Fredericton High School Auditorium (capacity 1,200), and plans to give two out-of-town concerts next season. Total attendance last season was about 1,100 for the main and 700 for the youth concert.

HALIFAX CONSERVATORY OF MUSIC[2] ORCHESTRA (amateur)

Conductor: Ifan Williams

This chamber music ensemble, made up of students of the Halifax Conservatory of Music and some professional musicians, was organized in 1920, but in recent years has been performing only sporadically.

[2]Now the Maritime Conservatory of Music.

HALIFAX SYMPHONETTE

Conductor: Alfred Strombergs

The Symphonette was founded in 1952 as the symphonic wing of the Nova Scotia Opera Association. It was first organized as a string orchestra but since 1953 has been expanded to a small symphony ensemble of about thirty musicians. During the regular season it performs six subscription and three youth concerts at the Queen Elizabeth High School Auditorium (capacity 1,200) with a total concert attendance of over 3,000. It also accompanies the Nova Scotia Opera Association productions, broadcasts about thirty-five programmes over CBC, and tours the province, giving some fifty concerts for school children and adult groups. It is partially subsidized by grants from the Province of Nova Scotia and the City of Halifax, with the remaining financing accomplished through CBC broadcasts, private donations and ticket sales. Early programmes featured eighteenth- and nineteenth-century string music, but last season for the first time the works of modern composers, such as Stravinsky, Copland and Bartok, were presented with very favourable audience reaction.

HAMILTON PHILHARMONIC ORCHESTRA

Conductor: Jan Wolanek

Established in 1949 as an amateur group, the Hamilton Philharmonic has, since 1950, grown into a semi-professional organization with a complement of sixty-five musicians. Its regular season has consisted of three winter concerts but three summer concerts were added in the 1953–54 season. Average attendance per concert at Memorial School Auditorium (capacity 1,400) has been 900. In May, 1953, the orchestra took part in the CBC broadcast series, "Orchestras in Smaller Cities." It receives a small grant from the City of Hamilton, plus private donations and some financial support from local industries. It is the orchestra's policy to feature Canadian guest artists as well as to present the works of Canadian composers.

NEW SYMPHONY ORCHESTRA OF KINGSTON (semi-professional)

Conductor: Graham George

Organized in January, 1954, this orchestra of forty players gives performances in Grant Hall, Queen's University (capacity 1,277). Its first concert attracted an almost capacity audience: two concerts are planned for the season 1954–55.

KITCHENER-WATERLOO SYMPHONY ORCHESTRA (amateur)

Conductor: Glenn Kruspe

Organized in 1945 by Dr. Kruspe and a group of interested musicians, this orchestra of about sixty-five instrumentalists performs four pairs of concerts and, since 1951, two youth concerts have been added to the regular season. The hall used for the regular series is the Collegiate Auditorium (capacity 750) and last season's average audience numbered about 650 per concert. Financing is done through public subscription, administered by an Association executive. The orchestra reports that it has benefited from an influx to this district of European musicians of German origin. Its programming is mainly classical in nature. Last season, two short pieces for orchestra by a Canadian composer were presented.

LONDON CHAMBER ORCHESTRA (amateur)

Conductor: Gordon Jeffery

Established as a chamber music ensemble in 1948, this group of fifteen musicians presents five concerts per year at Aeolian Hall (capacity 500), and for the past two years has taken part in the *St. John Passion* in Toronto, with the Aeolian Choral Society of London and a Toronto church choir.

LONDON CIVIC SYMPHONY (amateur)

Conductor: Martin Boundy

Originally organized in 1937, the London Civic Symphony was re-organized in 1949 under the auspices of the London Civic Symphony Association and numbers sixty-five musicians. It performs four winter concerts and two in the summer series at the H.B. Beal Technical School Auditorium (capacity 1,500), plus a short tour. It also takes part in annual oratorio presentations with massed choir, and broadcasts one concert over CBC and four over CFPL—the latter being rebroadcasts of winter programmes. Canadian artists are regularly featured as guest soloists.

MONTREAL SYMPHONY ORCHESTRA

Conductor: Guests

The Montreal Symphony was founded as Les Concerts Symphoniques de Montréal in 1934 by an interested group headed among others by Senator Athanase David and his wife, Fred Béique, Jean Lallemand

and Wilfrid Pelletier, who was its first Conductor. With a complement of seventy-five musicians, the orchestra currently presents a total of forty-five performances each season, consisting of twelve pairs of subscription concerts, eight pairs of youth concerts (English and French), as well as five concerts during the summer season. Sustaining broadcasts are also given over CBC. The concerts are given at Plateau Hall (capacity 1,308) and the approximate total attendance is 75,000 for the season. Canadian guest soloists and the works of Canadian composers are regularly programmed.

MONTREAL WOMEN'S SYMPHONY ORCHESTRA

Conductor: Ethel Stark

This first and only all-women orchestra in Canada was founded in 1940 by its Conductor, Ethel Stark. It has a present roster of about eighty musicians and gives four regular concerts per season at Plateau Hall (capacity 1,308). Average attendance per concert is about 1,200. Works by Canadian composers have been performed. The orchestra has appeared on tour in Canada and the United States.

MONTREAL JUNIOR SYMPHONY ORCHESTRA

Conductor: Lewis V. Elvin

This orchestra of seventy-five players between the ages of fifteen and twenty was founded in 1947 as an outgrowth of the Montreal Inter-schools Orchestra. It gives two concerts a year in Plateau Hall to a total audience of 800–1000, and in 1954 made a very successful tour of England including an appearance on BBC television. A group of business men, under the presidency of Douglas Jones, acts as an executive body for the group.

L'ORCHESTRE SYMPHONIQUE DE QUÉBEC

Conductor: Wilfrid Pelletier

The oldest registered orchestra in Canada, l'Orchestre Symphonique de Québec was founded in 1902 by Joseph Vézina, who was also its first President as well as its Conductor. The following year it received its charter, in which year it played for the Prince of Wales (later George V) during the celebration of the Tricentenary of Quebec. In 1942 the orchestra was reorganized as a corporation and many leading citizens of Quebec have become active members. During the winter season five regular and five children's concerts are given before capacity audiences at the Palais Montcalm (capacity 1,450). The soloists are 90 per cent Canadian and Canadian composers are featured each year. The orchestra is partly subsidized by the Province of Quebec and the City of Quebec.

L'ORCHESTRE SYMPHONIQUE DE TROIS-RIVIÈRES (amateur)

Conductor: Jean-Yves Landry

Founded in 1943, this orchestra has a current active membership of about forty, and presents two matinée concerts a year. These are held at the Capitol Theatre (capacity 1,200) with a total attendance of between 900 and 1,100.

OTTAWA PHILHARMONIC ORCHESTRA

Conductor: Eugene Kash

The Ottawa Philharmonic, founded in 1944 by Dr. Allard de Ridder, was incorporated two years later and is operated by a Board of Directors. Its season consists of six regular concerts and nine youth concerts, the latter initiated in 1945. The orchestra employs sixty to sixty-five musicians; attendances at performances (given at the Capitol Theatre with a capacity of 2,350) have been averaging about 2,000 persons per concert. It is a policy of the orchestra to perform at least one Canadian work on every programme. The orchestra is financed by private donations, an annual benefit performance, and through ticket sales.

REGINA SYMPHONY ORCHESTRA

Conductor: Knight Wilson

The Regina Symphony Orchestra, founded in 1927 by the Regina Orchestra Society, presents a regular season of four subscription concerts.

ROYAL CONSERVATORY OF TORONTO SYMPHONY ORCHESTRA (student)

Conductor: Ettore Mazzoleni

The original Toronto Symphony under the late Frank Welsman grew out of the Toronto Conservatory Orchestra around 1908. Prior to 1931 the Conservatory Orchestra had been mainly a string ensemble but since that date has been expanded into a symphony orchestra of about sixty student members, sometimes augmented by a few professional musicians. It has given many enterprising programmes, including first performances of several Canadian works; it also plays for most of the Toronto opera festivals.

ST. CATHARINES CIVIC ORCHESTRA (amateur)

Conductor: Jan Wolanek

This group of about sixty musicians, organized in 1948, gives three regular concerts and one youth concert per year at the Palace Theatre. It has also broadcast over CBC.

SASKATOON SYMPHONY ORCHESTRA (amateur)

Conductor: Victor Kveisis

This orchestra was founded in 1933 by the late Arthur Collingwood, Dean of Music of the University of Saskatchewan in Saskatoon. It performs four or five concerts each season with a guest soloist for each. Since 1937 some youth concerts have been added. Performances are given at the Capitol Theatre (capacity 1,400) and the average attendance per concert is 1,200. In recent years it has had the active support of the Rotary Club and a civic committee.

SYMPHONIE DE SHERBROOKE (amateur)

Conductor: Sylvio Lacharité

Founded in 1940, this orchestra presents four or five concerts a year.

TORONTO PHILHARMONIC ORCHESTRA

Conductor: Guests (since 1942 when Reginald Stewart, the original
         conductor, went to the United States)

The Toronto Philharmonic (originally called the Promenade Symphony Orchestra) was organized in 1934 by the Toronto Musicians' Association, on a share profit basis to conductors, members of the orchestra and the operating committee. Seventeen concerts are given during the spring and summer months in Varsity Arena (capacity 7,000) with a total attendance of about 156,000 over the past four years. The orchestra also appears on CBC sustaining television and radio broadcasts. Works by Canadian composers have been a regular feature of these concerts.

TORONTO SYMPHONY ORCHESTRA

Conductor: Sir Ernest MacMillan; Assistant Conductor: Paul Scherman

In 1906 Frank Welsman organized the Toronto Conservatory Symphony Orchestra, which two years later became the Toronto Symphony Orchestra until it was forced to suspend operations in 1918, due to the war and financial difficulties. In 1923 a group of local musicians reactivated the orchestra (first as the "New" and later as the "Toronto" Symphony) with Luigi von Kunits as its Conductor. Following his death in 1931, Ernest MacMillan was selected to replace him, and has been the moving spirit of this orchestra ever since. The orchestra employs approximately eighty musicians, and presents a season of almost eighty concerts, including twelve subscription pairs, twenty-six "Pops," and sixteen youth concerts, as well as benefits and out-of-town appearances. Performances are given in Massey Hall (capacity 2,764) and audience attendance is about 200,000 per season. One hour of each subscription programme is regularly broadcast by the CBC; the "Pops" have been broadcast weekly under the commercial sponsorship, first of the Robert Simpson Company and more recently of Canada Packers, Limited. Canadian guest soloists and composers are frequently featured. The Toronto Symphony Orchestra has given many concerts in other Canadian cities and has in recent years appeared in a number of cities in the United States. The orchestra is partly subsidized by a grant from the City of Toronto, but draws its chief support from private sources.

UNIVERSITY OF ALBERTA SYMPHONY ORCHESTRA (student)

Conductor: Arthur B. Crighton

This university orchestra was founded in 1945 and presents three concerts a year at Convocation Hall for an audience of approximately 300 per concert.

UNIVERSITY OF TORONTO ORCHESTRA (student)

Conductor: Professor Robert Rosevear

This orchestra, sponsored by the Students' Administrative Council of the University, provides orchestral experience for musically qualified undergraduates, including orchestral players in the Faculty of Music. The orchestra holds weekly rehearsals during the academic year and appears in students' concerts.

VANCOUVER JUNIOR SYMPHONY ORCHESTRA (amateur)

Conductor: Jean de Rimanoczy

The main purpose of this junior orchestra, founded in 1938 and with an active membership of forty-five, is to give an opportunity for the study of symphonic works. It gives two or three concerts a year in Point Grey Junior High School (capacity 850).

VANCOUVER SYMPHONY ORCHESTRA

Conductor: Irving Hoffman

The Vancouver Symphony has been giving a regular winter series of concerts since 1933 when Allard de Ridder was appointed Conductor. He resigned in 1942 and after a succession of guest conductors the policy of engaging a permanent conductor was re-established. The winter season consists of some ten concerts per year with a summer series of Sunday afternoon programmes, the latter subsidized by the British Columbia Electric Company. Since 1946 the Symphony has also been presenting youth concerts.

VICTORIA LITTLE SYMPHONY ORCHESTRA (amateur)

Conductor: William Bertsch

One of the most recent amateur groups to be formed, this orchestra gave its first performance in May, 1954. At present it has approximately thirty active members.

VICTORIA SYMPHONY ORCHESTRA

Conductor: Hans Gruber

Founded in 1941, this semi-professional orchestra of some seventy players now gives eight pairs of concerts and four youth concerts during the winter season and four summer concerts in the beautiful Butchart Gardens. The aggregate attendance at all concerts, summer and winter, is approximately 33,500.

WINDSOR SYMPHONY ORCHESTRA

Conductor: Matti Holli

Organized in 1946 by a concert committee, this orchestra presents twelve concerts a year.

WINNIPEG SYMPHONY ORCHESTRA

Conductor: Walter Kaufmann

The Winnipeg Symphony was organized in 1946 on the basis of a joint stock company with 1500 local citizens as shareholders. The orchestra is composed of sixty-five musicians; eight regular concerts are presented, plus two "Pops" and five student concerts. These are given in the Winnipeg Civic Auditorium (capacity 4,000) and the past season recorded an over-all concert attendance of 47,500. Eight one-hour broadcasts are tape recorded from actual concerts and given as delayed broadcasts by the CBC. The works of Canadian composers are extensively used. The orchestra is partly subsidized by the City of Winnipeg.

YORK CONCERT SOCIETY (Toronto)

Conductor: Dr. Heinz Unger

Established in 1952, this orchestra of thirty to thirty-five players gives four concerts per year at the Eaton Auditorium (Toronto) in the early spring; the average attendance is about 1,000 per concert.

To sum up, what can be said about the future of the symphony orchestra in Canada? In view of its steady growth throughout the country, particularly during the past decade, there can be no doubt but that symphonic music is taking its rightful place in the cultural life of Canada.

In this growth, both the orchestra and the audience must be considered. The repertoire of any orchestra is limited and influenced by the ability of its musicians, by the amount of rehearsal time at their disposal and by the responsiveness of the audience. These factors are inseparably linked. Simply stated, the better an orchestra performs the greater will be its chance of effective audience support. As far as the orchestras are concerned, there is now in Canada an increasing number of excellent musicians and, what is most important, because of the increased stature of Canadian orchestras these musicians are remaining in Canada and devoting their time and energy to raising the artistic level of those orchestras. It is good to note that Canadian artists and composers are now being regularly featured with the symphony orchestras. Also, the increased number of schools and conservatories of music, plus expanded scholarship programmes (in many cases subsidized by municipal and provincial grants), assure a steady flow of qualified musicians for the future and the continuous discovery and development of new talent.

In general, audience growth and support has paced the orchestral expansion. A large part of this success can undoubtedly be attributed to the extended use of youth concerts, which are soundly building the audiences of the future. Wherever they have been given, particularly when in close co-operation with the schools, results have been rapid and most gratifying. There are few more enthusiastic and receptive audiences in the world. And once again, the Canadian Broadcasting Corporation must be thanked for the splendid work it has done in promoting the very best in music—classical as well as modern—and making it available to all parts of the nation.

But in spite of these encouraging points, an orchestra still cannot exist without financial support. It is to be hoped that the future will continue to show an increase in financial assistance and encouragement on the part of municipal and provincial governments, augmenting the excellent work which has already been accomplished by individual citizens and local committees. It is erroneous to assume that an orchestra should be self-supporting. It can no more be self-supporting than a museum or an art gallery, and one trusts that not too long a period will elapse before the Canadian public will, as do the people of European countries, accept the principle of subsidization for orchestras.

CHORAL MUSIC

Ernest MacMillan

There is not any Musicke of Instruments whatsoever, comparable to that which is made of the voyces of Men, where the voices are good, and the same well sorted and ordered.

William Byrd

So wrote William Byrd almost four hundred years ago. Greatly though instruments have improved since, it still remains true that the singing of a great choir carries with it a thrill and an appeal hard to parallel in other musical experiences.

Choral music on a large scale is traditionally an amateur art and it is a happy circumstance that, in so many Canadian centres, its amateur status is still maintained. In an age when all performance tends to become more and more professionalized, when turning a disk or twisting a knob so often replaces the efforts (skilful or otherwise) of members of the family, and when outside distractions tempt us to forsake our hobbies, it is good to find so many enthusiasts still making music for its own sake, receiving and giving lasting pleasure and inspiration. Amateur music-making indicates a healthy communal life and helps to produce intelligent audiences; the most appreciative and discriminating listeners are usually those who can in some form create music for themselves. Perhaps it is no great loss if "monster" choirs of three or four thousand voices are practically a thing of the past, but many masterpieces demand choral forces which, if recruited from professional ranks and remunerated according to their professional status, would be impossibly expensive; we must be grateful to the amateurs for the chance to hear these still.

Disparity in quality is much less marked between amateur and professional choirs than it is between amateur and professional instrumental groups. Our larger choirs number among their membership many highly trained singers who find choral singing enjoyable and rewarding and other singers who, though they have renounced or never contemplated a professional career, have received good vocal training in their early years and would not willingly lose what they have gained. Wise vocal teachers encourage their students to enlarge their experience by singing in choirs; given this encouragement, many choirs are able to recruit some of their most valuable members from the student ranks. Many professional instrumentalists also recognize that singing great music in a fine chorus helps them in their own work.

Nowadays membership in a choir involves relatively greater sacrifices than formerly. Distractions and amusements for leisure hours are plentiful: movies, radio, television, the motor car and professional sports wean too many from indulging in pleasant activities on their own account. Offsetting improved means of transportation, the growth of our larger cities increases the difficulty of attending rehearsals. Many young couples lacking domestic service encounter an additional problem and expense in securing reliable "baby-sitters." The concert season itself, in most of our cities, offers enticing alternatives. It is not surprising therefore that large choirs are rarer now than in days gone by—very much rarer, indeed, in proportion to the population. Some notable choirs of the past are no more. Often this has been brought about by the retirement or death of a conductor around whose personality a group has been built and maintained: choirs as a rule feel a special loyalty towards their leaders. Other choirs have, through sustaining a similar loss, so declined in quality as to become unacceptable to the public. Yet the traditions of great choral music have on the whole been well maintained in Canada. Most of our larger cities, as well as a number of smaller ones, can boast of at least one body capable of rendering competently and sometimes with distinction the masterpieces of choral literature.

Of late years the smaller choir in Canada has come increasingly into its own. Small groups are very much in demand for broadcasting and a number have achieved professional status. Others have developed largely as a result of increased musical activity in schools or as an outgrowth of competitive festivals. Most of our universities, too, foster choral singing among their students and a number of commercial firms find it advantageous to organize choral bodies among their employees. Some of the latter devote their attention largely to productions of light opera; others are more active in the concert world. Among the notable choirs of this type are the Canada Packers Operatic Society of Toronto under E. R. Curry, Eaton Operatic Society (formerly Eaton Choral Society) under Godfrey Ridout, Cockshutt Male Choir of Brantford under Lansing MacDowell, Universal Cooler Male Choir, also of Brantford, under Frank Holton, and several others. The Motor City Choir of Oshawa owed its inception twenty years ago to the General Motors Company of Canada. This choir of sixty voices is now independent of this affiliation but still sings under the direction of its original conductor, Reginald Geen.

Though less numerous than choirs of women, male-voice choirs are still popular. Male church choirs with boy sopranos are the exception rather than the rule in Canada; fewer Canadian than English boys enjoy the advantage of early and thorough vocal training in church music. In our co-educational schools boys usually participate in choral singing but their numbers tend to drop off even before their voices approach the breaking stage. To be sure they often reappear as tenors and basses in the later high-school grades, but at this stage a boy is apt to be very self-conscious and his voice is immature. The best of our high-school choirs are generally composed of girls alone. As the late Lawrence Mason once remarked: "The female of the species is more choral than the male"; at least it is so in Canada, where even some of our most important organizations are apt to be a little top-heavy and where good tenors, in particular, are often at a premium.

Nevertheless the male choir continues to hold its own in many communities. Apart from our churches, choirs of boys' unbroken voices are found in Halifax (Y.M.C.A. *A Cappella* Boys' Choir under C. C. Underwood), Winnipeg (Winnipeg Boys' Choir under Donald Leggat) and several other centres. Adult male choirs are legion. The Winnipeg Male Voice Choir has a long and illustrious history and continues to do fine work under its present conductor, Donald Leggat. The same may be said of the Edmonton Welsh Male Chorus, founded in 1909 and long directed by W. J. Hendra, but now under Douglas Millson. Eldon Brethour, Supervisor of Music in the Toronto schools, has for eleven years past directed a chorus of about seventy male teachers, who give an annual concert in Massey Hall; its counterpart, the smaller Toronto Women Teachers' Choir, has been more recently formed. The experience of singing in these choirs, apart from the pleasure derived from the performances, must be invaluable to all members in their school work. Of a more professional type are The Songmen of Toronto under David Ouchterlony and The Shantymen of Halifax under Leonard Mayoh. A list of male choirs might be expanded to great dimensions; the fact remains, however, that choirs of women's voices are still more numerous and that in our mixed choruses women usually outnumber men.

LARGE CHOIRS

In past years it was not unusual to organize massed choirs of 2,000 or more voices—usually for patriotic or festal occasions. One recalls, for example, the Coliseum Chorus of some 2,500 voices which for many years sang annually at the Canadian National Exhibition in Toronto under the direction of the late Dr. Herbert Fricker and then of Dr. Charles Peaker. Nor was this by any means unique. Such a body of singers is naturally apt to be somewhat unwieldy: one conductor described the experience of directing a similar choir in England as being like "taking a jelly-fish for a walk on a string of elastic." Yet the "monster" choir, when its repertoire is judiciously selected from works of a massive nature, can undoubtedly produce a most thrilling effect and with the almost complete disappearance of such bodies we have lost something unique in our musical life. Our larger permanent choruses rarely number more than two hundred voices. The Kiwanis Festival Choir of London under Martin Boundy is an exception, being considerably larger. Like so many others this choir gives annual performances of Handel's *Messiah* and other standard oratorios in large arenas. The *Messiah* is frequently given also in Toronto under the auspices of the Canadian College of Organists by massed church choirs running to several hundred under Frederick Silvester, and in its annual performances of the same work, the Toronto Mendelssohn Choir of about 175 voices is augmented, in a few climaxes only, by an additional hundred or more voices. It remains true, however, that few permanent choirs exceed two hundred in strength and the majority are smaller. Among the choirs numbering one hundred and more in membership (other than those already mentioned) are the Halifax Choral Society (Leonard Mayoh), the Toronto Philharmonic Choir (Robert Hately), the Elgar Choir (Gifford Mitchell) of Montreal, the Ottawa Choral Union (no permanent conductor at present), the Winnipeg Philharmonic Choir (Donald Leggat), the Bach-Elgar Choir of Hamilton (Cyril Hampshire), the Victoria Choral Society (Graham Steed), the Mendelssohn Choir of Edmonton (E. A. Moore) and the Bach Choir of Vancouver (L. Cluderay). Among the universities with student choirs of similar strength are Mount Allison (Geoffrey Paysant) and Alberta (Richard Eaton).

THE CHORAL-ORCHESTRAL REPERTOIRE

With our larger choirs, the *Messiah* and to a lesser extent Mendelssohn's *Elijah* and Haydn's *Creation* continue to enjoy popularity, although many of the favourite oratorios of nineteenth-century England have tended to fall into oblivion. Where in Canada nowadays is one likely to hear adequate performances, with orchestral accompaniment, of *Israel in Egypt, St. Paul* or the once highly popular *Redemption* of Gounod?

On the other hand, the church cantatas and more extended choral works of J. S. Bach have, over a period of decades, met with increasing favour, although to the present writer's knowledge only on the radio has an extensive series of church cantatas been presented with orchestral accompaniment. The Bach tradition is being valiantly maintained by the Aeolian Choral Society of London which, under the direction of Gordon Jeffery, has since 1947 presented many of the church cantatas as well as the *St. John Passion*, the B minor Mass and other religious works. A number of church choirs, too, present church cantatas from time to time in the surroundings for which they were intended. Tribute was paid to the Master of Eisenach in 1950 (the two hundredth anniversary of his death) by the Toronto Mendelssohn Choir in a three-day festival which included performances of the B minor Mass, the *St. Matthew Passion*, the *Magnificat*, a number of cantatas, sacred and secular, as well as instrumental works. The same body presents annual performances of the *St. Matthew Passion*, continuing an almost unbroken tradition established in 1923. In 1954, both this and Handel's *Messiah* were given by the Choir with seventy players of the Toronto Symphony Orchestra in Carnegie Hall, New York. The name of the great Cantor is borne by many Canadian choirs: for example, the Bach Choir of Montreal, a professional group of thirty singers, established late in 1951 and conducted by George Little; the Bach Choir of Vancouver; and the Bach-Elgar Choir of Hamilton. Naturally these and other similar bodies include a due proportion of Bach's music on their programmes.

One cannot go into detail regarding the countless performances given from time to time of other standard works in the choral-orchestral repertoire: for instance, Brahms' *German Requiem*, the Mozart and Verdi Requiem Masses, Berlioz' Requiem and *Damnation of Faust*, Beethoven's Ninth Symphony and *Missa Solemnis* and various works of Elgar. Among lesser-known works, *The Children's Crusade* of Gabriel Pierné—first heard in Canada more than forty years ago under that genius among choral directors, A. S. Vogt (founder and, until 1917, Conductor of the Toronto Mendelssohn Choir)—has proved a perennial favourite, having been heard in

Hamilton, in Ottawa and quite frequently, in Toronto. The addition of a large chorus of children to the adult group lends to this work a special appeal; some of our school music supervisors have been most helpful in training these groups. The same composer's *St. Francis of Assisi*, also calling for a children's choir, was given its first Canadian performance some years ago by the Ottawa Choral Union under its former conductor, W. Allister Crandall.

Among modern works, those of English composers would seem to be the most favoured. Few of the choral compositions of Vaughan Williams have been neglected, many of them having been performed once and several fairly frequently. Among those which come to mind by other British composers are Arnold Bax's *St. Patrick's Breastplate*; Walton's *Belshazzar's Feast*; Delius' *Sea Drift*; Benjamin Britten's *Spring Symphony, Ballad of Heroes* and *A Ceremony of Carols*; Constant Lambert's *Rio Grande*; John Ireland's *These Things shall be*; Arthur Bliss's *Pastorale*; and many others. Most of Elgar's works have been performed, though they are now rather less popular than formerly; Parry is occasionally represented by *Blest Pair of Sirens* and *The Pied Piper of Hamelin*. Continental composers have perhaps fared less well, but Kodaly's *Psalmus Hungaricus*, Honegger's *Jeanne d'Arc au bûcher* and *Le Roi David* have, *inter alia*, received the tribute of at least one performance each, and works by other French composers, especially Berlioz, are frequently heard in Montreal and Quebec. Curiously enough, American composers have received much less than their due share of attention in the choral-orchestral field, but short works for *a cappella* choir appear not infrequently on Canadian programmes.

The Montreal Festivals have earned a special tribute through the presentation, in addition to their operatic productions, of a variety of great choral works under a number of distinguished conductors. In these they have the co-operation of one of Canada's major choirs, Les Disciples de Massenet of fifty voices, whose director is Dr. Charles Goulet. Another Montreal choir of equal size, Le Chœur Berlioz, conducted by Marcel Laurencelle, has an outstanding record in the presentation (sometimes with augmented forces) of major works as well as *a cappella* programmes.

Extended works for chorus and orchestra by Canadian composers are not numerous, but Canada includes among her adopted sons at least one who has shown genuine distinction in choral writing: Healey Willan, who has been resident in Canada for more than forty years.

His numerous contributions to *a cappella* music are most widely known, but we must not overlook his *Coronation Ode* (celebrating the Coronation of Her Majesty Queen Elizabeth II), his *Festal Te Deum* or his incidental music to E. J. Pratt's poem *Brébeuf and his Brethren,* which deals with the early Jesuit missions to the Hurons in the seventeenth century. Among other choral-orchestral works by Canadians, one might mention the oratorio *Esther* by Godfrey Ridout, the *Suite canadienne* and *Images du Canada français* by Claude Champagne and the setting of Swinburne's ode *England* by the present writer.

SMALLER CHOIRS AND A CAPPELLA SINGING

Without claiming to have covered more than a small part of the field of choral-orchestral music in Canada, we must pass on to smaller groups, most of which specialize in unaccompanied choral singing. Here we find a bewildering variety. In nearly all cities, towns and even villages in Canada one finds choirs, varying in size and in degree of excellence, which are able to present acceptable programmes of choral music. Highly experienced British and American adjudicators have expressed delighted surprise at the quality shown by the best of these groups, some of which function in quite small communities. The days of Elizabeth I are recalled by the singing of the English Choral Singers of Halifax, the Tudor Singers of Ottawa, the Coventry Singers of Peterborough, the University Mixed Chorus of the University of Alberta, or the Sherwood Robson Chorale of Vancouver—to mention only a few. On the other hand, the Studio Singers of Ottawa, a professional group under Dorothy Lampman McCurry, specializes in contemporary British works for chorus and orchestra. Both the Kingston Choral Society under Graham George and the Kitchener-Waterloo Philharmonic Choir under Glenn Kruspe also give oratorios and other extended works for chorus and orchestra.

French Canada has produced some of the most finished work in the country: the finest traditions of the Benedictine Order are preserved in the singing of plain-song by the monks at St. Benoît-du-Lac, in southern Quebec. The Palestrina Choir of Ottawa, under Father Martel, specializes in sixteenth-century polyphonic works and in folk-song arrangements. No less striking is the work done by the Chorale de l'Université Saint-Joseph (New Brunswick)—a male choir, formerly under the direction of Father Léandre Brault and now conducted by Father Soucie; this sometimes combines forces with the truly superb women's choir of Notre Dame d'Acadie in the neighbouring city of

Moncton, conducted by Sister Marie-Lucienne, singing plain-song and other religious music as well as folk-songs, chiefly French Canadian. The background of these and other similar choirs is described below in the chapter on the music of the Roman Catholic Church. French-speaking Canada naturally enjoys the advantage of a folk-song tradition rooted in Canada since the seventeenth century—an ever living source of inspiration. In Three Rivers, Quebec, Les Petits Chanteurs Trifluviens exploits this to the full; a male choir of some thirty voices, it gives most interesting programmes featuring French-Canadian folk-songs, seventeenth-century polyphonic works and more modern numbers, and has been heard in several cities of the United States. Continuing the work of the late Charles Marchand, the Quatuor Alouette of Montreal and similar groups present the folk-songs of their country and more sophisticated fare for delighted audiences. The Halifax Male Quartet, directed by Marjorie Payne, performs a similar service in presenting sea chanties and other songs of the Maritime Provinces over the CBC national network, as do The Shantymen already mentioned.

Indeed, from coast to coast, from St. John's Newfoundland, where the St. John's Glee Club, a group of over eighty under Mrs. Eleanor Jerrett, gives interesting *a cappella* programmes, to Comox on Vancouver Island, a small mining town which a few years ago was able to produce a men's choir that delighted the present writer, choral music seems to flourish to the evident enjoyment of participants as well as listeners. Halifax can boast of a great variety of choral groups, including the boys' choir and choral society already mentioned, and the charming Armdale Girls' Chorus, under Mary Dee Giroir. There is also much choral activity in other Nova Scotia centres. Of the Maritime capital cities other than Halifax and St. John's, Charlottetown and Fredericton, though smaller cities, are by no means lacking in choral activity. Charlottetown fosters the Charlottetown Chorale, which gives programmes of madrigals, folk-song arrangements and the like, under the direction of William Keith Rogers, a promising young composer, and Fredericton has a fine male choir, directed by David R. Howat, as well as the Cecilian Singers (women) under Rosalie Belyea. Choral music also holds an important place in the musical life of St. John and Moncton, while Edmundston, a largely French-speaking town in the northwest corner of New Brunswick, abounds in musical activities of which choral singing in the French tradition is by no means the least important. In Winnipeg, stimulated by one of the world's greatest competitive festivals, are a large number of choruses whose achievements are rooted in the finest traditions of English choral singing and whose work delights the ears of even the most sophisticated listener. There are several excellent choirs in Manitoba and the other prairie provinces where the competitive festival movement originated and still ensures high standards of singing. One may find flourishing choral groups in Brandon, Saskatoon, Moose Jaw, Medicine Hat, Calgary and Lethbridge, as well as in the capital cities.

Several Canadian choral groups have been heard in Great Britain. One might mention the Elgar Choir of Vancouver (C. E. Findlater, Director) and the girls' choir of Bishop Strachan School, Toronto (John Hodgins, Director) as well as the St. Joseph's University choir to which reference has already been made. In 1950 Les Disciples de Massenet made an extensive tour of France and in 1953 the Earle Terry Singers of London represented Canada at the International Conference on Music Education in Brussels. More recently the choir of St. George's Cathedral, Kingston, under George Maybee has been heard in the regular services of Westminster Abbey.

UNIVERSITIES

One could pay a lengthy tribute to the choral activities of our various universities. Mount Allison University, New Brunswick, for instance, boasts a choral society of 150 students which alternates, year by year, in giving oratorios and light operas, as well as taking part in church services. In the old city of Quebec, the Chorale Université Laval under the Abbé Fortier, gives programmes of madrigals and other works of classic polyphony, as well as folk-songs and occasional works with orchestra. Queen's University, Kingston, has a fine choral group directed by Dr. Graham George and composed largely of students. In the University of Toronto several choral bodies have been active over a period of years: one might mention in particular the University Choir (mixed voices), conducted by Richard Johnston, the Hart House Glee Club (male) and the Victoria College Music Club; the latter, under Godfrey Ridout, devotes itself largely to Gilbert and Sullivan operatic productions. Naturally many activities of the University of Toronto centre in the Royal Conservatory of Music, which is under its direction; a fuller account of this important institution will be given elsewhere in this book. Special mention must be made here of choral activity in the University of Alberta (Edmonton) where a mixed chorus of about 150 gives programmes of madrigals, folk-song arrangements and the like as well as more extended works such as Bach motets, under its conductor, Richard Eaton. To a greater or less degree, most Canadian universities foster some form of choral music among their students.

A REPRESENTATIVE PROFESSIONAL CHOIR

Some of the choral bodies of varying size which have been active of recent years have gained such success as to put them into the professional class. Probably the best known of these is the Leslie Bell Singers, whose conductor has shown not only outstanding ability in eliciting from his young female singers colourful and unusual effects but also in presenting to delighted audiences works ranging from Palestrina to negro spirituals and even quasi-instrumental arrangements of the latest "popular" hit-tunes. The Bell Singers have met with wide acclaim in many parts of Canada and the United States and rarely does a week go by when they may not be heard on the air. Other groups, in various parts of the country, have followed the example of the Bell Singers in staging their performances in such a manner as to appeal strongly to the eye as well as the ear through the resources of distinctive costumes and lighting. The most attractive of such groups suggest the loveliness of a flower garden; others, overstepping the mark, may savour a little of Hollywood. The purist might at times take exception to an excess of arrangements from instrumental works on programmes and to a too-frequent straining after instrumental effects but audiences as a rule appear to relish these and in technical finish many choirs of this type reach a very high standard. It might be added that the music is usually memorized and the eye of the listener is not distracted by the manipulation of unwieldy scores and the turning of pages.

SOME CHORAL CONDUCTORS

The activities of choral groups throughout the length and breadth of the country are so bewildering in number and variety that one cannot begin to do justice to all. Perhaps the writer may be forgiven if he pays a special tribute to a few men and women whose work has come prominently to his personal notice and who have in their respective communities exerted a wide influence on choral music in Canada. First and foremost comes to mind the name of the late Dr. A. S. Vogt; under his expert direction the Toronto Mendelssohn Choir reached a degree of perfection that won acclaim not only at home but in many cities of the United States, where it came to be regarded as without a peer on this continent. Other choral conductors of past years, such as the late H. K. Jordan of Brantford and Bruce Carey, founder of the Elgar Choir of Hamilton, acknowledged their debt to the example of Dr. Vogt. His successor, Dr. Herbert Fricker, carried on his work worthily until very shortly before his death, infusing into the singing much of the style of the best Yorkshire choirs. In recent years the Toronto Mendelssohn Choir has devoted itself chiefly to choral-orchestral works, although not neglecting unaccompanied singing. At present a smaller *a cappella* choir selected from its membership gives additional programmes under John Sidgwick; Mr. Sidgwick also directs an independent group of English Madrigal Singers.

Winnipeg owes a deep debt of gratitude to Ethel Kinley, formerly Supervisor of Music in the schools; she and her colleagues established a standard of school singing that has made its influence felt through-out the West; no one could hear a choir of young people under her direction without being deeply moved, and her students after reaching mature years have done much to continue the fine choral traditions of their community. Much the same can be said of the late Emily Tedd of Toronto. Among those still active, special mention might be made of Sherwood Robson (Vancouver), Richard Eaton (University of Alberta), George Little (Montreal), F. H. G. Wright (English Choral Singers of Halifax), Leslie Bell and Harvey Perrin of Toronto, Earle Terry and Don Wright of London and many others.

CHURCH CHOIRS

Reference is made elsewhere in this book to the many fine choirs in the churches of Canada. Here we are concerned with them only in so far as they enter other fields. In 1953, for example, the choir of Metropolitan Church, Toronto, under John Sidgwick, and the English Choral Singers of Halifax, under F. H. G. Wright, were jointly awarded the Lincoln Trophy for the finest choral singing heard in the competitive festivals across Canada that year. It is significant that this coveted trophy should be held by two choirs of so different a nature. Many other church choirs are heard frequently in concerts and broad-casts, one of the most notable being the choir of St. Mary Magdalene's Church, Toronto, under Dr. Healey Willan, which specializes in six-teenth-century and other *a cappella* works, chiefly of a religious char-acter. The all-male choir of St. Simon's Church, Toronto, is also heard outside its own *milieu* (particularly around Christmas time) in concerts of mixed sacred and secular music. The choir of the Schola Cantorum of Toronto and several other choirs from Roman Catholic churches and schools are also heard from time to time in concerts and broadcasts. It might be added that several of our larger choral bodies owe their origin to church choirs of which they are an expansion. Special broadcasts of religious music by groups of professional singers are regularly heard over the air, two of the most notable being those conducted by W. H. Anderson (Winnipeg) and Dalton Baker (Vancouver).

SPECIAL NATIONAL GROUPS

Apart from the fundamental differences of British and French traditions, the population of Canada represents to a great extent what the late John Murray Gibbon aptly termed a "mosaic." It was Dr. Gibbon who, as General Publicity Agent of the Canadian Pacific Railway, organized some twenty-five years ago a series of folk festivals in the chief cities, the nature of each festival being largely determined by the local resources. Naturally the long-established German community centring in Kitchener and Waterloo has been exceedingly active in its musical life. Of the many German groups in other parts of Canada, one might mention the Harmonic Male Choir of Toronto under Hans Kamus. But many other ethnological groups contribute their share. The Jewish Folk Choir of Toronto under Emil Gartner has been most enterprising in presenting contemporary works of varying origin, many of them with full orchestra. Russians, Ukrainians, Poles and Czechs bring a Slavic touch to our choral life. In Toronto alone Poland is represented by at least four choirs, including the St. Cecilia Choir under the Rev. Bernard Kopec. One has also heard delightful singing from groups of Icelanders in Winnipeg and, particularly since World War II, refugees from the Baltic States have made significant contributions. The Lithuanian community of Toronto, for example, has organized not only a choir of seventy but also a small orchestra.

Canada numbers among its population many of Italian origin; these add much to our musical life, though perhaps less noticeably in the choral than in other fields. The negro, of course, is often a born singer, but has been less musically prominent in Canada than in the United States, representing as he does only a small proportion of our population. Although one cannot say that the Oriental as such has noticeably affected choral music in this country, it is delightful to see the faces of Chinese and Japanese children in so many of our school choirs, especially in the West, and to note how enthusiastically they sing.

A pleasing feature of "Music Day" at the Canadian National Exhibition in Toronto is the open-air singing, in various parts of the grounds, of small and medium-sized choruses. Probably about 40 per cent of these are national groups, most of them dressed in the colourful costumes of their respective countries.

One regrets having to leave so much unsaid; in a book of this nature much of significance is bound to be overlooked. Even as this chapter was being written the writer received fresh information regarding other choral bodies—information impossible to classify in a short time. Naturally he is unable to speak at first hand regarding the quality of work done by more than a fraction of the choirs named. However, if this brief review has done something to indicate that Canada is a singing nation—indeed increasingly so—it will not altogether have failed in its purpose.

OPERA AND BALLET

Colin Sabiston and Pearl McCarthy

Come, my dear girls, as we shall bid adieu to London on Monday, I will take you to the opera this evening.
To the opera? O how delightful! then we shall hear Mdm. C. in some of her finest songs.
Be quick, then, for the carriage is at the door.
To me everything will be new and interesting, for I never was at the opera.
Hush! the curtain rises.

Rev. Thomas Vivier—*French and English Dialogues upon Several Subjects; Exclusively Adapted for the Use of Young Ladies,* 1814

It is the thesis of this chapter that there is, in Canada, an active demand for both professional and amateur performances of opera and ballet; that groups in each field have reached high standards and have developed a surprisingly wide repertoire; but that we are, for the moment, stuck fast at that crucial turn in the road where efficient amateurism should go on to self-sustaining professionalism of a permanent sort. We do not deprecate amateurism in any of the arts. Where there is informed amateurism there is enthusiasm in the search for excellence. But the turn cannot be made until some circumstances of our lingering national immaturity are altered. For opera and ballet are essentially co-operative social pursuits.

In none of the other musical arts is it so necessary to have a nation-wide, social view. A violinist may conceivably find the full worth of his labour if stationed in a far lighthouse. A chamber music ensemble may find satisfaction playing for itself on a remote island. But opera and ballet are in their nature popular. Their music is for the people, or they die. As Verdi reminded Gatti-Casazza, opera houses are meant to be full.

It is imperative, therefore, to consider some socio-economic factors which are temporarily impeding the progress of opera and ballet. The first is geographic distance. The second is that the development of communities in the Maritimes, Central Canada, the Prairies and the Pacific coast has differed in character owing to regional variations in economic activity. Differing economic foundations led to differences in the social structure of communities; and this variety in structure alters regional emphasis on cultural objectives, notwithstanding some tastes and preferences which may be common to all. In a general way, all these communities may think alike about Canadian culture. But they do not think together. Within the context of this chapter, then, there are three distances to be conquered: the geographic, which separates physical communities; the economic, which varies the structure of these communities; and the social, which creates different stresses on cultural values.

Contrary to some other opinions, we do not believe that our cultural barriers—if that is not too strong a term—arise from differences in either race, religion or language. They are of socio-economic origin. The underlying factor of geographic distance is being overcome. The cultural barrier is harder to deal with. Opera and ballet are universally popular in all communities but the nature of the support varies widely. Hence the need for national opera and ballet organizations.

A word concerning the functions of national opera and ballet companies should be introduced here lest it seem that we seek undue centralization or a flat sameness. Briefly, such national companies should establish standards, not exercise a monopoly. The traditions created by La Scala did not impair the functions of opera houses in Vienna, Budapest, Prague, Berlin, Paris, Riga, or even the minor provincial houses. So also of ballet. The Russian Imperial Ballet set the standard. Its effect was to encourage the founding of French, English, German and Central European ballet companies. All acknowledged, in the graceful spirit of the art they shared, the source of their inspiration, although moving on towards more distinctly regional expressions. The case for strong opera and ballet companies in Canada is more than analogous. It is identical. They must be built up in centres where talent is developed and trained. They must be strong in their financial sinews as well as in their artistry. They will then lead regional development but will be dominant nowhere except upon their own stages.

Both opera and ballet are well established in Canada on a non-professional basis. Local groups frequently find sufficiently strong sponsorship to warrant annual productions, sometimes including limited tours in local areas. Difficulties of financing and the inadequacy of theatres themselves across the Dominion have made the going rather harder for professional groups. Ballet alone has progressed more nearly to national status, as will be outlined later. Opera has not yet reached any similar national status although, significantly, some productions (notably those by the Royal Conservatory Company) have been more artistic than one might see in any but the front-rank opera houses of the international scene.

On the whole, there is more activity at amateur, semi-professional and professional levels of opera than of ballet. But no national opera has emerged. More singers and more orchestral players are engaged in rehearsals and in performances. But their efforts are spent within narrow orbits, so far as theatre performances are concerned. The costs of operatic sets, travelling and staging are so far prohibitive in relation to earning possibilities. And the lack of proper stage accommodation is an even greater barrier to tours by opera groups than it is to ballet companies.

To a degree, the Royal Conservatory Opera Company, still intimately associated with the Opera School of the Royal Conservatory of Toronto, has been successful in meeting the challenge in all respects except extended tours. It has passed its fifth annual festival in Toronto, with short tours in a limited repertoire in Ontario. It is fully professional now but operates within a limited season, and all performers must seek other means of living for the remaining months of the year. It wisely stresses music rather than staging until capital may be available for more elaborate productions.

When and how the Royal Conservatory Opera, with its great artistic resources, may develop into a securely established national opera, is a problem not solved at the moment. It is farther on its way than any other company in the field. But without adequate capital it cannot acquire all the expensive appurtenances of production on a scale to assure permanence; and without permanence it cannot sustain the burden of its capital requirements.

That opera and ballet companies have reached high levels of competence has been owing in part to broadcasts over the CBC's radio and television networks. In addition to such contributions as it has made by presenting its own programmes, the CBC has aided the survival of artists trained for our lyric theatre. From coast to coast, both opera and ballet groups have been engaged for programmes ranging widely in variety and of generally high standard. These engagements have had two effects: they have sustained well-founded professionalism, and they have developed an audience that is nation-wide and that would welcome live performances if civic accommodation were available. Both broadcast and theatre audiences would grow together.

The above synoptic view of opera and ballet in Canada is a hopeful picture, but not a satisfactory one for a nation which ranks third in world trade. It shows the two great lyric arts, with histories reaching into the distant past, assiduously developing talents—but yet lacking national status. However if we hold our gaze on the well-laid foundations, confidence in the future is justified. As the opposing socio-economic factors are challenged and defeated, Canadian culture will reach full maturity.

Some details of the broad picture are startling, some are poignant. It is startling to find that an enjoyable performance of Gluck's *Orpheus* was given by amateurs, trained by a native son, in a fairly remote Nova Scotia mining town. It is poignant to learn that ballet groups from Vancouver have financed their own tours up the coast to fishing centres and inland to lumbering centres in the Rockies. But these could not be made to pay, and one company has been re-located in Montreal to concentrate on television programmes.

At the amateur level, however, there are many examples of well-rooted opera groups, some of which have progressed so far as to perform such works as *The Magic Flute*. A few of them operate on a profit-sharing basis to the extent of paying nominal fees to principals. But if scenic sets instead of drapes are used, these emoluments are either dropped or added to the deficits. Broadly speaking, the deficits are readily underwritten by willing subscribers. These established opera companies occasionally claim semi-professional status, especially when choristers share the divvy. But they do not stress the point except when they feel that standards are professional, although the groups are not commercial.

As senior amateurs, these well-established groups are doing exactly what the frankly amateur groups are doing—using their own musical talents and energy to present opera music to audiences that want it and gladly pay for it either at the box office or as special subscribers. Once in Canada every county town had an opera house, but no opera. Now we have opera, but no opera houses. But the amateurs are filling such town hall auditoriums as remain, school assembly halls and even gymnasiums. They are renting sports arenas, and returning, too, to the parish halls from which opera emerged. For both oratorio and opera had their ultimate origin in the church. The Metropolitan Opera Company of New York now comes annually to Toronto to present several works from its repertoire, with full orchestra and ballet, to the largest indoor audiences for opera anywhere in the world—in the Maple Leaf Gardens, built for sport but now adapted most satisfactorily for presenting this composite of all the arts at reasonable prices. It has also accommodated great ballet companies visiting Toronto.

It is necessary to remember, without delving into historical detail, that opera and ballet in Canada never had a chance to develop and take over the old theatres. The three types of distance mentioned earlier intervened. In addition, when we began to benefit by the great post-war migrations, some of our new Canadians could be forgiven for thinking first of running hot water; and, while many of the highly cultured became servants, some former slum dwellers struggled to affluence in strange occupations. Our cultural development has been contrapuntal in character, with too much stress on one theme, minor attention to second themes, and total neglect of others. We have trained good singers and dancers without providing them with professional employment on the legitimate stage. We have developed a demand for new opera and choreography without developing audiences and theatres. And without these, librettists, composers and choreographers have little chance of being paid for their work. In short, we have yet to establish a satisfactory affinity between our cultural lives and our socio-economic preoccupations. But we are entitled to feel some pride for having tackled a problem that has had no counterpart in its complexity since the great migrations of 700 A.D. The social and economic confusions then and now are similar, the cultural problems of the same type.

This is the place, while stressing the building of audiences, to note such felicitous co-operation as has come from the Rotary Clubs, acting on their own initiative and, in the first instance, concerned with raising money for social service projects. Bringing the Metropolitan Opera Company to Toronto, the Toronto Rotary did make some money for such causes. But its members themselves have been surprised by the accrual of profits of another kind. They have given large numbers of people the idea, for the first time, of travelling for the express purpose of attending opera. And they increased the potential audience of their own community. Peterborough Rotary also has sponsored operatic entertainment. Branches of the Ontario Registered Music Teachers' Association, the "Christian Culture" series of Windsor, the Forest Hill and Etobicoke community organizations in Toronto are other examples of organizations widening the public.

The panoramic view of operatic activity reveals that about 1,200 performers, including instrumentalists, were engaged during the

1953–54 season in about 200 public performances of some 50 works ranging from serious opera through Gilbert and Sullivan to lighter operettas. Several thousand citizens across the country have active membership in a series of associations whose function it is to foster and promote support by publicity, personal canvass and ticket sales, or—when the red has to be faced—to pay the deficit.

The performing groups include fully professional companies, such as Vancouver's Theatre under the Stars, Toronto's Royal Conservatory Opera Company and Melody Fair, each with extensive repertoires, frequent rotation of singers and sometimes inconsistencies in box office results. There are semi-professional companies with less extensive repertoires, shorter seasons and, as they operate in smaller centres, a more constant complement of soloists. The first group employs performers identified with their respective professional guilds or unions; the second, a combination of full professionals, students and student-artists, and outright amateurs. A final group is wholly amateur, and its typical companies, while enjoying a certain continuity, are dependent upon an energetic conductor for the regularity of annual productions. Most of them prepare one show per year; others, two or more. They are seldom reimbursed for out-of-pocket expenses.

Answers to questionnaires on which this survey is based, plus direct knowledge, news reports and interviews, agree on the details of a picture which shows the above people rehearsing earnestly under a variety of difficulties, performing creditably, and always conscious of their artistic shortcomings. The mass of data also includes evidence of capacity or near-capacity audiences which are selective where a choice offers. Where there is no choice, as in most places, the audiences are large and enthusiastic notwithstanding. Their attitude is that no performance resulting from sincere effort is so bad that it fails to give some idea of the interest and the beauty of the music.

All such activity represents the first beginnings of a national opera and indeed a national ballet, as ballet groups frequently are associated with productions at all levels. The slow break into professionalism, it should be remembered, has been out of a long and mostly forgotten era of amateurism. For some oldsters, now confirmed patrons of the lyric theatre, first experience of opera consisted of hearing a fantasia from *Faust* for four hands on the piano, or the sextet from *Lucia* on trombones in a vaudeville house. And in collegiate and church assembly halls there were intermittent performances of *The Mikado* and *The Geisha Girl*, with casts sweating alternately over the stage carpentry and the scores, the performances being held together more by gusto than by skill. Such amateurism, naturally on a higher level, still persists. It may be seen in Toronto in the Canada Packers and the Eaton Operatic Societies, or in smaller places where the only available Buttercup may weigh in at upward of twelve stone, or the only tenor who can sing the role of Nanki-Poo be somewhat over the age limit. The great recommendation of such entertainments was that the performers undertook the productions for the fun of it.

Always, of course, there were serious artistic enterprises. Montreal boasted a fine opera company before World War I. Sir Ernest MacMillan's productions between the wars of Vaughan Williams' *Hugh the Drover*, *Hänsel and Gretel* and other operas, with Canadian singers, were milestones which had parallels, even if not counterparts, in other provincial centres.

Of opera by Canadian composers there has been very little, a natural circumstance in the absence of opera established on a permanent basis. Dr. Healey Willan's radio operas *Transit through Fire* and *Deirdre of the Sorrows* (libretto by John Coulter), were commissioned and produced by the Canadian Broadcasting Corporation and were highly regarded as serious music in this field. At Queen's University, Kingston, Dr. Graham George has produced his opera *Evangeline*. Herman Voaden has been the librettist for *The Prodigal Son*, composed by the American Jacobi. In lighter vein, Keith MacMillan wrote the amusing score for *Saints Alive*, performed at Hart House by a cast from Trinity College. Mavor Moore wrote both the words and the music for the CBC musical called *Mariposa Belle*, based on Stephen Leacock's *Sunshine Sketches*; the New Play Society early in 1955 presented the stage version under the title *Sunshine Town*. It reproduces much of the Leacock humour and atmosphere, with not much more jingle than the basic text warranted.

A most interesting venture was the 1950 production in Duncan, B.C., on Vancouver Island of an opera *Tzinguaw*, based almost entirely on west coast songs and dances and presented by a cast of Cowichan native Indians. Written by an enthusiastic amateur composer, Frank Morrison, it met with great success, being repeated over a period of more than three years in Victoria, Vancouver and four or five other centres, recorded and broadcast by the CBC and even relayed (in Spanish and Portuguese) to all countries of South America. Some of the melodies are imitations rather than genuine folk-songs but the whole work preserves much of the atmosphere of the totem-pole country with its striking landscape so graphically pictured by Emily Carr and other painters.

Scanning the scene from one side of Canada to the other, one may imagine that Verdi, with his feeling for the popular character of great art forms, would like Canada's pioneering in opera, and the persistence of both performers and listeners even where there are no opera houses. We recall the story of his walking with his prima donna on the Mediterranean shore when they came upon a fisherman returning from his work, singing a miscellany of Verdi's airs. The trio sang together into the early hours.

He might feel that another shore, that of Nova Scotia in Canada, was likely to become the setting for a similar scene. There, people have heard his music performed by the Nova Scotia Opera Association, occasionally in a theatre, more often in school halls in Halifax, Sydney, Glace Bay, Truro or Wolfville. Or they have heard it broadcast from tape recordings over the CBC's Maritime network. The repertoire has gone beyond Verdi. In recent seasons they have performed *Don Giovanni, The Marriage of Figaro, Tales of Hoffmann, Traviata, Madame Butterfly, Countess Maritza, Cavalleria Rusticana,* and a local folk opera, *The Broken Ring.* Mariss Vetra, now of Toronto where he conducts an opera workshop, started this company on its way so well that it is continuing with Feodor Brilts as conductor. It is not alone. Local amateurs of New Glasgow have presented *Orpheus,* under the direction of Charles Underwood. The CBC also bought broadcast rights and sent its recordings to wider audiences. This group is known as the Pictou County Opera Guild Company.

We have given these ventures more space than can be spared for others equally worthy, for several reasons. The Maritimes are not economically abreast of the rest of Canada. Mr. Vetra is Latvian-born; Mr. Underwood was born in Glace Bay, studied abroad and made a career elsewhere, but returned to give his people opera. And across Canada we see the same situation—conductors, directors, soloists, instrumentalists, some from Europe, some from our own towns, all Canadians making opera as best they can for Canadian audiences.

But the choice reason for our stressing Nova Scotia touches another question. Private effort by the Nova Scotia Opera Association, of which Mr. Justice Currie is President, has been assisted by provincial and civic grants. In other words, the beginnings of governmental co-operation have come, not where treasuries are most fat, but where the regional economy is difficult. We hear too often in Canada that there is nothing wrong with the arts that a million dollars would not cure. The point is rather that when the will of artists is complemented by a public will to support them, progress is possible.

The stage and the audience (always including the top gallery) must complement each other. Until this is achieved, we shall have what we see now. When it is, we shall have a national opera and ballet. Audiences may not be limited to the *élite*, the cognoscenti, the well-to-do. Opera shares that democratic quality which marks the British Derby. One can no more enjoy opera and ballet privately than the toffs who frequent the Royal Enclosure can enjoy the racing classic in the seclusion of their well-hedged estates. The easily caught up slogan of "doing something for the young" has tempted many into a cruel stupidity. Scholarship dancers and singers too often have little beyond a few weeks' employment per year on the stage for which to thank donors who meant to be generous. Some who think slowly and in ruts believe all would be well if tickets were cheap enough. Is it not sometimes forgotten that value on the stage is a better draw than cut rates at the box office? And is it not too often overlooked that sound business management must accompany production enterprise on a basis that is efficient as well as sympathetic? Sponsoring committees sometimes seem to think that an excess of enthusiasm is a substitute for prudent management.

After leaving the Maritimes, our survey must make a halt at Montreal where the Opera Guild was founded by Mme Pauline Donalda in 1941. It has developed a repertoire of fifteen productions, seven of which were firsts in Canada; other operas are so rarely heard that the Montreal performances could claim an important place in Canadian operatic pioneering. These latter included *Otello* and *Louise*. Their firsts included *Coq d'Or, The Magic Flute, The Abduction from the Seraglio, The Consul, Love for Three Oranges.* Casts have been overwhelmingly Canadian with a few imported soloists. The Montreal Festivals have, over a long period of years, been responsible for many fine operatic productions, chiefly in the summer months.

It is significant that a city with a less heterogeneous population, Ottawa, reports "not in the red." If it has not led in adventurous enterprises, neither has it built beyond what the foundations will carry. Ottawa steadily rises as a music centre, therefore. The Ottawa Grand Opera Company, founded in 1948 with 50 active members, is completely self-supporting and not in debt. It has presented some eight operas, most of them from the standard repertoire. The Orpheus

Operatic Society, founded in 1917, but incorporating the old Glee Club founded in 1906, owns its building, gives light opera and is self-supporting. The Civil Service Operatic Society gives Gilbert and Sullivan, and is self-supporting. All are amateur.

The Edmonton Civic Opera Association, chartered in 1935, occupies a unique niche of its own. It is an amateur group with fifty members, whose musical director and conductor is Mrs. J. B. Carmichael. The company has given two performances annually of either light or grand opera—and has never received any donation of any kind from civic or provincial sources or elsewhere. Out of its profits it has given annually a major scholarship of $300 for a vocal student, and three junior scholarships of $100 each. During the war its profits went towards buying an ambulance and other comforts for the armed forces. Its last two productions were *The Red Mill* and *The Vagabond King*, and it now has *Brigadoon* in preparation for early in 1955.

On the west coast, the University of British Columbia has established, as an extension feature, summer courses and productions of opera, usually in concert form. Vancouver's Theatre under the Stars must be given high credit because it has made one branch of stage music, light opera, professional and self-supporting. Playing to audiences in Malkin Bowl, Stanley Park, with seating capacity of 4,276, it has gained steadily since its establishment in 1939.

Coming to central Canada, one finds that the Royal Conservatory Opera Company of Toronto must face responsibility because much of the hope for a national opera lies in this company, whose members represent some of the best talent that has emerged across the country. The human responsibility is indicated by a glance at the names of places from which some of its singers come: St. Boniface, Man.; Weyburn, Sask.; Windsor, Ont.; Quebec, Que.; Bridgewater, N.S.; Calgary, Alta.; Vancouver, B.C.; Montreal, London, Ottawa, Hamilton, and so on.

The Royal Conservatory Opera Company, although not first in the field, has developed into a position of leadership since it grew out of the Opera School founded in 1946. And, in addition to productions under its own flag, it has given major resources to radio. CBC's television, gallantly essaying such operatic projects as *Fidelio* and *Don Giovanni*, has also drawn heavily on the same resources.

Obviously the steady build has been due to correct pride on the part of executives and teachers in attaining a standard, and that is still the company's basic asset, although the Toronto Opera Festival

Association has taken over from the Conservatory the practical task of trying to make ends meet when the last curtain goes down on the festivals. The presence of Edward Johnson as Chairman of the Board of Governors of the Conservatory has been an inspiration. Dr. Arnold Walter, to whose energetic efforts the establishment of the present Opera School at the Conservatory largely owes its inception, is now chiefly engaged in other fields. The Musical Director, Nicholas Goldschmidt, together with the Stage Director, Herman Geiger-Torel, and their able staff work within the Conservatory's School of Music of which Dr. Ettore Mazzoleni is Principal. All have made valuable contributions to the training of students and to the success of the productions.

The Royal Conservatory Company has a repertoire of some twenty works, plus some one-acters and an extensive list of excerpt programmes which are in demand as special engagement offerings. Opera followers may debate the Royal Conservatory productions—indeed one of the finest signs that opera is now an institution in Toronto is that there are enough people of varied tastes in opera to start an argument at any intermission. But any person whose experience extends beyond rare recordings and an occasional visit to the greatest opera houses, knows that there has been entertainment and often startling excellence in the festivals which have been offered to Toronto audiences and which have included *Orpheus, Hänsel and Gretel, La Serva Patrona, Gianni Schicchi, Rigoletto, Don Giovanni, La Bohème, Madame Butterfly, Faust, The Marriage of Figaro, The Magic Flute, Manon, The School for Fathers, Suor Angelica, The Bartered Bride, Così fan tutte, The Consul, Angélique, The Old Maid and the Thief.* Some singers who have become widely known in this company are Lois Marshall, Louise Roy, Marguerite Gignac, James Milligan, Mary Morrison, Theresa Gray, Irene Solemka, Joanne Ivey, Andrew MacMillan, Elizabeth Benson Guy, Gilles Lamontagne, Ernest Adams, Pierre Boutet and Jan Rubes.

When you find an old friend of Puccini's, Father Dante, coming up from his Brooklyn parish to hear *Madame Butterfly*, or opera executives travelling from South America to scout the Toronto productions, or when you discover that this company is included in the *Book of Knowledge*, you may take it that it is no mere native pride which makes Canadians feel that they see the basis of more than a local institution in the Royal Conservatory Opera Company.

But there we are—with a basis. Either longer seasons in Toronto or these in combination with more extensive touring are needed to give the company that institutional unity and integration which is the mark of experienced professionalism. It needs the certainty of combined public and private endowment.

It is interesting to note in passing that with a few exceptions all Canadian companies so far have by-passed Wagnerian opera and the Russian classics. These present production problems beyond the present scope of the best and most prosperous companies in our still young lyric theatre.

The light opera field in Toronto supplies one professional establishment, Melody Fair, now playing in the Mutual Street Arena, with seating capacity of 5,300 and with the largest theatre-in-the-round installation on the continent. They have audience problems to work out but, in addition to pleasing entertainment, they give scope for talent. Hundreds take auditions, and value the Equity cards they get if they join the company.

Ballet is a more meteoric story, has made more sensational news, has had the most hair-raising griefs and the most sudden successes. It has progressed more nearly to national status than has opera. The National Ballet, with Celia Franca as Director, has not only completed three coast-to-coast tours but has made successful forays into American cities near the border. For its 1954–55 season, tours east and west of Ontario will be abandoned, since long jumps are necessary to pass cities where audiences undoubtedly exist, but where there is no proper theatre accommodation. However, in addition to touring Ontario, the National Ballet, including an orchestra for the first time, will make extensive visits to the United States, performing in Detroit, Chicago, Pittsburgh, Philadelphia, New York, and other centres. A full-length *Swan Lake* will be its main feature. Also included in its repertoire this year is a new Canadian ballet, *Barbara Allen*, with an excellent score by Louis Applebaum and choreography by Joey Harris.

The Royal Winnipeg Ballet, directed by Gwyneth Lloyd, putting greater stress on contemporary themes, also has toured Canada and penetrated the United States. Its financial backing has been less secure, however, and a disastrous fire in Winnipeg this past season destroyed all its physical assets. The company will be inactive until the spring of 1955 as a result. Its many friends hope it will be fully rehabilitated by then, as its most successful repertoire has complemented rather than conflicted with the National Ballet contribution.

Several Canadian composers have of late years taken an interest in ballet. Among the works produced in various localities are Eric Wild's *The Shooting of Dan McGrew*, John Weinzweig's *The Red Ear of Corn*, Louis Applebaum's *Dark of the Moon*, Robert Fleming's *Shadow on the Prairie* and Hector Gratton's *Le Premier*.

Stability in the field of the dance is indicated by the organizing of the Canadian Dance Teachers' Association, with branches in Toronto, London, Calgary, Edmonton and Vancouver. Their aim is to maintain standards as well as a high level of ethics in the profession. The fact that there can be such an organization recalls that, as in opera, a host of studios and non-professional endeavours across the country have formed the organic basis from which a national ballet may grow strong. Boris Volkoff, still active in Toronto, may be mentioned as having done notable pioneering in central Canada to have ballet recognized as an institution.

As in opera, there is a panorama of effort across the country. The Halifax Theatre Ballet, directed by Hilda Strombergs, is sponsored by a guild and, in addition to its own programme, has taken part in operatic productions in the Maritimes. The Montreal Modern Dance Company, directed by Yoné Kvietys, is professional, has produced major works and has used Canadian music, including that by François Morel. Montreal now has the Heino Heiden Ballet, also professional, formerly of Vancouver, but remaining in Montreal because there is demand there for its work in television. Their heavy engagements for the future months include *Petrouchka*, *Ondine*, and about fifteen other programmes for Montreal CBC.

In Toronto, several studios have totalled many hundreds of students. The Janet Baldwin Ballet fills professional engagements. The Willy Blok Hanson Dance Group is completely professional and gave seven stage, plus sixteen TV performances last season. The company's art is based on Dalcroze rhythmics. Their Canadian numbers have included *The Loon's Necklace* and *Maria Chapdelaine*, with music by Calvin Jackson. These two companies, as well as the Toronto Festival Dancers, the Ottawa Classical Ballet and the Volkoff Classical Ballet, were among the many who participated in the sixth annual Ballet Festival of 1954.

Geographic distances in Canada, which have been mentioned

already in several connections, render it difficult for any ballet group in this country to see the work of international companies or to observe the activities of Canadian companies located in other cities. For this reason, the annual Ballet Festival, which is attended by groups from all regions of Canada, has provided a welcome opportunity for dancers, choreographers, composers, designers, working in classical or modern manner, to present their repertoire and receive comment upon it from critics and fellow-performers.

Every leading dance studio in Canada can point to dancers it has trained but who are now in companies in other countries because there is no permanent ballet here. Those who have young "finds" (such as little Judith Dornis who has been offered dance scholarships in Paris, London, Moscow and New York but is now with Celia Franca and Betty Oliphant in Toronto) are wondering, Will the national ballet situation mature in time? Or will Canada lose such prime material for distinguished ballet?

It has been said in the course of this essay that the lyric theatre in Canada has not reached national stature. But there is a very real sense in which its components represent the nation. Its best performers come from all parts of the Dominion. Its artistic achievements are known in London and New York. Some of its productions are even more widely familiar through CBC broadcasts and the international distribution of National Film Board moving pictures. It has sent some of its leading singers and dancers abroad to perform with major companies.

What is the next step? Certainly not to settle down at the present level of performance. Who knows how soon some individual patron, syndicate or government may be prepared to endow a Canadian Glyndebourne, a Sadler's Wells? Even the Canadian National Exhibition may raise its sights for the Grandstand Show. It could do worse, for instance, than to commission a panoramic production of Aïda, complete with ships afloat, camels, elephants, military bands and troops on the march. And of course our best operatic and ballet talent. That would be a fresh chapter in New World history. The next step is to be ready.

SOLO ARTISTS

Ettore Mazzoleni

I think I know the reason why music, more than any other art, is subject to the changes of which it is accused: it depends all the time on those who perform it.

Grétry, *Mémoires, ou Essai sur la musique*, 1789

Good performers who will give to the musical life of a country a distinction of its own are produced only when certain conditions are fulfilled. These conditions are talent, training and opportunity.

The performer, like the composer, is as much a craftsman as an artist. He may have talent—and it has been proven again and again both at home and abroad, particularly abroad, that we have an abundance of talented young people in Canada—but this talent must be trained and exercised. There must be teachers to develop it and a public ready and willing to give it a chance. There must be informed criticism of a kind which can have meaning for the public and the performer, and there must be an audience with confidence enough in its own judgment to be able to recognize talent for what it is worth.

These conditions are not likely to be met in the culture of a comparatively young nation. But Canada is rapidly coming of age, and the history of performance in the last half-century is a perfect reflection of this growing state and of the improvement in those conditions necessary to performance.

To begin with, we imported most of our music and musicians from England, France and other European countries with long-established musical traditions of their own; and we exported to those same countries many of our finest young musicians who had been brought in touch with the art of music. Later we lost them also to the United States because there, in well-endowed institutions and large centres, they could get the scholarship training they needed and the opportunities and recognition which were their right.

A glance back at certain Canadian-born performers who made an international name for themselves is very telling. Let us take a few examples. Just over a hundred years ago, Marie-Louise-Cécile-Emma

106

Lajeunesse, later known to the world as Emma Albani, was born at Chambly, Quebec, the daughter of a musician who played the organ, violin, harp and piano. Taken to Albany, New York, while still in her teens, she was urged to go to Europe for study and funds were raised for this purpose. She studied in Paris and Milan, adopted the Italianized name of Albani and was then launched on a spectacular career both in Europe and in America as an operatic singer.

Edward Johnson, whose career as a singer belongs to the first thirty years or so of the twentieth century, was born in Guelph, Ontario. He was interested in music from childhood, but it was only after he had completed a year of university life that he was advised to go to New York for study because of the unusual promise of his voice. The pattern was clear. Despite his early success in operetta he realized that he must go to Italy. He studied in Florence, changed his name to Eduardo di Giovanni and started a brilliant operatic career which eventually led to his becoming General Manager of the Metropolitan Opera in New York.

Lynnwood Farnam, the organ virtuoso, was born at Sutton, Quebec, in 1885. His early lessons were taken at home, but he soon won a scholarship which took him to England to the Royal College of Music. He returned to Montreal for a few years, but then moved to posts in Boston and New York, touring extensively as a recitalist and teaching in addition to his duties as a church organist.

Kathleen Parlow, born in Calgary in 1890, was taken as a child to San Francisco, and later to St. Petersburg to study with Leopold Auer. She had already made a successful *début* in England, and now toured in Russia, Scandinavia, Germany, Holland and Belgium. She settled in the United States in 1910 and, after many tours which included Oriental countries, finally returned to Canada where she is still active.

The pattern was thus only too often the same: a brilliant young student had to go abroad for his training and then, having succeeded, was absorbed into the world market and in danger of being lost to his own country. To a point, that was as it should be; talent of this high order is so rare that it belongs to the international concert stage. At the time when these careers were being made, scope for performance in Canada was in any event very limited. But unfortunately the pattern had been set for that body of good young native artists which grew larger as Canada itself developed and as musical life here took on a more vigorous and active character. They not only went overseas or to the United States for their training because the opportunities for advanced study and performance were not yet sufficiently developed in this country, but they soon lost their connection with Canada and became instead a part of the musical life of their country of adoption. It is interesting to note, by way of example, that at one time nine of the eighteen string players in the famed Boyd Neel Orchestra were Canadians who had gone to England on valuable scholarships offered by the Royal Schools. Many of them remained in England or settled elsewhere, including Frederick Grinke who was leader of the orchestra for ten years and a distinguished soloist and chamber music player. The "lost legion" of Canadian musicians during the first half of this century must surely be an unnecessarily large one.

What is the situation today as it affects the performer? We have seen a remarkable growth of interest and activity in serious music during the past twenty or thirty years, partly as the result of mechanical inventions such as the phonograph, the radio and now television which have made the literature of music readily available to every individual, partly as the outcome of the recognition by educational authorities of the high value of the study of music, rightly undertaken, and partly as the product of the leadership given by a few outstanding musicians who chose to give their abilities as performers, educators and administrators to their country of birth rather than go abroad or to the United States where they would have been more adequately rewarded. The influence of these teachers together with that of a number of fine musicians who were brought to this country to fill certain posts or who decided to settle here, has developed a high standard of performance which our audiences are quick to recognize.

It was this high standard which prompted Arthur Benjamin on his return to England at the end of World War II, after spending some years in Canada and touring the country many times as an adjudicator, to issue a warning which might well have been heeded by our immigration authorities. "Woe betide any European who hopes to make a living in musical Canada if his standards are not sufficiently high." He went on to speak of the excellent teaching of young people up to the age of fifteen, teaching which was more adventurous and less hide-bound than that in England, for instance, but he did feel that there was a scarcity of the sort of teacher who could put a final polish and the stamp of maturity on performance.

There was some measure of truth in his criticism but there is less now, when the major music schools are at last offering scholarship training at an advanced level and of a kind which before could only have been obtained abroad. Technical standards in Canada, as in many other countries, are now so high that each new generation seems to begin where the last left off. It is not unusual to hear young players with a skill that would have been considered quite unique if not impossible one hundred, even fifty years ago. And the standard is still rising. Of course, only the rare talent will achieve permanent success. That is inevitable, but from the many good students we are now finding who might never before have had a chance will emerge the few who will become outstanding artists.

The last few years have seen more than one example of such young musicians, trained entirely or almost entirely in Canada, beginning to establish for themselves a reputation in their own country despite all those geographical and other natural handicaps from which the musician suffers as much as any other artist, and then finding or making for themselves the break which will give them an international career. Lois Marshall, that remarkable young singer who carried on all her musical studies in Toronto, was on the way to becoming known to the whole country when she won the Naumburg Prize in New York. This gave her a Town Hall *début*, which led at once to a contract with Columbia Artists Management, one of the dominating agencies in the concert field. This led in turn to auditions which resulted in her engagement by such conductors as Toscanini and Munch, and to tours in Canada as well as the United States which should serve to establish her as one of the finest young artists any country has produced. Betty-Jean Hagen, the violinist, was trained almost solely in Canada. A series of awards, the Naumburg in New York, the Pathé-Marconi in Paris, the Carl Flesch in London, and the Harriet Cohen Medal (1952) for the outstanding woman violinist in the British Commonwealth, carried her through that precarious passage from student to professional; during the season 1954–55 she will travel for the eleventh time to Europe for a concert tour. Glenn Gould, surely one of the most remarkable of young musicians and pianists, was trained entirely in Canada. For some time he has confined his performances to this country. In Canada we have a basic distrust of our own ability to produce anything really outstanding, and as a result we either pay the artist a wholly meaningless and harmful lip-service or treat him with condescension until he has been accepted in New York or London or Paris; nevertheless in this case shrewd guidance and management have given proof that a native artist can build for himself a national reputation. If it can be accomplished in this particular instance, the moral is obvious.

It might seem invidious to mention only these three young performers who are on the threshold of what might well be great careers, and not to mention the many others who have already made a place for themselves at home or abroad, or who would also seem to have an exciting future before them. They have been chosen simply because they show the change which has of recent years come over the Canadian scene.

The change, however, is not being brought about as yet without very serious handicaps and limitations. In the first place, the Canadian concert-goer is in a much happier position than the Canadian performer. Being a neighbour of the United States we have most of the great artists of the world close at hand. Consequently American agencies, together with certain national agencies and local musical societies, can offer us a constant supply of "name" material at what for the concert-goer is a very moderate price. While no one would wish to deny the musical public the chance and the right to hear the incomparably great performers, there can be no doubt that a great deal of our own talent is as a result never given the opportunity it deserves. This is particularly true in the case of those cities whose musical life is largely dominated by the series of Community Concerts organized by American agencies.

Because as yet we have developed no national agency of our own which can begin to rival these American agencies in organization and financial resource, those of our artists who would like to earn a living by performance alone must often face not only the usual handicaps of a public which does not want to hear them until they are known and critics who in some cases are quite unqualified to judge them, but also the crippling costs of travelling long distances for comparatively few engagements. It is sometimes difficult for them to do more than meet expenses, simply because artists from the United States have crowded them out of so many of the centres which would have helped to make up a satisfactory circuit. What is even more disturbing—and it has been the cause of some bitter controversy—is that often the series of concerts arranged by the agencies will include with the "name" artists one or two others who are not as well known as and indeed in some cases are actually inferior in talent and experience to Canadians who are looking for opportunities in the concert field.

It is not surprising then that so many of our finest young musicians even now leave the country feeling that they have been spurned, when all they asked was a fair chance and a reasonable livelihood.

But there is a brighter side to the picture. Increasing demand for Canadian artists, which seems to be a sign of our national maturity, has led to a number of Canadians being added to the lists of Community Concerts Service and other agencies of American origin; more recently it has led to the establishment of a new agency in Toronto, Community Concerts of Canada, Ltd., to direct the business affairs of Canadian artists and organizations. Those who make the major circuits will have the chance to enjoy the career of a successful concert-artist, doing the sort of thing they would most want and are perhaps most fitted to do. Those who do not may never rise above the level of the struggling artist. Sooner or later these will be disillusioned and will probably abandon a concert career, hoping to teach, or throw themselves on the mercy of the already burdened CBC. But that is part of the magnificent gamble of talent, which demands of those who take part in it relentless study and concentration on doing the best of which they are capable.

The American agencies, however, are not alone in recognizing the demand for Canadian artists. For some seasons now certain musical clubs and societies, particularly in Toronto, Montreal and Winnipeg, have consistently included Canadians in their series. Several concert managers are working on behalf of Canadian artists. Each year brings the announcement from various communities of new series dedicated solely to Canadian artists. Unfortunately the response of the public is still very disappointing, especially in those crowded centres where the concert-going public at best is only a small fraction of the potential audience, and where the highly competitive nature of the enterprise is a handicap in itself.

For the young artist in any country at the beginning of his concert career and very much in need of public appearances the problem has always been considered acute. However, there have been a number of notable efforts to promote the interests of the beginner in certain parts of Canada. Something like fifteen years ago a "Young Artists Series," with promotion by the Federation of Music Teachers, was initiated in the western provinces largely through the efforts of that splendid teacher and idealist, Lyell Gustin of Saskatoon. It has now grown so successfully that twice a year three soloists chosen from the four western provinces are sent on tour from Winnipeg to Victoria. In addition, the Saskatchewan Arts Board has organized for some years a

"Young Musicians Series" of Saskatchewan-born or -trained soloists who tour the cities and towns of the province. The Ontario Department of Education organizes and subsidizes in much the same way tours in smaller places where concerts are given in school halls. These tours, directed since 1946 by Major Brian McCool, have in some seasons engaged as many as seventy-five individual artists for more than 150 concerts. Les Jeunesses Musicales du Canada, founded in 1949, is now a member of a federation representative of fifteen countries and already includes in its circuits thirty-eight towns in the three provinces of Quebec, Ontario and New Brunswick. Not only does it promote concerts by young Canadians, but it also arranges exchange concerts with European countries. In Ontario the Concert Associations of Canada organize concerts on a co-operative basis for a closed membership. Since their formation in 1951 they have promoted the interests of some of our most outstanding artists.

One of the most hopeful signs of improvement in the situation is the appearance within recent years of gramophone companies dedicated largely to recording Canadian artists. These are still in their infancy but have already succeeded in bringing to the notice of a wide public much of the fine work being done in this country. During the 1930's and 40's, when serious music was recorded in ever increasing amount and when many an artist won much of his fame through the medium of the gramophone, it was a serious handicap to the Canadian performer that his work was so seldom available in this medium. Let us hope that the new companies, of which a more detailed account is given elsewhere in this book, will help him in the future to win ever wider acclaim.

There have been many other enterprises of the kind, too numerous to list but all indicative of the fact that we are at last awakening to our own resources and taking some pride in developing our own performers. Two radio programmes, for example, "Singing Stars of Tomorrow" and "Nos Futures Etoiles," have done much to find new talent and to give it a chance, but more than that they have made a fair proportion of the public realize something of the unusual wealth of material which is ours.

It is still difficult in Canada to make a living solely as a performer, except as an orchestral player or through the opportunities offered by radio and television. Many of our performers, as soon as they reach a certain level of excellence and experience, are still apt to be lured away by better rewards and larger scope than we can offer. It is to be hoped that the Canadian public will not remain indifferent to our own artists until they have received the stamp of approval from abroad.

One problem remains: how can our potential performers survive the period when their talents are maturing—the period between graduation and professionalism—without having to pursue some occupation which will distract them, or having to accept work which is not relevant to their aims as artists? The old argument is that if they have genuine talent they will win through anyway. In some cases it is a valid one, and we can quote examples to prove it. But how many have been lost because they could not afford to take the gamble?

CHAMBER MUSIC

Marcus Adeney

Mark how one string, sweet husband to another,
Strikes each in each by mutual ordering;
Resembling sire and child and happy mother,
Who, all in one, one pleasing note do sing:
Whose speechless song, being many, seeming one,
Sings this to thee: "Thou single wilt prove none."

Shakespeare, *Sonnet VIII*

For the Western world generally, including a minority of Canadians, chamber music is not just a part of our European heritage; it is essentially a means of communication. In its classical form this was house music like radio or television. It came into existence as an aristocratic recreation, after instrumental techniques had been brought to a kind of perfection in the larger forms employed by Bach and Handel. While the early Canadian scene was unsuitable, our ways of living not propitious for the transplanting of chamber music, there has always been a friendly welcome here for the newcomer bearing cultural goods. This hospitable attitude towards things new or even strange derives from the fact that although only a part of the European heritage could be expected to flourish in pioneering times, persons with exceptional talent or training were not altogether lacking. The amateur violist could not rest until he had gathered other string players about him and initiated them into the glories of Haydn, and the one-time concert-goer was naturally unwilling to drop his enthusiasm and judgment into a pool of silence.

From a *History of Galt*, published in 1880, we learn about "Mr. James S. Glennie, who was Clerk of the Division Court, and had been a stock-broker in the city of London, England. His favourite instrument was the violincello [*sic*]." Mr. Glennie not only played but also composed music. Among his friends was John Kennedy, an old Highlander "who followed the occupation of a limeburner. He was excellent at strathspeys and reels. A third was John Garrison, an

American by birth. Garrison made his living by hunting, trapping, and fiddling, but chiefly the latter. The three formed themselves into a band, and frequently met at Barlow's tavern in the afternoon, where an audience would soon collect, and they would discourse those sweet sounds which 'sublime emotions kindle,' until the close of the day, and often far into the night." This was in 1838. Seventy years later similar events were taking place only a few miles down the Grand River in the town of Paris, Ontario. Here three executives of the Penman Company formed the nucleus of a chamber orchestra. They were C. B. Robinson, trumpet, O. R. Whitby, viola, and W. H. Adeney, piano. The writer's mother, an excellent violinist, was pressed into service with her more promising pupils, and thereafter quite serious music, for instruments in various combinations, was heard at parties and in concerts. Thus in small towns as well as large centres, wherever musically trained people came together, the more accessible chamber music of the masters was kept alive by string players; arrangements for two pianos or for piano-four-hands took the place of symphonies or concerted performance. The pervasive amateur, for whose pleasure so many masterpieces were written, cherished "the tradition" not only in his heart but in Peters' great editions and with lusty performances whenever occasion allowed. So did the few professionals, for whom there was only sporadic employment in the early days.

While the beginnings of recognizably professional chamber music in Canada are, and perhaps always will be, obscure, we look to Quebec for the first ensembles. A famous early organization, Lavigne's Septuar Haydn, was well established in 1871. It derived from two famous clubs, the Quintette and the Septette, and consisted of a string quintet, flute and piano. It participated in the Boston Peace Jubilee (1872) and gave hundreds of performances in public. This group, which owned a large and valuable library, was dissolved only upon formation of the Société Symphonique de Québec. Most chamber music recitals till the end of the century must have consisted of arranged numbers, or individual movements from original works, interspersed with vocal or instrumental solos. This situation, judging from collections of programmes from Toronto and smaller Ontario centres, seems to have been paralleled in English-speaking Canada.

An internationally famous violinist, Jehin-Prume, who settled in Canada in 1867, helped to establish Montreal's first effective chamber music organization, L'Association Artistique, a string quartet appearing with the pianist Maria Heynberg. In 1885 a wealthy citizen, George Drummond, engaged a quartet led by Reichling for weekly concerts at his home before invited guests. This had its equivalent in Toronto at a much later date when musicales were given by Miss Mc-Cormick at "Oaklands," first with expensively imported players, then with local musicians under the direction of Karl Ondricek. A programme dated February 27, 1919, notes the performance of a Mendelssohn quartet by Mr. Ondricek, Oswald Roberts (cellist), Dr. Wagner and Mr. Louden. The last two named were accomplished amateurs.

John Ellis (born in Norfolk, 1795) came to Canada in 1836, bringing with him a Peter Walmsley cello. From that time onward, there were chamber music clubs in Toronto where he made his home, for this excellent musician was indefatigable "and never to be seen without his bass." When the Philharmonic Society gave its first concert (1854) a "Serenade Trio" by Beethoven was offered by F. Griebel, a professional violinist who had left Jenny Lind's touring company, Mr. Childs, violist, and Mr. Ellis, who insisted on the word "amateur" appearing with his name on every programme. With Mr. Noverre these three formed a String Quartette Society and gave many public performances, adding one or two flutes to the ensemble as occasion required. Also notable at this time was a Piano Quartette with Carl Pieler, piano, Ernst Pieler, cello, Mr. Noverre, violin, and Mr. Thomas, viola. By 1878 when the *Mail* published an article on music in Toronto, "members of such groups were too numerous to mention."

About the year 1875 the Beethoven Quintette Club of Boston was highly favoured by Toronto audiences. This consisted of a string quartet together with W. Reizel, who played viola, flute, or cello as occasion demanded. The Beethoven Quartette of Buffalo, assisting "a chorus and orchestra of 200 performers," opened the New Pavilion in the Horticultural Gardens in 1879. The season of 1885–86 was memorable for "Popular Quartet Concerts," given on alternate Monday nights at the Horticultural Gardens by Jacobsen, Bayley, Fisher, and the cellist Ludwig Corell, especially brought out from Germany. Attendance reached a high of 1,400, and works as serious as Mozart's Clarinet Quintet were featured. In Ottawa there was a string quartet as early as 1884, and an Ottawa String Quartet was formed on a more substantial basis in 1914.

It would seem useful in the space at my disposal to indicate by several instances the steps by which performances of chamber music have been able to gain a nation-wide, if limited, public acceptance. Undoubtedly the European musicians who came to Montreal or Toronto were responsible for an impetus still to be found among amateurs, and for a reliable critical audience. Wide diffusion and a larger public had, of course, to wait upon the coming of radio and accessible recordings.

Notable in the early years of this century was the Toronto String Quartet, which played under Frank Blachford's direction from 1905 until after World War I. Concerts were given on a subscription basis and proved to be self sustaining. The Academy String Quartet was established shortly after the violinist Luigi von Kunits settled in Toronto in 1912. The membership of both groups changed from time to time, but some fine chamber players of the period should be mentioned: violinists Roland Roberts, Arthur Ely, Nora Hayes; violists Frank Converse Smith and Alfred Bruce; cellists Henry Saunders, Frederick Nicolai, Leo Smith and George Bruce. Longest lived of all Canadian chamber music groups is probably the Hambourg Trio. Founded in Europe by the three famous brothers Mark, Jan and Boris in 1905, it was re-formed shortly after their father, Professor Michael Hambourg, with Jan and Boris, came to Toronto in 1912. A recital at Massey Hall celebrated the occasion of Mark's visit to Canada in 1915. In 1935 the original (European) trio after appearing with the Toronto Symphony Orchestra, embarked on a "Gala Tour," giving ten concerts. Many well-known musicians have belonged to the Hambourg Trio: pianists Grace Smith Harris, Reginald Stewart, Clement Hambourg; violinists Geza de Kresz, Elie Spivak, Vino Harisay and Harry Adaskin. At the time of his sudden death in 1954, Boris Hambourg was planning a series of trio concerts with Pearl Palmason, violinist, and Earle Moss, pianist.

Montreal made history in 1910 with the provincially endowed Dubois Quartette: A. Chamberland, A. Dansereau, E. Schneider, and J.-B. Dubois. Although this excellent group may have suffered from lack of popular support in the early days, it did not break up until 1920 when Chamberland founded his own quartet. For some candid comment on the level of public taste in 1913 we are indebted to Arthur Laurendeau: "In dealing with the subject of chamber music in the city of Montreal, the critic finds very little material, since this branch of the musical art might almost be put down as non-existent. Our prevalent taste for the noisy keeps it in perpetual exile from us, and most efforts in this line have led to dismal failure. There is no doubt that what we lack is an educated public, open to this highest manifestation of music."[1] Beside this, however, should be placed the

[1]"Chamber and Church Music in Montreal," in *Year Book of Canadian Art,* 1913 (Toronto: Arts and Letters Club).

impressive list of J.-B. Dubois' chamber music activities. At the end of the century Montrealers were attending concerts by the Haydn Trio: Emery Lavigne, pianist, J.-J. Goulet, violinist, and M. Dubois. In 1904 the first McGill Quartette was formed with Alfred De Sève, J.-J. Goulet, A. Chamberland and the same distinguished cellist. Again we hear of Dubois in connection with the Beethoven Trio (1908–10).

Even before the early thirties, changes impended for performing musicians in this country. We must remember that during and for several years after World War I, leading moving picture theatres maintained large orchestras. Toronto's Allen and Regent "symphonies," which raised many a dull film to almost operatic stature, required the full-time services of our best players. At this time touring artists held the stage; unforgettable concerts were given by the Flonzaley, London and other famous quartets. Then came radio, with its ambiguous promise of world audiences for music and entertainment; and suddenly the prospects for frequent performances by two, three or four musicians revived. Finally, after the setbacks of the depression, prosperity came to Canada bringing with it a new sense of pride and responsibility.

In 1924 the present Governor-General of Canada, the Right Honourable Vincent Massey, established the Hart House Quartet on the basis of a twenty-year grant from the Massey Foundation. In addition to giving concerts to the students at Hart House and Convocation Hall (University of Toronto), this distinguished group, whose original members were Geza de Kresz, Harry Adaskin, Milton Blackstone and Boris Hambourg, toured successfully abroad and introduced essential chamber works to a whole generation of Canadians. It survived until 1945 although the war years were unpropitious and competition in the concert world severe. James Levey, former leader of the London String Quartet, replaced de Kresz in 1935, Adolf Koldofsky replaced Adaskin in 1938, and Blackstone's chair was taken by Allard de Ridder in 1940. Other changes followed, but it will be noted that Boris Hambourg played for the lifetime of the Quartet and of the Hambourg Trio, except for one season when the Hart House Quartet was on tour. At that time his place in the Trio was taken by the present writer.

Elie Spivak came to Toronto in 1925 as violinist, teacher and (later) Concertmaster of the Toronto Symphony Orchestra. In 1929, with Harold Sumberg, Donald Heins and Leo Smith he founded the Toronto Conservatory Quartet which gave regular concerts, often of unusual music, wisely supplementing the work of the Hart House group. Those were promising years for chamber music, partly because a generation of young Canadians had come to maturity. These players did not carry the obvious credentials of their European elders, and they found it even harder to gain patronage. Products of local teaching and theatre orchestras—with at most a few years' study abroad—they were ambitious, realistic, prepared to play ball with the sponsors of advertising. In a country new to its own opportunities and to the cumulative riches of a musical tradition, they could only work hard, honour great men and further such essential matters as chamber music without hope of much tangible reward. Joyce Hornyansky's notable series of "Fireside Concerts" in Toronto depended largely upon these strenuous youngsters. Their need for recognition in a concert field of their own making was exemplified in Samuel D. Hersenhoren's New World Chamber Orchestra, a group of six strings with piano. Lacking endowment, it was inevitable that these players should finally go their own ways, each bending his talent to whatever economic wind might blow. The thirties, as everyone knows, were bad years for non-essential industries. In the Canadian West excellent musicians acknowledged a park bench as home.

But another change was impending. In Montreal the Société de Musique Euterpe, organized in 1933, had, only a year later, given thirty-six chamber music performances over Radio-Etat. At the same time (1933) Joseph Shadwick, one of the best violinists ever to leave Canada for greener fields abroad, returned to Winnipeg for one memorable season. His radio-sponsored quartet (the other members being John Sutter, Eugene Hudson and Isaac Mamott) was so successful that the CBC continued a weekly series for about five years afterward, with Isaac Mamott, cellist, directing the Tudor Quartet. Radio has since been the mainstay of chamber music in Canada, and its adoption of that role in the mid-thirties was one reason, no doubt, why Murray Adaskin announced (1936) that an ensemble hitherto sponsored by the Royal York Hotel of Toronto would give concerts as the Toronto Trio. The other members were Cornelius Ysselstyn and Louis Crerar. Thanks to the interest of the Canadian Pacific Railway in music, similar developments occurred in Vancouver, Regina and Calgary.

It is not surprising that serious musicians should have gravitated to Montreal or Toronto. We might indeed wonder at the extent of talent and training found in Winnipeg but for the fact that in 1913 a full military band was brought out from England for the forming of the 106th Battalion, Winnipeg Light Infantry. A year later these men—highly trained, versatile musicians—were sent to France with the 10th

Battalion; but many settled in the West after their army service and provided a sound basis for teaching and performance. Since that time Winnipeg has given to Canada a succession of fine string players, most of whom acknowledge a debt to teachers W. G. Rutherford or John Waterhouse. High standards of chamber music performance were set by the Cherniavskys (like the Hambourgs of Toronto represented by a father and three sons) and by the Nelsova family (father and three daughters). Winnipeg is, of course, associated with the rise of cellist Zara Nelsova to world eminence. In the early 1940's was formed the Canadian Trio, all members of which—Kathleen Parlow, Zara Nelsova and Sir Ernest MacMillan—were born in Canada. This trio continued to function for two or three years, giving concerts and broadcasts in Toronto and other cities and appearing (in the Beethoven Triple Concerto) with the Toronto Symphony Orchestra. About the same time a series of sonata recitals was given over the air by Miss Parlow and Sir Ernest.

It remains only to indicate new directions and to speak briefly of those professional artists who are maintaining the standards of chamber music demanded in Canada today. In the writer's opinion LP records, by expanding the horizons of our listening enjoyment, must affect every phase of concert performance. While the string quartet, surely the most intimate and eloquent form of classical music, will hold its place so long as men delight in the refinement and rationalization of emotion, earlier and later groupings of instruments, dealing with other subject-matter on other terms, now claim our liveliest interest.

In this context the importance of Madame Celia Bizony's Musica Antica e Nuova in Montreal could hardly be exaggerated. Since 1951 this group has presented music of different periods and styles from the twelfth century to the present time, much of it the product of research in Europe. Madame Bizony, as singer and musicologist, collaborated with Boris Ord at King's College, Cambridge, in founding the original Musica Antica e Nuova in England. In addition to the Sunday recitals of this society, various concerts and broadcasts indicate a new range of musical interest in Montreal. Five chamber music programmes given in connection with the Montreal Festivals for 1954 include rarely heard masterpieces such as *The Art of the Fugue* by J. S. Bach, conducted by Alexander Brott, and a whole group of novelties, from Telemann to Alban Berg, presented by the Musica Antica e Nuova.

The concerts given at Strachan Hall, Trinity College, Toronto, as part of the annual Earle Grey Shakespeare Festival, are no less timely. In this connection Wolfgang Grunsky's Quintette of Viols, using the famous Hart House collection, should be mentioned as succeeding a group established by the late Leo Smith. Employing modern instruments, a quartet under my own direction, with Hyman Goodman, Berul Sugarman and Eugene Hudson, twice presented Elizabethan music for the Earle Grey Festival. Very different programmes were given by Glenn Gould at the Royal Conservatory of Music, Toronto, in October, 1952, and January, 1954, with Victor Feldbrill conducting. At the first of these Schoenberg's *Ode to Napoleon* was declaimed by Barbara Franklin supported by a group of younger string players, and songs by the same composer were sung by Elizabeth Benson Guy. The second concert featured works by Webern and Berg, the players being Morris Weinzweig (saxophone), Morry Kernerman (violin), Ezra Schabas (clarinet) and Glenn Gould (piano).

Interest in unusual music and in the work of young Canadians is exemplified in the offerings of the Hamilton Chamber Music Society. Programmes for 1953–54 included a performance by outstanding chamber players from Toronto, in solo and in combination, and an appearance by the Royal Conservatory Quartet, composed of younger practising musicians. I wonder how many of the music-lovers who attended these admirable concerts recall that some forty years ago Hamilton possessed one of the finest civic choirs in the nation and, thanks to the Bartmann family, had excellent chamber music of its own. Gordon Jeffery of the London (Ontario) School of Church Music has a record of five years' production of chamber music of the baroque and pre-baroque era with the organ as an integral part of the ensemble. Along with this goes music of today—by Hindemith and modern American composers such as Barber and Porter. For those who favour the Haydn-to-Brahms era there is the fifteen-year-old London Chamber Music Society, an amateur group which gives four or five concerts a year.

Two well-established quartets in the West have shown, each in its own way, how limiting circumstance may be turned to advantage. The Knight Wilson Quartet in Regina plays largely for its own pleasure (let us not forget that some of the greatest music was written with this purpose in mind) but also gives recitals. The Edmonton String Quartet, made up of part-time players with the exception of violinist-leader Edgar Williams, broadcasts weekly from a local station and gives annual concerts. Also at Edmonton, the Women's Musical Club sponsors a chamber music recital by members of the local symphony orchestra.

In Vancouver The Friends of Chamber Music have since 1947 presented a succession of famous ensembles. Similar programmes were provided in Toronto by The Friends of Great Music. Perhaps even more important are such groups as the Kitchener-Waterloo Chamber Music Society which presents five concerts each year, four being given by local musicians, the fifth by artist students from the Royal Conservatory of Music of Toronto. Internationally famous quartets also appear under concert management. The "Pro Musica" series of Montreal, like that of the Women's Musical Club of Toronto, helps to create a discriminating audience by making something of a social event out of concerts heard at regular intervals during winter months.

No Canadian university supports a string quartet, but when chamber players like Harry Adaskin, or composers of chamber music like Jean Coulthard, are appointed to the staff of the University of British Columbia, when Murray Adaskin accepts a post at Saskatoon or Alexander Brott is established at McGill in Montreal, a step in that desirable direction has perhaps been taken. Yet unless a resident quartet can be provided for, cities other than the few largest afford an insufficient base on which to build ensembles.

The Banff School of Fine Arts, where in the summer months Clayton Hare gives a course in string playing, and the Otter Lake Festival in Quebec are instances of how leisure time may be spent on music study and performance under ideal conditions. The Banff School, established by the University of Alberta in 1933, stresses student-work-in-progress; the Otter Lake Festival, concerts of unusual music presented by distinguished artists. Both encourage a serious and properly social approach to the playing of stringed instruments.

One of the liveliest of our contemporaries, Alexander Brott, founded the McGill Quartet in 1939, with Mildred Goodman, Edwin Sherard and Lotte Goetzel. This group was recently absorbed into the McGill Chamber Music Society, now in its sixteenth season. Present programmes range from Telemann to Schoenberg, whereas until three years ago they were definitely classical. As a notable composer Mr. Brott may have helped to direct the trend—in line with Madame Bizony's group—in favour of new music and deserved revivals.

Other quartets have formed and re-formed, to meet occasions or to broadcast special series. Founded in 1943, the Parlow Quartet of Toronto (present members Kathleen Parlow, Andrew Benac, Stanley Solomon and Isaac Mamott) has made extensive tours and given many radio recitals. Violinist John Dembeck, with a representative group which has included Robert Warburton, Stanley Kolt and Cornelius Ysselstyn, has done as much as anyone to maintain CBC Toronto's high repute for string playing. Elie Spivak, long associated with chamber music in Toronto, as we have seen, established his own quartet in 1952 with Francesco Fusco, Jack Neilson and Philip Spivak. The return of Albert Pratz to the scene of his earliest triumphs as a violinist saw a revival of chamber works with variously combined instruments. The Festival Trio (Pratz, Mamott, Gould) appeared at the first Stratford Shakespearean Festival and has since been heard on the national networks. Leo Barkin, accompanist to a generation of concert artists, has contributed as pianist to the success of very many of Toronto's chamber groups. More recently George Brough and Mario Bernardi have done notable work in the same field, while John Newmark of Montreal, a musician of wide interests and accomplishments, has with his Clementi piano recalled the charm of early keyboard music to listeners across Canada. His new programme (1954) brings chamber music informally and intimately into the realm of television.

The somewhat novel approach of the Solway Quartet was partly due to its first appearing in smaller centres under the auspices of Ontario's Department of Education. Two steps were taken to overcome any sense of strangeness in an audience new to string quartets: first, the programmes selected were as various as the form traditionally allowed; secondly, both the composer and the music were introduced by informal but informative remarks. Founded in 1948, the ensemble now consists of Maurice Solway, Berul Sugarman, Eugene Hudson and Marcus Adeney.

In the far West the name of Jean de Rimanoczy overshadows all others. This excellent violinist has given Vancouver prominence throughout Canada in the field of chamber music by imposing the stamp of his personality upon a number of organizations, including his string quartet. Associated with him have been the English cellist, Audrey Piggott, Smythe Humphries, violist, and the best of string players resident in British Columbia. Albert Steinberg, John Avison and Eugene Hudson have at various times directed chamber groups there. No doubt the presence of that remarkable pianist-composer, Arthur Benjamin, for several years resident in Vancouver, affected the programmes as well as the performance of chamber music.

Since January, 1954, Dirk Keetbaas, formerly of Toronto, has been providing a series of programmes (CBC Western Network, from Winnipeg) featuring his own instrument, the flute, with an otherwise flexible group. This, reports Mr. Chester Duncan, has had a rejuvenating effect on chamber music in that city, so varied and interesting are the works performed. John Waterhouse, violin teacher, and Ronald Gibson of the School of Music, University of Manitoba, should also be mentioned for their encouragement of group playing in music education.

In Montreal, as we have seen, the unusual and the new has been stressed by musicians and their supporters alike. At the same time classical concerts, provided by some of the world's finest ensembles, have kept the tradition very much alive. Audiences and performers will be recruited from the fortunate youngsters who have attended the concerts of Les Jeunesses Musicales, which employ much of the best Canadian talent for a series of concerts and lecture recitals in several provinces, notably Quebec. A high degree of co-operation marks chamber music activities in Montreal. Hyman Bress (from Cape Town) and Walter Joachim (German cellist) with pianist John Newmark, formed a trio which has given concerts and broadcasts, and has appeared at the Otter Lake Festival. Mario Duschenes, flautist, has devoted numberless hours (like the cellist Rowland Pack of Toronto) to developing a recorder group which has already broadcast with great success.

The name of Rowland Pack reminds us that Mr. Pack, his wife Carol Wright, pianist, and violinist Joseph Pach, now form a trio which has toured extensively in Ontario and Quebec. Another generation of Canadian musicians, with interests related to a rapidly changing environment, is engaged in the presentation of new works by Canadians. Recently the Packs introduced a sonata for cello and piano by Leslie Mann. As far back as 1948, with Andrew Benac and James Petaki, Pack and Pach were heard over the CBC in a quartet by Clermont Pépin. Perry Bauman, oboist, established in 1951 a wood wind quintet with Arlene Nimmons as pianist. Other members of the group, all of the younger generation, were Edward Hutchings (oboe), Norman Glick (clarinet), Anthony Antonacci (flute) and Nicholas Kilburn (bassoon). In Montreal the celebrated Masella brothers and

Arthur Romano have effectively introduced orchestral brass and saxophones into chamber music. Excellent pioneering along these lines should be credited to Reginald Barrow (French horn) in Toronto. As a final note: two unusual concerts of chamber music were heard at the Royal Conservatory in the spring of 1953, when trios for clarinet, flute and cello were played by Leslie Mann, Anthony Antonacci and James Hunter.

All in all, Canada, with its short cultural traditions, has done well in providing opportunities for chamber music performance; adequate support for chamber organizations has, however, in most cases been conspicuously lacking. This means that in almost every instance the groups which we have mentioned can give only part-time service to an art which every serious musician knows to be highly specialized. The literature of chamber music, it need hardly be said, is of permanent interest. It is also a living form to which contemporary composers substantially contribute. In their days of prosperity Canadians have shown themselves to be, as a writer to the *Manchester Guardian* put it, "culturally evasive," and chamber music players have as a result been compelled to earn a living in other ways. Such musicians should not be thought of as entertainers or artisans. As we said at the outset, chamber music provides an essential link in our chain of communications.

MUSIC AND RADIO

Geoffrey Waddington

*The importance of national radio programmes is not limited
. . . to the enjoyment of the audience, but includes the influence of the radio programme on those who take part in
it.*

Report of the Royal Commission on National
Development in the Arts, Letters and Sciences

An unusual relationship exists between music and radio in Canada,
largely because of the unique character of our national radio system.
It is generally recognized that the national radio system is in no small
measure responsible for bringing Canadian music to its present high
pitch of development. Any examination of this relationship, therefore,
must first take into account the conditions of broadcasting in this
country.

It has been stated: "The Canadian national broadcasting system
is the result of ingenious improvisation to provide speedily an extensive service in a country where adequate coverage is perhaps the
most expensive and the most difficult in the world. . . . One station
in New York City can reach a population equal to that of Canada.
Britain reaches a population of 50 millions with 975 miles of land-
line; Canada requires 15,000 [23,000 in 1954] miles of telegraph or
telephone line to provide a national broadcasting service to her 14
[15] millions."[1]

This national service was established in its present form in 1936.
It was apparent as early as 1923, when the Federal Radio Commission of the United States (later the FCC) allocated its stations
every wavelength on the broadcast band, including those occupied by
Canada, that American radio would exert a powerful influence on
Canadian life and culture. From that time until the present it has
been a preoccupation of the Canadian government to maintain both
the technical and the cultural identity of its radio system.

The year 1927 saw the first International Radiotelegraph Conference
in Washington and good progress was made in settling disputes over
the allocation of wavelengths in adjacent countries in order to avoid

[1]*Report of the Royal Commission on National Development in the Arts, Letters
and Sciences* (Ottawa, 1951), p. 27.

unnecessary interference. But, by 1929, the increase in the number of radio receivers was so phenomenal that the government began to take an interest in programme content as well as wavelength allocation. "Advertising was becoming increasingly strident, most of the programmes came from sources outside Canada, and broadcasting stations were concentrated in urban centres leaving other large areas unserved."[2] It was the feeling of a number of people, both in the government and outside, that if advertising alone were to take over control of broadcasting, certain important aspects of our cultural life might be overlooked. Also, since there should be "something for everybody" on the airwaves, some form of recognition of the rights of minority groups and interests seemed to be required.

At that time no group of private broadcasters, supported wholly through advertising, could be expected to give long-range consideration to such matters. In spite of this, in the final analysis, through public service broadcasting at the local level, such stations have made a notable contribution to community life and welfare. In fact, over the years a system has been worked out which is peculiar to Canada, whereby private and public radio work side by side.

The government, in 1929, felt that it was in the public interest to set up a Royal Commission on Radio Broadcasting, "to inquire into the existing situation in Canada and to examine the different methods adopted in other countries." The report of the now celebrated Aird Commission, with Sir John Aird as Chairman, became the blueprint for the system of broadcasting which Canada enjoys today.

Before studying conditions in Canada, the Commission made a detailed examination of existing and embryonic radio systems in other parts of the world. "Everywhere in Europe," it stated, "we found inquiries being conducted under government auspices for the purpose of organizing broadcasting on a nation-wide basis in the public interest." Once again the phrase "in the public interest" predominates.

When it had completed hearings throughout Canada, and gathered opinions from all segments of the public, the Commission was able to recommend:

(a) That broadcasting should be placed on a basis of public service and that the stations providing a service of this kind should be owned and operated by one national company; that provincial authorities should have control over the programs of the station or stations in their respective areas;

(b) That the company should be known as the Canadian Radio Broad-

2*Ibid.*, p. 24.

casting Company; that it should be vested with all the powers of private enterprise and that its status and duties should correspond to those of a public utility.

In all there were some thirteen points in the report. These were not substantially changed when the Canadian Radio Broadcasting Act of 1932 set up the Canadian Radio Broadcasting Commission, guided chiefly by the recommendations of Sir John Aird's team of experts.

By 1936, however, technical and programme expansion had been so great that many of the provisions of the 1932 Act were already obsolete, and radical changes were necessary. The Parliamentary Committee of that year recommended the scrapping of the Canadian Radio Broadcasting Act of 1932, and the founding of "a corporation with an honorary board of nine governors chosen to give representation to all parts of Canada, this board to operate through a general manager and an assistant general manager who would be responsible to the board for the conduct of all business of the corporation." The Committee's report received unanimous approval, and, in 1936, the present Canadian Broadcasting Corporation replaced the Canadian Radio Broadcasting Commission.

Broadcasting policy in Canada is based on the Canadian Broadcasting Act of 1936. The CBC is responsible not to the government of the day, but to Parliament, and it reports to Parliament every year. Thus the CBC is responsible directly to the people of Canada. The Board of Governors of the CBC is made up of eleven Canadians from all parts of the country and from many walks of life. Except for the Chairman, the members serve without salary as trustees of the national interest in broadcasting. It is their job to see that Canadians, wherever they may live, are well served by publicly owned and privately owned broadcasting stations alike, and to this end the Board makes regulations that apply equally to both types of stations. As in other countries, the power to issue licences to broadcast rests with the federal government.

It will be quite apparent, then, that in a country covering an area of more than 3,600,000 square miles, a country of two official languages, populated by only some 15 million people, the publicly owned Canadian Broadcasting Corporation is playing a unique and important role in the unification and cultural development of that country. Its contribution to the cause of music is a significant one. Operating three networks, two in English and one in French, in a system which includes both commercial and non-commercial broadcasting, the CBC has endeavoured to provide its listeners with as comprehensive a programme of music as is possible within the limitations of time and financial resources.

Recognition of these forces at work in the field of national radio prompted the Royal Commission on the Arts, Letters and Sciences to comment in 1951: "The national system . . . has constantly kept in view its three objectives for broadcasting in Canada: an adequate coverage of the entire population, opportunities for Canadian talent and for Canadian self-expression generally, and successful resistance to the absorption of Canada into the general cultural pattern of the United States."[3]

"Adequate coverage of the entire population" means attention to minority, as well as majority, interests. It means that those people who are interested in chamber music or opera will have the opportunity to hear music in that form. It also means that majority tastes are served in the matter of programmes of light music. An equitable programme balance which will please all kinds of musical taste is of course virtually impossible. Whatever programme planners produce as a "balanced" schedule is subject to the criticism of whichever group feels that its interests are not being adequately served. Experience over the years, however, has provided sufficient background information to permit programming which will appeal to average tastes and provide programmes of interest to minority audiences and specialized groups.

In the field of serious music the CBC endeavours to provide the listener with the best of this kind that is being produced in all parts of Canada in a broad programme policy which takes into account music that has been created in the past and that is being created in the present.

With the demise of the NBC Symphony, the CBC Orchestra has become the only full-scale symphony in North America to be maintained by a broadcasting organization. Located in Toronto, the orchestra has no permanent conductor. Instead, outstanding Canadian and foreign-born conductors are invited to lead it. The policy, which has proven popular with listeners, has been to present the best symphonic music, including contemporary works of all periods and countries. In this way, listeners frequently hear works which are rarely included on symphony programmes in the normal course of events.

The Little Symphony Orchestra of Montreal, with programmes de-

[3]*Ibid.*, p. 40.

voted mainly to the music of the eighteenth century, has been broadcasting concerts weekly for the past six years and has gained much
favourable recognition in both Canada and the United States. Other
CBC orchestras of varying proportions and types, originating in production centres from Vancouver to Halifax, serve to round out the
over-all plan of studio presentations.

Regular broadcasts of concerts are provided by the major symphony
organizations in Canada. These include those of the Vancouver Symphony Orchestra, the Winnipeg Symphony Orchestra, the Toronto
Symphony Orchestra and, from Montreal, the orchestra of Les Concerts Symphoniques. Arrangements are made through the department
of International Exchange and the International Service of the CBC
to bring to the Canadian radio audience performances of distinguished
orchestras in the United Kingdom, Europe and the United States.

Programmes of chamber music are presented regularly on the national networks. Because of the geographic and economic problems
involved in arranging concert tours in this country, many of the chamber music organizations mentioned elsewhere in this book have been
largely dependent upon broadcasting for national recognition.

Choral music is presented in many shapes and forms, ranging from
broadcasts of church choirs, various ethnic groups and groups especially organized for radio, to those of such nationally known organizations as Les Disciples de Massenet in Montreal, the Winnipeg
Philharmonic Choir, the Bach Choir of Montreal, and the Toronto
Mendelssohn Choir. Performances over the years of Handel's *Messiah*
and Bach's *St. Matthew Passion* by the last-named Canadian organization have become a national tradition.

Recitals both vocal and instrumental constitute another important
phase of the national programme policy. More than 500 recital periods
are scheduled each year providing opportunities for distinguished
Canadian and foreign artists. Regional programmes are arranged to
encourage the young and promising.

The CBC Opera Company, formed six years ago, presents seven or
eight full-length operas each year. It has been referred to as a logical
and effectual alternative to a state-supported national opera. Designed
for radio presentation only, it cannot of course be considered a permanent alternative but it has brought about a national awareness of
this particular art form and has proven that opera can be performed
at a high professional level by Canadians. In addition to these productions, broadcasts of the Metropolitan Opera direct from New York

and performances by United Kingdom and European opera companies by tape recording are made available to the radio audience.

The Canadian composer must not be overlooked, for it is no exaggeration to say that he regards the CBC as one of his foremost benefactors. Largely through the efforts of the CBC, Canadian music is becoming known both at home and abroad. The International Service of the CBC has made an invaluable contribution, not only in broadcasting original compositions by Canadian composers in regularly scheduled programmes, but also in providing recordings which are brought to the attention of music-lovers in other countries through Canadian diplomatic missions (see also the chapter on recordings later in this book). The CBC has commissioned original compositions for special occasions. It gives many first performances of new music by Canadians, and presents entire series of programmes featuring original Canadian works.

A very wide range of light music is presented on the three networks. The programmes originate at many points across the country featuring various types of instrumental groups and popular singers. These, together with broadcasts of the nation's top dance bands and choral groups specializing in the popular idiom, and the performances of light operas and musical comedies, provide the listener with varied and colourful fare in light entertainment.

Programmes for children occupy an important place in network and local schedules and in many of these the younger listener is introduced to music in an entertaining but informative way. The programmes referred to here are planned for out-of-school listening. CBC school broadcasts, listened to in 12,000 schools throughout the country, are described in another chapter by the Supervisor of School Broadcasts, Mr. R. S. Lambert.

In these days of mass communication, the influence of radio upon the intellectual life and cultural character of a community can be said to be of unusual importance in Canada, by reason of its small population in an extremely thin distribution. Assuming that music is a vital and necessary element in the growth of our society, it requires little imagination to grasp the significance of radio's contribution to this development. In making this contribution, the CBC has met the basic need of all musicians, that of employment. Annual disbursements in excess of $2,500,000 a year to musical and dramatic artists provide a very large number of orchestral musicians and singers with the major portion of their income. Quite apart from the direct material benefits to the musical profession is the support, financial and otherwise, given to the major symphony societies. In large measure the CBC's broadcasts of programmes by choral organizations have helped to keep alive a tradition which, though it provided the focal point of the cultural life of communities throughout the country in earlier and simpler times, has dwindled considerably in the present day and age.

The Canadian composer faces more than the usual number of problems and handicaps in Canada. Among these is the infrequent public performance of his works. It is understandable, but nevertheless regrettable, that for "box office" reasons works by Canadian composers appear too seldom on the regular programmes of large symphony orchestras. In this field, however, the CBC has been able to fill the gap by giving frequent broadcast performances of Canadian music. Works are commissioned for special occasions and much of the best that is being written today is recorded for distribution abroad by the CBC's International Service.

In conclusion, it may be said that the national system of broadcasting has done much to encourage, promote and perform music in its many aspects across the nation and has brought about a greater knowledge, understanding and appreciation of it among Canadians. If we agree with Herbert Spencer that "music must take rank as the highest of the fine arts, as one which more than any other ministers to human welfare," this must be regarded as one of the most notable and worthy contributions which broadcasting has made.

EDUCATION IN MUSIC

Arnold Walter

Let such teach others who themselves excel,
And censure freely who have written well.

Pope, *Essay on Criticism*

Until 1900, music was a European monopoly. Europeans still regard it as such, out of ignorance and understandable pride; nevertheless, it is a most obvious fact that what we call Western Music is neither European nor Western any more, that it has conquered the East like science or technology, that its dominion is extended over the whole world. In Ankara they sing *Bohème* in Turkish, in Tokyo they perform the *Messiah* as regularly as in Manchester, in India native scholars are frantically trying to save the remnants of indigenous *mélos* before the oncoming tide of that music which, till so very recently, we regarded as our own.

These facts conflict with the widespread belief (ultimately derived from German sources of the early nineteenth century) that every nation has (or ought to have) its own music, with roots in the soil, influenced by folk-song, based on tradition and formed by history. A typical nineteenth-century theory, an extension in fact and adaptation of the tenets of nationalism. Music historians were so obsessed by it, that they went out of their way searching for local characteristics, for peculiarities, dissimilarities, disregarding the fundamental truth that 90 per cent of all music performed and taught anywhere in the world is startlingly alike; they were acting like travellers on the look-out for picturesque details, being profoundly bored by whatever reminded them of home.

But the facts are there, staring us in the eye: from Moscow to San Francisco, from Rome to Melbourne, opera houses, orchestras and soloists play the same repertoire, conservatories teach the same techniques, millions of listeners act on the assumption that there is only one kind of music that can be enjoyed by everyone who has ears to hear. Contemporary composers follow international trends: the dodecaphonists sound much the same in Italy or Canada; the followers of

133

Hindemith have more in common with each other than with those countrymen of theirs who profess different ideals.

So it would seem that the most important factor to start with is not the assumption of infinite variety determined by national characteristics, but a very powerful common denominator binding all countries. Differences exist, they should be defined and described; such studies, however, should not result, as it were, in a volume of essays on highly diversified subjects, but rather in a set of variations on a common theme.

Let us agree, then, that there is a main stream of music enriching the soil of many lands. Some were cultivated sooner than others: what interests us here, are the problems of comparative late-comers in musical aspirations and achievements.

Canada, as Vincent Massey so aptly put it, is the meeting ground of a geographical axis from the South and an historical axis from the East. She is both a North American and a British Commonwealth nation: her whole civilization is determined by the two sets of threads in her national fabric. In music, British influence is by no means negligible: many outstanding musicians are British trained; music schools and university departments started out by imitating the British pattern; the examination system, the Festival movement are British in origin. Still, it is probably fair to say that by and large Canada shared her musical experience, the problems, the mode and tempo of her development with the United States to such an extent that it might not be a waste of time and valuable space to trace the growth of music and music education on the North American continent as a whole.

Until World War I, the whole continent was, musically speaking, a colony of Europe. The nineteenth century had been an era of large-scale importation: the repertoire itself, as well as many performers and teachers, came from abroad. Such performances as were given concerned relatively small sections of the population: the rich and idle, the diamond horseshoe of the Metropolitan Opera House, the ladies' clubs in leading cities. Native talent was usually exported, to be educated in Vienna or in Dresden, in Paris or Milan. There was no give and take between indigenous music (which of course existed as it always does) and the imported goods from abroad. Music education in schools was in its infancy; universities took little interest in the subject. Conservatories could in no way be compared to European institutions bearing that name. Writing in 1902, Lavignac (*L'Education musicale*) dismisses them rather contemptuously: they are really not conservatories at all, he says, but "écoles libres," schools composed of a body of teachers each acting on his own accord, associated only with the aim of attracting a large clientèle. . . . North Americans admired Europe's musical achievement, and rightly so; if the Europeans admired anything North American at all it was the rapid expansion of the continent, its industrial power, its technology; certainly not its civilization, which was thought of as third rate and superficial in the extreme.

Few people realize how utterly, how completely all this has been changed in the unbelievably short time of a few decades. Page after page could be filled by listing North American achievements in the field of music, without stressing quantity at the expense of quality. Suffice it to say that import and export of talent are beginning to show a favourable balance; that schools on all levels, from the kindergarten to the university, are vitally concerned with music; that it has been taken out of the hands of the few, affecting now impressively large sections of an ever growing population; that there is a wholesome fusion between folk-music, popular music and serious composition; that professional music education is as good as, and perhaps better than it is anywhere else.

The achievement is there for all to see. It was made possible by a rapid increase in population, by an unprecedented economic development, by an unshakable belief in the power of education and by a peculiarly North American aptitude (a passion almost) for organization, administration and mass production. But the motor power behind all this must most certainly have been a genuine love for music. In America, music may be "big business"—but you can't have big business if your product is not widely in demand.

The achievement is there, but it has its detractors. It is mushroom-art (they say), too rapidly grown, too polyglot, too much at the mercy of every fad and fancy fashionable in New York; not rooted in the soil, not linked with traditional song; too much dependent on media of mass communications which help to destroy the transmission of culture in the home. Which is true. But most of it, unfortunately, is true now for every country under the sun: similar complaints reach us from Paris, Salzburg or Rome. Our repertoire is polyglot by definition; genuine folk-song is dead or dying all through the Western world; mass communications dominate us all. These are consequences of an industrial, technological and managerial civilization which none of us can escape.

Once more: the achievement is there: it needs evaluation. A rather important lesson can be learned from the incontrovertible fact that the North American people were able to acquire a musical civilization at top speed and in record time. The fact quite clearly contradicts those endlessly repeated statements that cultural growth (in music at least) must be indigenous—local at first and parochial, national later— before it can ever hope to aspire to international significance: that it needs a great deal of time, centuries in fact, before it can mature.

The truth of the matter is that music is capable of being transplanted. Like the gospel, it can be preached everywhere; like science, it can be adopted by any nation. In fact, this Western music as we know it is a surprisingly independent phenomenon, a self-contained system almost like mathematics. If we compare the relative simplicity of that system with the myriad changes in spiritual outlook, in political life, in the social organization of the nations who created it, we must come to the conclusion that it is far less sociologically determined than we were led to believe.

If that is true, how can it be the business of a young nation, of a "new" continent to begin at the beginning again and to develop, slowly and painfully, a musical culture all their own? Do we expect them to present us with a new religion, a new science or a new alphabet? Is it not rather their business to partake in a common good, to share the labours of a common civilization whose boundaries are widening constantly? Because of its terrific speed, the North American development is in plain flux. There is nothing static about it, nothing permanent. Its present stage is like a given point on a steeply rising curve; tomorrow, the co-ordinates will have lengthened, the point described will have risen again.

It is in that light that the following remarks must be understood.

To a very large extent, Canada has shared the development traced above with the United States. The two countries have much more in common than the celebrated undefended frontier almost four thousand miles in length. Media of mass communication, for instance, of singular importance to a vast and thinly populated country: broadcasts and films, records and periodicals; operatic experience (which means largely broadcasts from the Metropolitan Opera House); also concert management, almost exclusively centred in New York; labour unions (Canadian musicians being affiliated with the American Federation of Labour); and Teachers' Federations such as the MENC and MTNA. (B. K. Sandwell has pointed out how few Canadians realize that these foreign media are foreign at all. They are taken for granted as an intrinsic part of Canadian life.)

There are differences of course. Geographically the country is larger than its southern neighbour; but it has only one tenth of its population, and even proportionately less wealth. Canada is a bilingual country sheltering two distinct cultures; but since an overwhelming majority of Canadians live near the border, cultural transmission is easier, quicker and more effective following the axis from the South than the axis from the East. Montreal and Toronto are in closer contact with New York than with each other; Winnipeg feels a greater affinity to Minneapolis and Chicago than to Toronto.

When music comes to a new country, its various aspects develop in a definite sequence. First the performer makes his appearance; the teacher is second, the composer last. The present stage of musical development in Canada could perhaps be defined by saying that performance is a universally accepted fact; that education, though far from having reached its climax, is progressing vigorously; while the composer is just finding his bearings.

Music itself is older than history; music education a comparatively recent arrival. Its primary task has always consisted, and still consists, in training skilled craftsmen (a musical labour force as we would say); since the Renaissance it has been given the additional assignment of training the amateur, the educated layman. Traditional training centres (Scholae Cantorum, cathedral schools, guilds and *Stadtpfeifereien*) became obsolete around 1800; it was at that time that the conservatory as well as the private teacher appeared on the scene.

The nineteenth-century conservatory was a very different affair from the older *conservatorio* in Italy (actually an *ospedale*, a foundling home, traditionally taking a special interest in the musical accomplishments of its inmates). The new—or reorganized—conservatories were first and foremost training centres for young professionals; but when their numbers increased all through the century, some of them acquired a mixed clientèle, opening their doors to gifted amateurs. Private teaching had started modestly enough, with aging artists giving instruction for a pittance if there was nothing else for them to do. But when great virtuosi (from Chopin and Liszt to Bülow and Busoni) formed circles of pupils and disciples, who in turn formed circles of pupils and disciples in studios of their own, private teaching became a very important thread in the fabric of music education. This, then, was the situation in which music education found itself in the early twentieth century, at the time when it was transmitted to, adopted and adapted by the North American continent: it aimed at training the professional and at instructing the amateur; it flourished in conservatories and private studios, assisted by traditional music-making in the home, without much help from schools and universities.

The pattern underwent considerable change during the last half century, particularly on this side of the Atlantic. To begin with, the home, for untold centuries the most efficient, and psychologically the most important, custodian of musical tradition, ceased to function. "The transmission of culture in the home," so B. K. Sandwell tells us, "from older to younger generations . . . which fifty years ago was of the first importance in the cultural processes, is now almost extinct. . . . The school is now almost the only person-to-person cultural contact which is left in full operation." And even the influence of the school, he goes on to say, is greatly diminished by such things as radio and movies: "Culture, in other words . . . is transmitted by Hollywood and Radio City, and by books and magazines which are more and more becoming accessories of those institutions."[1] From the educator's point of view, a desperate situation. It was fortunate indeed that the schools grasped the emergency and answered the challenge. Music education in the schools is certainly one of the brightest features of North American civilization. It deserves a chapter of its own, and has been dealt with elsewhere in this volume. Work done in schools is happily supplemented by children's concerts (particularly flourishing in Montreal, Ottawa and Toronto); by high school concerts; and finally by youth concerts, the latter being organized by Les Jeunesses Musicales du Canada. The international movement bearing that name started in Belgium in 1940, linked with the Resistance. Subsequently it spread to fifteen different countries and took root in Canada in 1949. At present, it serves the provinces of Quebec, Ontario and New Brunswick; offers a minimum of four annual concerts to its members (who must be under thirty) and publishes a special magazine, *Le Journal musical canadien*; it has also succeeded in establishing a music camp, and in organizing record clubs where specially selected programmes are introduced by commentators—a feature which is common to all youth concerts mentioned.

It would be unjust, ridiculous even, not to recognize the tremendous service rendered to the cause of music education by the various media

[1]B. K. Sandwell, "Present Day Influences on Canadian Society," *Royal Commission Studies* (Ottawa, 1951), p. 3.

of mass communication (they, too, are described in detail in this volume). Nevertheless, there is too much "broadcasting" in all this and the mass element creeps in almost everywhere; technology replaces the person to person contact of performer and audience, of composer and community, of teacher and student, sometimes even of mother and child: when a carefully selected children's record takes the place of an old-fashioned lullaby. . . .

Still, there are unprecedented opportunities for the average citizen to become acquainted and familiar with musical tradition, to enrich his life through artistic experience. But where do we stand with regard to professional music education?

The first half of the nineteenth century saw the establishment (or reorganization) of European conservatories of renown; the first half of the twentieth century witnessed similar establishments in the Americas. Many of these institutions, far from being operated for profit, are heavily endowed, like Juilliard or the Eastman School of Music: Mr. Lavignac himself would have to take them seriously. In Canada, the Province of Quebec founded the Conservatoire de Musique in Montreal; the Toronto Conservatory of Music, now the Royal Conservatory, was thoroughly reorganized. These are by no means the only Canadian conservatories to be taken into consideration. There are many that could be mentioned with approval, particularly those connected with universities (McGill, Western Ontario, Saskatchewan, Mount Allison, Montreal, Laval—the list is by no means exhaustive). The Conservatoire, however, and the Royal Conservatory are the leading institutions in the country. They are focal points in a rapidly expanding musical civilization, of greater consequence perhaps than educational institutions possess in a more static environment; of particular interest also as embodiments of musico-educational ideas characteristic of the two distinct cultures they represent.

The Conservatoire de Musique in Montreal follows as closely as possible the example of the Conservatoire National de Musique et de Déclamation in Paris. It is state-supported, that is, it operates under a substantial grant from the Province of Quebec. (Education being a provincial matter, Canadian schools must look to provincial governments for assistance.) Tuition is free of charge. A "Prix d'Europe," offered by the Province, is a welcome substitute for the historically famous "Prix de Rome." It usually leads to postgraduate study in France. The establishment of a branch institute in Quebec City reminds one of the French procedure (already adopted by Sarette) of founding succursalia in provincial towns. Teaching methods are decidedly French; years of training in *solfège* give students a better grounding perhaps than any other method can provide. The institution as a whole is dedicated to the upholding of French tradition—dedicated to the ARS GALLICA as understood by Franck, Fauré, by d'Indy and Debussy, in all its purity of style, sincerity of expression and lucidity. Here, where ancient France still lingers, traditional values are more highly regarded and more powerful perhaps than anywhere else on the North American continent.

Situated in cosmopolitan and Americanized Toronto, the Royal Conservatory is a very different kind of institution. Founded in 1886 as an independent music school, it has been governed and controlled by the University of Toronto for more than thirty years. It enjoys financial assistance from the Province of Ontario through the University, but it is far from being a scholarship school like its sister institution in Montreal. A recent reorganization divided it into two constituent parts, the "School of Music" and the "Faculty of Music."

The School of Music offers both vocational and avocational training, the former leading to the associate diploma; it also acts as an examining body of national importance: eleven branches, scattered throughout the city, help to take care of a student body more numerous than that of any other music school in the British Dominions.

The Faculty of Music offers diploma courses for performers and private music teachers; degree courses for composers and school music teachers; graduate courses with concentration in Composition, Theory, Musicology and Music Education; and the doctorate in Composition. In addition, it fulfils the function of a music department in a liberal arts college by instructing students in an Arts course with honours in Music, and also by offering electives to the general student body of the University.

In other words, the Royal Conservatory provides tuition for every conceivable kind of music student: the gifted amateur, the practically minded professional, the academically minded, and the graduate student. It is the "Faculty of Music" which, more closely linked with the University, profits most from the financial assistance granted to the institution as a whole; both departments, however, depend on privately donated scholarships for their often impecunious clientèle.

As constituted now, the Royal Conservatory follows no known pattern of organization. There is a good reason for that. It attracts students from all parts of the Dominion; it must, in turn, be mindful of the needs of the entire country. These needs have changed considerably since the war. A great increase in population and an expanding economy have led to an upsurge of musical interest: new orchestras are being established, broadcasting is adding new features, television is being introduced—more performers are needed, more teachers. In the past, Canada imported much of what it needed musically and exported most of its talent, which gravitated towards greener fields abroad. Now she needs all the talent she can find—a fact which curiously enough has not yet met with universal recognition. In such a period of transition and adjustment an educational institution may well be justified in doing more than cater to established needs. Apart from discovering and training talent, it may suggest, may even search for, new ways of using it, thus giving direction to the development as a whole. The Royal Conservatory's contribution to opera is a case in point, leading to the establishment of an annual Opera Festival, to nation-wide opera broadcasts, to civic sponsorship. Here again we are not dealing with an isolated event; schools like Eastman and Juilliard, universities like Columbia and Indiana have made similar contributions. The movement may be likened to the establishment, in 1828, of the Société des Concerts du Conservatoire in Paris: American schools are doing for opera in the twentieth century what the great French school did for orchestral music in the nineteenth.

To revert to our comparison between Toronto and Montreal, it cannot truthfully be said that Torontonian teaching follows British tradition. The Conservatory's teaching staff is rather cosmopolitan in origin and outlook; teaching methods stem largely from Continental and American sources. The influence of the Royal Schools, of Holst and Vaughan Williams, of Walton and Britten is still felt of course, but it is less conspicuous than it was twenty or even ten years ago: here again, the North-South axis exerts its pull. No doubt Toronto is less faithful to her own background than Montreal.

A decidedly British feature in Canadian musical life is the holding of local examinations throughout the Dominion. As far back as 1889 the Royal Academy and the Royal College of Music joined forces in creating a single examining body, the Associated Board of the Royal Schools, to conduct examinations in the various centres of the United Kingdom. The scheme was soon extended to the Dominions and is still flourishing in Canada. It is a significant fact perhaps (and a sign of coming of age) that the Royal Schools themselves have, as of 1954, ceased to be an examining body in this country; at present, examinations are being conducted under the auspices of McGill University; of the University of Western Ontario; of the Universities of Manitoba, Alberta and Saskatchewan. The most influential examining body is undoubtedly the Royal Conservatory, whose steadily growing number of candidates exceeded 35,000 in 1954: an enviable achievement in a highly competitive field. The value of such examinations is often debated, is debatable perhaps. The system aims at unification and improvement of standards; it is decidedly a help in sifting students and discovering talent; and adds a competitive element to music study, a powerful incentive to many a youngster. Yet it is precisely this competitive element which is being questioned as a suitable psychological foundation for artistic endeavour on whatever level; it also happens quite frequently that music study is narrowed down to preparation for a certain grade. Still, as long as the wide open spaces of the Canadian sub-continent are not supplied with enough good music teachers to answer the needs of the entire population for better educational opportunities, the examination system will in all likelihood remain in force.

This brings us to private teaching, of particular importance in a country like ours where (in spite of all the heartening progress reported in this chapter) countless communities are still without an adequate supply of well-trained teachers. There is no law prescribing certification; there are as yet no unified standards; but a great deal has been accomplished by the establishment, in eight of the ten provinces, of Music Teachers' Associations, banded together in the Canadian Federation of Music Teachers. Adequate training is the prerequisite of membership; the associations aim at educating the public, at upholding and raising standards, at developing a code of ethics. Provincial news letters and a C.F.M.T.A. bulletin provide information, educational conventions facilitate the interchange of ideas. Members must be holders of a diploma equivalent to the Associate or Licentiate diplomas issued by the Royal Conservatory, McGill Conservatory, the Western Board of Music or similar institutions. Most of these diplomas are granted on examination. There are two notable exceptions: a two-year course (diploma: Mus.G.Pad.) offered by the University of Western Ontario; and a three-year Licentiate course under the Faculty of Music of the Royal Conservatory.

Universities have repeatedly been mentioned in this report; it will be necessary now to assess their contribution as a whole although it may be difficult to find a common denominator for the varied activities conducted under their auspices. They offer professional courses for music students, credit courses for Arts students, or both. They own and operate conservatories or music schools; conduct examinations; are connected with provincial and local music festivals. It has been argued that some of these activities are not the proper domain of the university; that there should be a clearer distinction between music departments and music schools, between academic study and practical application. The fact remains, however, that conservatories and music schools find it more and more impossible to continue operations on a self-supporting basis. If they are not endowed (and our tax tables are not conducive to large-scale endowments) they have no alternative but to seek government assistance: and affiliation with a university is still the most effective means to that end. Also, we are again dealing here with a field determined by the North-South and East-West co-ordinates. In British universities, music study is largely based on the assumption that "applied music" (or preparation for performance) should be left to conservatories or private instructors; that a university should concern itself exclusively with the provision of historical background, theoretical knowledge and analytical skill. In the United States, on the other hand, we find many music departments accrediting practical as well as historical and theoretical study "apparently confirmed in the belief that music, if adequately presented, cannot be divided into self-contained compartments but must be presented in its full and splendid vitality as a living art."[2]

The Canadian pattern (if we can call it so) is influenced by both trends of thought. On the undergraduate level, our universities offer three distinct kinds of music courses: those leading to the degree of Mus.Bac.; Arts courses with Music as a field of concentration; and music courses with Arts credits.

Those leading to the degree of Bachelor of Music are essentially courses for professional musicians, concentrating "on one branch of music in a setting of other musical subjects." Usually of three years' duration, they are available in the Universities of Toronto, McGill, Montreal, Laval and Bishop's University; Mount Allison, Dalhousie and Acadia Universities offer four-year courses. Curricula are commonly based on theory, history, form and analysis. Acadia admits applied music as principal subject; Toronto offers an option between

2Randall Thompson, *College Music* (New York: Macmillan, 1935), p. 705.

Composition and History and Literature of Music. Both Toronto and McGill present teachers' training courses as variants of the courses just described. McGill offers the degree of Mus.Bac. in education, adding practical work to the usual fare of historical and theoretical subjects. Toronto offers the Mus.Bac. degree in Music Education: historical and theoretical studies are supplemented by vocal and instrumental classes, choral and band work, while "arranging" takes the place of the former "exercise"—the name given to a composition or thesis. In view of the fact that school music courses are frankly vocational, calling for a wide range of subjects and the acquisition of special skills, the emphasis laid upon practical preparation seems fully justified.

Arts courses in Music have a different function. Whether a student chooses it as an elective or as a field of concentration, he will experience music in relation to other Arts subjects instead of specializing in one of its branches. Arts courses with a "major" in Music are rather rare in Canada—an honour course in Music, offered by the University of Toronto, is the outstanding example. Planned to provide a balanced programme, striving to maintain an intelligent equilibrium between primary and auxiliary studies, such courses are destined to contribute a great deal to the development of personality and the enjoyment of the art.

As electives, music courses are available in almost all universities possessing music departments. They are usually restricted to lectures and classes in theory, history and form (British Columbia, Saskatchewan, Alberta, Queen's); in some cases (in Mount Allison, for instance) applied music or "practical subjects" are added to the programme.

It has already been mentioned that a surprising number of our universities control, or are affiliated with, conservatories (or Ecoles de Musique) which provide the necessary teaching for whatever courses the university chooses to offer (e.g., Toronto, Western, McGill, Laval, Montreal, Dalhousie, Mount Allison). Such an arrangement makes it possible for university faculties to offer performers' and teachers' courses, usually leading to Associate and Licentiate diplomas (Toronto, McGill, Dalhousie, etc.)—with the result that the distinction between conservatories and university faculties proper tends to disappear. A new entity is in the ascendency, the University School of Music, a typically North American form of organization, unknown in Europe and the British Isles, but flourishing in the United States.

Graduate studies, leading to the doctorate in Music (Mus.D.) are offered by approximately one-third of the universities mentioned. The doctorate is essentially a composer's degree, the main requirement being a large-scale composition to be presented as an "exercise." Until very recently, no provision was made for graduate study involving musical scholarship. At the time of writing (session 1954–55) the University of Toronto is introducing for the first time graduate courses leading to the degree of Master of Music with concentration in the fields of Composition, Theory, Music Education and Musicology proper.

To summarize the foregoing, we would say that in the last few decades Canadian music education has changed beyond recognition. It has grown in quantity and improved in quality. It offers a great many opportunities to the gifted amateur. On the professional level it is not handicapped by unemployment—on the contrary, there is a shortage of talented performers and teachers. In the North, and particularly in the West, there is still a frontier awaiting the musical pioneer. Commercially minded music schools ("more interested in augmenting their receipts than in elevating the level of national art" as Lavignac had it) are a thing of the past. Newly founded or reorganized conservatories have no reason to be afraid of comparisons with similar institutions abroad. The universities are increasingly more active in the field, organizing Schools of Music in the American sense of the term, and acting as channels for government assistance.

A bright picture altogether. True, there are negative features to be considered. For geographical and demographic reasons, there is no even distribution of educational facilities throughout the Dominion. A vast "hinterland" is dominated by powerful centres like Montreal and Toronto; they in turn are influenced by New York, Montreal perhaps less so than Toronto. Tempo and dynamics of the development described are decidedly American—a good thing in itself, yet it tends to weaken Canada's own heritage of French and British tradition. Still, the positive features are infinitely stronger than the negative ones: looking down from heaven, Monsieur Lavignac must be vastly astonished about the changes wrought in the North American wilderness.

MUSIC IN THE SCHOOLS

G. Roy Fenwick

Musical training is a more potent instrument than any other because rhythm and harmony find their way into the inward places of the soul.

Plato, *The Republic*, Book III

In Canada, education is in the hands of the ten provincial governments, not the federal government. For this reason there is considerable variation in the organization of the school systems. The public schools are co-educational except in the case of some of the Roman Catholic schools in Quebec and Ontario, and are divided into Elementary schools (Grades I to VIII) and Secondary schools (Grades IX to XIII). In some of the provinces there are three divisions, Elementary (Grades I to VI), Intermediate (Grades VII to X), and Senior (Grades XI to XIII). In Ontario, separate elementary schools are provided for Roman Catholic pupils, both English and French-speaking, and in Quebec for English Protestant children. The secondary schools are academic, commercial, technical or a combination of these divisions. There are many private boys' and girls' schools in all the provinces. The courses of study prescribed by the Departments of Education vary to some extent, but music is provided for in all ten provinces as a regular part of the programme in elementary schools and as an optional subject in the secondary schools.

Musical training in Canadian schools emphasizes the cultural rather than the vocational side of the subject. It is true that the performance of music has become the livelihood of many people, and the schools have a duty to perform in discovering and encouraging those who, by reason of exceptional talent, are likely to find their life work in music. Elementary training in singing and playing is quite justified, and the schools attempt, with considerable success, to develop correct singing habits. In many cities and towns they also provide for class instruction in piano, violin and other instruments, as will be described later. The Canadian Bureau for the Advancement of Music has been active in promoting instrumental classes in schools. Individual instruction is usually given outside of regular school hours, the pupils paying a small fee to private teachers who are given access to school facilities by the local authorities. It seems to be agreed, however, that there are agencies outside the school which are better equipped to give advanced individual training in this art, and public education does not assume the work now being done so well by conservatories and private music teachers. In general, the schools are concerned chiefly with developing interested and discriminating listeners, and the courses of study in use in Canadian schools are designed to bring the young people into contact with beauty, assist them in self-expression, give them an outlet for their emotions and provide them with a rewarding means of using their leisure time.

These aims are achieved by activities which fall into three groups: making music, reading music, and hearing music. The normal, healthy child craves activity and learns best by doing. It is important that his introduction to the study of music should be through music itself, and not through facts about music. Singing of songs is the first and at all times the most important approach to music, because it may be performed by any group, regardless of size or grading, and because it touches a responsive chord in every child. Canadian schools emphasize the singing of folk and art songs, within the understanding of the pupils, to develop taste and good singing habits and to correlate music with other school subjects and the daily experiences of the children. Special mention should be made of kindergartens which are part of the school system in most of the graded schools. Here the children receive their first introduction to music through rhythmic response and the singing of many songs. Considerable freedom is allowed in the choice of song books and it is not usual to authorize any particular books. Among the commonly used texts are the *High Road of Song* (Gage), *Singing Period* (Waterloo), *Canadian Singer* (Gage), *Music Horizons* (Gage), *Youthful Voices* (Thompson) and similar books published by Ginn, Dent, Oxford University Press and others.

Rote singing, however, does not provide for the future. The songs that are suitable for children of school age will, in many cases, have little appeal in later years, and if our young people are to continue to engage in musical endeavours they must be given some independent power in the language of music. Sight singing is the key which unlocks the door to future participation. In the Canadian schools, music is treated as a second language, no more difficult than any other, but more useful to many students than some other languages. When the subject is presented with skill and with proper respect, most of the pupils acquire reasonable facility in the singing of simple music at sight. Except in the French schools of Quebec, where the fixed doh system is followed, some derivation of the movable doh system, originated by John Curwen, is employed. The tonic sol-fa syllables are in general use in the earlier grades, but these are applied to staff notation from the beginning.

Children develop musicianship to a certain degree by listening to their own performances and to the performances of others, but in addition to this they must be given an opportunity to become familiar with music which is beyond their performing ability; this, for their highest development, must represent the best in musical literature. The capacity for enjoyment of music is with children always in advance of the capacity to perform. In most provinces a well-defined course in listening is followed, beginning with rhythmic response and quiet listening to short classics and parts of larger works, and proceeding, in the secondary schools, to a serious study of the development of music including the instruments of the orchestra, elementary form and the lives and works of many of the great composers. Most of the training in listening is carried on by means of gramophone recordings, but many schools use sound films, film strips and tape recorders to good advantage. The educational radio programmes which are available in almost all parts of Canada are received with enthusiasm by the children, and are of great assistance to the music teachers. Students are also encouraged to attend local concerts, and performing artists are invited to visit the schools. In 1946 the Ontario Department of Education initiated a scheme for taking concert parties into the smaller cities and towns of the province. This had a twofold purpose: first, to give secondary school pupils in smaller centres the same cultural advantage enjoyed by those in the large cities; second, to give young professional musicians, most of them graduates of the Canadian schools, an opportunity to gain experience in concert work. Each year about 125 concerts are given in 40 towns by 75 artists. Students are charged a very small fee, and the public are admitted when seats are available. In towns where there are large halls the concerts are usually self-sustaining, but where the only auditorium is too small to accommodate a large enough audience to pay expenses, the Department subsidizes the concerts by meeting any deficit.

The Toronto Musicians' Association has provided free concerts by groups of professional musicians in many of the secondary schools of Metropolitan Toronto, and the Toronto Symphony Orchestra each year presents a series of youth programmes in Toronto and elsewhere. In

Nova Scotia the Halifax Symphonette visits some of the schools, and in other provinces similar schemes are carried on where possible.

While it is true that the only economically possible way of reaching all the children is through vocal music, Canadian schools recognize the fact that instrumental music may be taught successfully in classes. The majority of secondary schools have orchestras for ensemble training of the pupils of private music teachers, and an increasing number of schools, both secondary and elementary, are teaching band and orchestral instruments as part of the regular curriculum. It is generally realized that this instruction should commence in the lower grades, especially in the case of stringed instruments, so that the pupils will have developed some facility by the time they reach the secondary school level. In some of the provinces considerable use is made of pre-band instruments, such as percussion bands, recorders, tonettes and melody flutes. Even in schools where there are no bands or orchestras these simpler instruments stimulate interest in playing and reading music, and in some of the more sparsely populated parts of the Prairie Provinces, where vocal training is difficult, these instruments are widely used as a substitute for singing.

In Ontario some seventy-five secondary schools have already introduced instrumental classes as part of the curriculum with instruments supplied by the schools. Students in these classes are given usually at least four periods a week of intensive instruction, and it has been noted that scholarship pupils naturally gravitate to the music classes. Groups under instruction are of course from the same grade, and take all their other subjects together; they vary from twenty-four to thirty-six in number on assorted violins, violas, cellos and basses in one class, and on all the various brass and woodwind instruments in another. Teachers qualified to give instruction on all instruments are difficult to locate, but the University of Toronto has graduated approximately sixty experts who are now in charge of the seventy odd schools mentioned at the beginning of this paragraph. In some schools instrumental music is so popular that it is offered as a special privilege, and only pupils with an average of at least 65 per cent on all other subjects are allowed to register in the music course. To assist in the initiation of instrumental courses the Department of Education in Ontario makes generous grants. Only those who have seen the results are able to realize the incalculable value to the pupils and to the schools of this new subject on the curriculum.

Music, by its very nature, demands an opportunity to be heard, and it is not advisable that hearing be confined to the classroom. Extra-curricular activities in music are very important. These, which take the form of choirs, orchestras, bands, concerts, operettas and festivals, serve to motivate the pupils' efforts, stimulate public interest and improve the standard of performance. They also provide, for the more talented children, a richer musical fare than is possible in the classroom. The competitive festival particularly, which started in the Prairie Provinces, and reached a high standard of performance in the Winnipeg Festival, due in part to the fine leadership of Miss Ethel Kinley, has spread throughout the entire country, and is having a marked effect upon school music in Canada. Extra-curricular groups developed in the schools also serve their communities by frequent performances at church services and public gatherings of various kinds. An interesting example of extra-curricular activity by students is the Sir Ernest MacMillan Fine Arts Clubs in British Columbia. This organization, which has chapters in many of the schools, has through the enthusiastic and indefatigable work of Miss Marjorie Agnew and her associates, had a considerable influence not only in music, but in the other arts as well. It has raised considerable sums for the endowment of scholarships and each year holds a music and arts festival of its own. In Toronto, the Junior Council of the Toronto Symphony Orchestra is representative of most of the secondary schools of Toronto as well as the private schools.

The organization of school music varies to some extent in the different provinces. Ontario, Saskatchewan and New Brunswick have each a provincial Director of Music whose duty it is to promote, co-ordinate and stimulate the work in the schools. In the other seven provinces the Department of Education encourages the subject financially and otherwise. In the elementary schools, except in a few cases where a special music teacher is employed, the responsibility for progress in music, as in other subjects, rests with the regular teacher. Usually the local School Boards employ one or more supervisors to direct and assist the teacher. Even in the smallest rural schools, this co-operative effort seems to be the most effective way of obtaining satisfactory standards. The supervisors visit each classroom regularly, giving model lessons and conferring with the teachers. Classes for instructing the teachers are common, and in some places teachers' choirs are organized. The Toronto Men Teachers' Choir, under the direction of Eldon Brethour, is one of these organizations which enjoys a more than local reputation. There is no doubt that music has greater prestige in the eyes of the pupils when their teachers take some active part in the public performance of music. In the secondary schools music is usually taught by a music specialist who, in most cases, is a regular member of the staff and who teaches some other subjects as well.

Elementary school teachers receive some instruction in music at Normal Schools and Teachers' Colleges. The music supervisors are trained at summer schools which are conducted by the Departments of Education in many of the provinces. The secondary school music specialists are trained at the summer courses or at a few of the universities. The University of Toronto offers in the Faculty of Music a special three-year course for School Music specialists leading to the degree of Mus.Bac. These specialists proceed to the Ontario College of Education, where in one additional year they obtain a High School Assistant's certificate. In most of the provinces music is the only subject which may be taught by a person who is not a qualified school teacher. These musicians, having taken the required summer courses, are employed full or part time in the teaching of music only. The largest summer course for school music teachers is conducted annually at Toronto by the Ontario Department of Education. This has been in operation continuously since 1913 except during the war period 1941 to 1944. An average of four hundred teachers take one of nine five-week courses in vocal and instrumental music. These courses include class methods, practice teaching, sight singing, music appreciation and vocal or instrumental training. One period daily is devoted to choral training for the entire school and at the end of the course this choir has appeared each year for some time back with the Toronto Philharmonic Orchestra at one of its Promenade Concerts.

Although music is now recognized as a school subject in all of Canada, the history of its development varies greatly in the different provinces. In Ontario the Toronto Normal School (now the Teachers' College) has had a music instructor continuously since 1848. Music was first taught in the public schools of Hamilton in 1853, London in 1856, Toronto in 1872, Ottawa in 1906 and Windsor 1909. The development of music in the rural schools and in the secondary schools of Ontario dates from 1935. At the present time 80 per cent of all elementary schools and 65 per cent of all secondary schools have a well-organized vocal music programme, and instrumental music is taught in 21 per cent of the secondary schools. In the other provinces music has held a respected place in the curriculum for many years, and today it is spreading to even the smallest communities. Reports received from all provinces show that interest in school music is growing every-where.

The character of school music in Canada has been affected by in-fluences beyond its borders. In the earlier days music teachers were recruited from those who were trained in the mother countries, and it is natural that Quebec has retained many of the ideas and ideals of France, while the English-speaking provinces have adopted proced-ures similar to those of the British Isles. The proximity of the United States and the similarity of the educational systems in the two adjacent countries have also left their marks on music in Canadian schools. Canada today is developing a philosophy of music education which combines the thoroughness and artistry of England and France with the enthusiasm and organizing genius of our neighbours to the south.

In several of the provinces certain certificates from accredited ex-amining bodies are accepted as an option for the secondary school graduation diplomas and for entrance to Canadian universities. These include certificates from the Royal Conservatory of Music, Toronto; McGill University, Montreal; the Montreal Conservatoire de Musique et d'Art Dramatique; the Western Board of Music; the Associated Board of the Royal Schools of Music; and Trinity College, London, England.

The active interest shown by organizations outside the school sys-tem has always had a part in the development of music in the schools of Canada. The influence of these organizations has had a salutary effect upon the attitude of school authorities, and has given strength and encouragement to those actively engaged in teaching music. Women's Institutes have encouraged music contests at rural school fairs; in some cases they have paid the salaries of music teachers and have purchased equipment. Home and School Associations have pur-chased equipment, organized music clubs in the schools, formed music auxiliaries to provide entertainment and transportation for performing groups, and through mothers' choirs, set an example for their children to follow. The service clubs and other organizations have sponsored music festivals. Conservatories of music, the Registered Music Teach-ers' Associations, radio stations, the Musicians' Union, and the music publishers and dealers have all shown a spirit of co-operation and sympathy with music in the schools.

MUSIC IN SCHOOL BROADCASTING

R. S. Lambert

Music . . . is the best mind-trainer on the list.
Charles W. Eliot

Music plays an important part in broadcasts to the schools of Canada, in programmes designed directly to cultivate appreciation of music, and in a special use to heighten indirectly the force of the dramatic presentation characteristic of most school broadcasts. It is not easy to say which of these two approaches, the direct or the indirect, has the greater influence. Undoubtedly, however, the cumulative effect of school music broadcasts is to enlarge and make more responsive the potential adult audience of the future for music in all forms.

It should be remembered that in the distribution of powers made by the British North America Act education was allotted to the provinces. School broadcasts in Canada are therefore a joint presentation of the Canadian Broadcasting Corporation and the Departments of Education of the ten provinces. Each province provides its own schedule of school broadcasts planned to tie in closely with the local curriculum. In addition, all the provinces co-operate in planning, on one day of each week, National School Broadcasts designed to promote the sense of united and common citizenship among our young people at school. Both provincial and National School Broadcasts are planned by committees of educational experts, headed by the National Advisory Council on School Broadcasting. This body consists of representatives of each Department of Education, of the teachers, school trustees, universities, and Home and School Federations, and also of the Canadian Education Association. Its present chairman is Dr. H. P. Moffatt, Deputy Minister of Education for Nova Scotia.

All programmes are heard over facilities provided by the CBC. In a broad division of function, the educators make themselves responsible for the content and planning, the CBC for the form and presentation of school broadcasts. This means that, in musical matters, the CBC School Broadcasts Department is responsible for hiring the musicians and producing the programmes in which they take part.

Music Appreciation is a regular feature of the school broadcasting schedule of each province. Usually the courses are given at three student levels: Primary (Grades I-III), Intermediate (Grades IV-VI) and Senior (Grades VII-VIII). The purpose and form of the broadcasts vary from province to province in accordance with local teaching techniques and local musical resources.

For junior grades the programmes often (e.g., in the Atlantic provinces and Ontario) take the form of teaching songs already listed in provincially prescribed song books. For more senior grades, they usually take the form of exposing the students' ears to "good" (i.e., classical or semi-classical) instrumental (including orchestral) music; generally this is presented with explanatory comments. In this type of programme, there are three governing factors: the music curriculum of the province; the availability of commentators with the right "microphone personality" for the classroom audience; and the availability of live talent (instrumental and vocal) for performance. The usual duration of a school music broadcast is 15 minutes for the junior grades, and 30 for the senior grades.

Where circumstances permit (e.g., in Ontario) live orchestras, some of them nationally famous, as well as instrumental ensembles, individual instrumentalists and singers are employed on these broadcasts. For instance, the Ontario music appreciation series ("Music for Young Folk") regularly includes short concerts specially arranged by the provincial Director of Music and performed by the Toronto Symphony Orchestra. In some provinces, however, recordings are used, because live talent is not available or the cost involved is too great.

In Saskatchewan a novel approach to school music broadcasts is made. In accordance with the provincial music education policy, stress is laid on the making and playing of simple musical instruments, as a first step towards combined training in appreciation and performance.

Choral singing receives considerable encouragement through the opportunities afforded by school broadcasts. In Manitoba, where substantial German and Ukrainian elements form part of the population, the standard of choral singing, especially in high schools, is exceptionally high—and this is reflected in the local school broadcasts. In Ontario also, each spring, a choral festival ("Ontario Sings") is given by selected school choirs (usually high school) from different centres, urban and rural. Each week for five or six weeks one or more such choirs go on the air, and are listened to in the schools of other parts of the province, and of English-speaking Quebec. The result is to give a powerful stimulus everywhere to good performance. In Alberta, elementary school choirs have been used to demonstrate how certain songs should be sung. This form of teaching has proved very popular and has given an impetus to singing and listening, especially in rural centres and among senior grades.

In the National School Broadcasts, music appreciation is dealt with rather differently than in the provincial broadcasts. In this case, the aim is to provide the boys and girls of Canada as a whole with outstanding musical experiences which they would be unlikely to enjoy through the resources of their own province alone. For example, symphony concerts have been broadcast by the Toronto and Vancouver Symphony Orchestras.

A sustained effort has been made, over a period of three years, to introduce opera to the school radio audience. This included complete performances (in serial instalments) of Gluck's *Orpheus*, Britten's *Let's Make an Opera* and Gilbert and Sullivan's *The Pirates of Penzance*—in a form suitably adapted for classroom listening. A feature of these broadcasts was the attempt to make it possible for students to learn some of the principal songs, and so participate themselves, in their classrooms, in the performances.

In 1953–54, a fresh experiment was tried. Under the title "Music in the Making," a series of half-hour programmes was given explaining how and why a composer composes music, and how it comes to be performed. Haydn's "Surprise" Symphony (No. 94) was taken as an example. Each movement was analysed in turn and played complete, and in the last broadcast the symphony as a whole was played. "Papa" Haydn himself was introduced as commentator and expositor, and each broadcast included brief dramatized illustrations of episodes from his life bearing on his music. In this way a proportion of drama was blended with listening to music. Experience has shown that for elementary classroom audiences about seven minutes represents the maximum period of uninterrupted listening to serious orchestral music possible without boredom, unless the music has been led up to by careful preliminary sampling and analysis.

Judging by evaluations received from teachers in every province, "Music in the Making" proved the most successful music appreciation series ever broadcast to schools in Canada. Ninety per cent of the evaluating teachers praised the programmes in every respect, and many teachers emphasized that it had an appeal to the very young, as well as to the more senior students. "It is impossible," reported one Ontario teacher, "to measure how far-reaching the educational value of such a program can be. Children take the new interest [music] into the home, and parents become interested, and so it grows. Apart from the musical value, a new relationship is fostered between child and home; between home and school." The general listener's point of view was typified in a letter from a Calgary lady. "When I came to Calgary 45 years ago, after having spent the first 30 years of my life in a near professional musical atmosphere on the European continent, I never dreamed of ever hearing a program such as your school broadcast on CBX yesterday afternoon. I was moved to tears at the realization of what Canada had achieved in the last quarter century, and I am happy for our young people (and old) and want to express my admiration and gratitude for what you are doing in that line."

In choral singing, the National School Broadcasts assist the impetus already given in provincial series, by providing, at the close of the Christmas term each year, an opportunity for a selected school choir to give a concert of carols and Christmas music. Each province takes its turn in supplying this pre-Christmas broadcast.

In many school broadcasts dealing with subjects other than music appreciation, music is used extensively as part of the dramatized form in which they are presented. In literature and social studies broadcasts, in particular, place is found for appropriate songs (especially ballads and folk-songs) and tunes, often performed live by professional musicians and artists. Recorded versions of such music are also used for this purpose.

Radio is an emotional rather than an intellectual medium of expression and communication. Listening to a good school broadcast is an experience that should stimulate the students' imagination. Music is an essential tool for this purpose. For this reason, original "bridge" and "mood" music is often composed and performed as an integral part of school broadcast dramatizations. In this form compositions by Canadian composers reach the ears of the classroom audience, which is otherwise not sufficiently trained musically to appreciate contemporary compositions for instruments or orchestra when offered in concert form.

Music also plays an important part in CBC's daily "Kindergarten of the Air," a highly popular programme designed to give pre-school training to children of from 3½ to 6 years of age in their homes. This programme is also extensively used in Grades I and II at school, and in kindergarten and nursery school groups. Each broadcast includes songs which the children learn to sing with their radio teacher, as well as rhythmic movements and dances which they are also taught. They are trained to listen for very short periods of, say, one or two minutes to "quiet music" played on the piano. In this way, these very small youngsters are made familiar with music in its active and receptive aspects.

The CBC has only this year (1954) begun experimenting with educational telecasts, to determine their utility in the classroom. It is too early to say how far TV can be used as an aid to music teaching; but possibly identification of instruments of the orchestra, and instruction in playing a solo instrument, may come within the range of the new medium.

RECORDINGS

John Beckwith

Momentany as a sound . . .

A *Midsummer Night's Dream*, Act I, Scene i

The radio and the phonograph—one by projecting sound through space and the other by preserving it through time—have wrought the greatest of revolutions in our musical life. No longer is sound "momentany"—or as we would say, momentary. Since the invention of musical notation the work of the composer has been capable of preservation; until the twentieth century that of the performer died with him—indeed died, in a sense, with each performance. What would we not give to hear the singing of Jenny Lind, to listen to Bach on the organ, Paganini on the violin or Chopin on the piano? The fine singers and instrumentalists of today, however, will live on and continue to delight posterity. The composer too can, if he will, give his stamp of approval or express his censure of this or that interpretation; with the works of the past, on the other hand, even the best informed interpreter finds a margin of conjecture. Finally the potential audience of all musicians has been widened beyond what our forefathers could have imagined. These observations may seem platitudinous but they bear frequent repetition lest we take our blessings too much for granted.

Canada's production of phonograph records is, like her production of books, considerably lower than one might expect in a country of her population and cultural attainments. The comparison to book publishing will help explain some of the reasons. Although most Canadian literary works of merit written each year reach publication, many of the successful ones have to be published in New York or London and imported (in some form) for sale in Canada. The same is true when it comes to recordings of Canadian musical performers and composers. Both fields, book publishing and record manufacture, are dominated by Canadian subsidiaries of leading English and American firms, which means that activities are largely concentrated on reproducing what is done elsewhere. This has its advantages, but it also means that there are fewer independent Canadian firms than might be expected, and that the work of these is of smaller proportions than might be felt desirable from the cultural viewpoint. However, in both fields, it is fair to add, there are signs that this state of affairs is changing. This is especially so with recordings.

As a point of history, records were being made in Canada almost as early as in the United States. Herbert Berliner, son of the founder of "E. Berliner's Gram-O-Phone," and still living now in Montreal, came to this country about the turn of the century to form the Berliner Gramophone Company of Canada. By 1907 this firm was issuing Victor Records. Today, Capitol, Columbia, Decca (London), and RCA Victor are among the chief international recording companies operating directly in the Canadian market. Columbia opened its own Canadian office in 1954, having previously operated through an agent, Sparton of Canada, Limited. Sparton, with studios in London, Ontario, has since entered the recording field as an independent, both of its American namesake and of the Columbia organization. Capitol, established here in the mid-1940's, entered into closer relations with its American headquarters in 1954, becoming Capitol Record Distributors of Canada. Decca has been established in Canada since the 1920's, and its twin, London Records, since 1948.

Some recordings are cut by these firms in Canada, but only a very limited number are of serious music. In the experience of the company executives, Canadian sales alone will seldom cover the cost of such recordings, and the wider American and European markets are highly competitive ones to break into. Also, a recurring *leit-motif* in talks with company executives is the complaint that minimum union fees for recording fixed by an American union as applying to the American recording situation, are unduly high when applied in Canada. While this may be true, unionists seem justified in protecting artists in this way, considering the unpredictable uses sometimes made of recordings and the fact that, unlike composers, artists do not hold copyright on their performances.

The bulk of these firms' activity today consists of importing matrices from their international head-offices, arranging for records to be pressed from these, packaging and distributing them to the Canadian market. Again there is the parallel to the many book publishers in Canada who import plates from the United States or Britain, have books printed from these, and bind and distribute them. Thus these companies are often essentially book-keepers and co-ordinators of the specialized work of others. Retail prices could probably be cut considerably on both books and records if all the many tasks involved could be performed by a single company. Victor has its own pressing plant, at Smith's Falls, Ontario. Capitol hopes to have one quite soon. The others "farm out" their work, as do most of the smaller companies. The chief record-pressing concerns in the country engaged in this sort of job-work are Compo Records in Montreal and Quality Records in Toronto, although the Victor pressing plant also handles quite a volume of it. Distribution, too, is often handled by Canadian firms acting for the large international companies.

The few Canadian independents recording serious music are of fairly recent establishment, and include Beaver (1950) and Hallmark (1952) in Toronto and Orfeo (1954) in Montreal. Information regarding these important ventures will be given later in this chapter. Canadian "popular" recordings are manufactured more extensively and appear in Montreal, Toronto, and Vancouver, under such labels as Alvina, Aragon, Dominion and Gavotte, to mention only a few. Two New York firms, Debut and Discovery, have been active in recording Canadian jazz musicians. Several music publishers (among them Chappell and Company, B M I Canada Limited, and Boosey and Hawkes of Canada) manufacture and distribute transcriptions for the use of radio stations; these are mostly of light music.

Of recordings by Canadian artists, whether made in Canada or elsewhere, among the earliest examples still available are Edward Johnson's pre-electrical recordings for Victor of several operatic arias. Some of these have been re-recorded. Cylinder recordings of the fabulous Emma Albani are collectors' items nowadays. Canadians who made big popular successes in the early days of recording include the ballad singer Henry Burr, born in New Brunswick, who is reported to have made over 12,000 records in his day; and the cornet virtuoso and band conductor Herbert L. Clarke, who, though not Canadian-born, was closely associated with musical life in several Ontario centres in the 1880's and 1890's and again following World War I. The earliest of Kathleen Parlow's many violin solo recordings for Columbia date from the second decade of this century. Eva Gauthier and Pauline Donalda, sopranos, both recorded for Victor about that time. Ellen Ballon, Mona Bates and Reginald Stewart, pianists, all made recordings for the Duo-Art (pianola) Company in the 1920's. The Hart House String Quartet, in its heyday, made a number of recordings for Victor, both in the studios at Camden, New Jersey, and in Montreal. The Montreal recordings, made in the early 1930's, include the Haydn Quartet in F minor, Opus 20, No. 5, and Two Sketches by Ernest MacMillan on French-Canadian tunes. Boris Hambourg, cellist of the quartet, made several fine solo discs in the 1920's. Several Canadian popular performers have been recording since those "early" days, one of the pioneers being Don Messer (Decca).

Among Canadian-born artists and artists associated with the Canadian musical scene whose recordings, mostly made abroad, are now generally available, are Ellen Ballon, pianist (London); Mary Bothwell, soprano (Royale); Rosario Bourdon, conductor (Victor); Désiré Defauw, conductor (Victor); Jeanne Dusseau, soprano (HMV); Reginald Godden, pianist (London); Jeanne Gordon, soprano (Victor); Frances James, soprano (Lyrichord); Raoul Jobin, tenor (Victor); Adolf Koldofsky, violinist (Dial); Ida Krehm, pianist (Paraclete); Arthur Leblanc, violinist (Victor); Gordon Manley, pianist (New Records); Lois Marshall, soprano (Victor); Alan Mills, folk singer (Folkways); Zara Nelsova, cellist (London); John Newmark, accompanist (Allegro, London); the Quatuor Alouette (Victor); Ernest Seitz, pianist (Victor); Ernest White, organist (Mercury). Several of these have also recorded in Canada for Beaver and Hallmark. It is worth mentioning in detail the several cases where Canadian artists have recorded contemporary works under the supervision of the composers, or, sometimes, in direct collaboration with them. Among these are Zara Nelsova's recordings of Samuel Barber's Cello Concerto, and two works by Ernest Bloch, *Schelomo* and *From Jewish Life*; Ellen Ballon's recordings of a piano concerto and other pieces by Villa-Lobos; the recording of Hindemith's song cycle *Das Marienleben* by Frances James and George Brough; and the late Adolf Koldofsky's recording of the Schoenberg Fantasy for violin. It is also a matter of pride that Lois Marshall was Toscanini's choice to record the soprano solo part in his version of the Beethoven *Missa Solemnis*. In January, 1955, it was announced that the pianist Glenn Gould had signed a contract with Columbia Records (U.S.) for some Bach recordings.

Several artists now active in Canada made recordings before settling here. Quentin Maclean's organ recordings for English Columbia, Heinz Unger's recordings with the National Symphony Orchestra (a British recording orchestra) of several Mendelssohn works, and Lubka Kolessa's versions of piano works by Mozart, Beethoven, Schumann and Brahms, may be mentioned.

The first Canadian choir to make recordings was apparently the

Toronto Mendelssohn Choir under the late Dr. H. A. Fricker, for Brunswick. Two Canadian choirs were among the contributors to the large Gregorian chant collection issued by Kyriale Records in the United States: the Choir of the Sulpician Seminary of Philosophy, Montreal, and the St. Augustine's Seminary Choir, Toronto. Even more widely known are the recordings of plain-song by the choir of the Benedictine monks of St. Benoît-du-Lac, at Lake Memphremagog, Quebec.

Two fine Canadian bands made recordings during World War II: the Canadian Grenadier Guards' Band of Montreal, under the late Captain J. J. Gagnier, for Victor, and the RCAF Overseas Band for HMV. The recording of Canadian orchestras was undertaken, apparently for the first time, by Victor in the early 1940's. The Toronto Symphony Orchestra, under Sir Ernest MacMillan, recorded the Elgar *Pomp and Circumstance Marches*, Nos. 1–4, a William Byrd Suite arranged by Gordon Jacob, four movements from Holst's *The Planets*, and the *Serenade* from Haydn's Quartet, Opus 3, No. 5. The Montreal Festivals Orchestra and the choir of Les Disciples de Massenet recorded Fauré's *Requiem*, with Wilfrid Pelletier conducting. These discs were made in Canada and distributed internationally by the Victor organization. It is perhaps surprising that so few recordings of the Montreal and Toronto orchestras have been forthcoming since the introduction of long-playing records in the late 1940's.

However, an important phenomenon which dates from the beginning of the "LP" era is the formation of Canadian companies for the production of long-playing records of serious musical content. Beaver Records has issued recordings of Handel's *Messiah* and Bach's *St. Matthew Passion* by the Toronto Mendelssohn Choir and the Toronto Symphony Orchestra under Sir Ernest MacMillan. By arrangement with Victor, these discs are being distributed in the United States under that company's "Bluebird Classics" label—both in complete three-record sets and in shorter "Highlights" on "extended-play" discs (45 rpm). They are apparently enjoying widespread popularity there with record-buyers: in their first season 20,000 records of the *Messiah* and 3,000 of the *Passion* were reported to have been sold. According to its President, Mr. F. R. MacKelcan, Beaver was formed primarily to record the Mendelssohn Choir but does not by any means confine itself to this function. Further recordings of works from the chorus-and-orchestra repertoire may be expected from this company. A recording by the Toronto Symphony

Orchestra of Tschaikowsky's Fifth Symphony, made for Beaver, has also been taken into the Victor "Bluebird" catalogue; further works have been recorded and will probably be released by the time the present book appears in print.

Hallmark Recordings Limited has an arrangement with Decca covering foreign distribution of its records. The Hallmark catalogue is an enterprising, off-the-beaten-track classical list, including performances by some outstanding Canadian artists, among them Lois Marshall, soprano; Greta Kraus, harpsichordist; Glenn Gould, pianist; Albert Pratz, violinist; and John Newmark, pianist. Hallmark claims to be "the only Canadian recording company producing and cutting its own high-grade long-playing records." Its most successful release from a commercial viewpoint has been a recording of Miss Marshall singing Falla's *Seven Spanish Popular Songs* and the Purcell-Britten *Three Divine Hymns*. A release which has been very highly praised is that of Mr. Newmark playing Haydn, Emmanuel Bach, and Clementi on a piano actually built by Clementi about 1810. Obviously Hallmark is not competing in the Tschaikowsky Piano Concerto market; thus with the above-mentioned and other comparatively rare items—for instance, Bach's *Variations in the Italian Manner*, Alban Berg's Piano Sonata, and the *Pastorale* for voice and orchestra by the Cleveland composer, Herbert Elwell—all now listed in the Hallmark catalogue, one feels justified in expecting that some attention will eventually be paid also to the many worth-while but so far unrecorded works by Canadian composers.

The third and newest Canadian firm to enter the recording field is Orfeo, a concert managing organization in Montreal, whose initial release, awaited at the present writing, is of special significance because it includes a work by a Canadian composer, the *Eglogues* of Jean Papineau-Couture. Orfeo is apparently intending to sell this and later releases through Hallmark.

It is sad to have to report that the number of recordings of works by our composers has not kept pace with the quantity and quality of the available music. In the mid-1940's an album containing the Piano Concerto in C minor of Healey Willan and the *Suite canadienne* of Claude Champagne was issued by the CBC and distributed as a presentation set. The Willan work was later distributed internationally by Victor under its own label, and was evidently a commercial success. Subsequently an album containing works for small orchestra by John Weinzweig, Jean Coulthard, G.-E. Tanguay, and Ernest

MacMillan was issued by the CBC, without being taken up by Victor, under the title "Canadian Album No. 2." French recording companies have brought out, more recently, works by André Mathieu—*Quebec Concerto* (Parlophone) and *Trois Etudes* (Boîte à Musique). Barbara Pentland's *Studies in Line* and Kenneth Peacock's *Bridal Suite*, both for piano, were recorded by English Decca and are distributed in Canada on the London label. A major work of Claude Champagne, his *Symphonie gaspésienne*, was recorded by the CBC and later issued commercially by Polydor. However, the tale is not long in the telling. Clearly, Canadian composition is virgin territory for most of the recording companies, whether large or small, affiliated or independent. When asked his opinion about the prospects, one executive said: "Any company that didn't do something of that sort in the long run—say, twenty-five or fifty years from now—would just not be living up to its responsibility." One agrees with the sentiment, of course, but one hopes the estimated time proves at least a decade or two too long.

Folk Songs of Canada, the music collection edited by Edith Fowke and Richard Johnston (Waterloo Music Company, 1954), contains a short list of records of Canadian folk-music; an editorial note points out that "at present very few recordings of Canadian folk songs are available." The National Museum at Ottawa has some thousands of recordings and tapes of folk-music; one would welcome the release of some of this valuable and fascinating material and the growing band of folk-song enthusiasts in Canada would probably ensure a good sale.[1]

One very important recording activity in the country remains to be mentioned. The Canadian Broadcasting Corporation has taken a leading part in the recording of serious music for the past decade or so. Its activities in this field have mostly been undertaken by its International Service, whose music producer was Miss Patricia Fitzgerald and is now Mr. Roy Royal. In 1949 the International Service initiated a transcription library. Transcribed Canadian musical programmes were, and still are, pressed in lots of 150 each and distributed to Canadian embassies, consulates and trade representatives throughout the world, as well as to 48 foreign radio stations (or, in some cases, net-

[1]Since the above account was written a start has been made in this direction with the appearance of volume VIII (*Canada*) in Columbia's recorded World Library of Folk and Primitive Music. This material has been re-recorded from the National Museum collection and the release contains extensive notes by Marius Barbeau.

works) and 15 Canadian ones. The foreign radio stations include 18 in South America, 14 in Europe, 7 in the Far East and Australasia, 6 in the West Indies, and 3 in Africa and the Near East. The absence of United States radio stations and networks from this list has been remarked. The catalogue of these transcriptions lists 100 programmes, issued at intervals between 1949 and 1954. Another fifteen were announced as being in preparation in the fall of 1954. The programmes are fifteen, or more often thirty minutes in length; some are longer. In content they include performances by Canadian entertainers, among them Giselle MacKenzie, Alan Mills, the Leslie Bell Singers, Oscar Peterson, and the "Prairie Schooner" company; works from the standard repertoire (Beethoven, Schumann, Brahms, Debussy) performed by Canadian artists (Zara Nelsova, Eugene Kash, Ross Pratt, and others); and a large number of serious works by Canadian composers. These last make up 34 of the first 100 programmes (including 85 works by 41 Canadian composers), and are especially worthy of comment.

There are some surprising omissions, and, inevitably, some unevenness in the representation; but the aim is eventually to include representative pieces by every important composer in the country. Record quality in the early stages of this CBC transcribing was a bit rough, but the later programmes are of the very highest quality from the standpoint of reproduction. Orchestral pieces constitute the bulk of the programmes in this category, though there are choral works, songs and instrumental solos as well. It is possible to complain that opera, operetta, chamber music and organ compositions are either under-represented or not represented at all, and that the prepared scripts which are distributed with the pressings are not always well written or accurate. In the main, however, this project deserves high praise—especially since virtually no one else in Canada has made available publicly, even in this restricted and non-commercial form, the music of our composers.

To what extent are the CBC's transcriptions used after their distribution? How frequently are they broadcast? I am told there is definite evidence that all the radio stations or networks provided with the programmes actually relay them—at least once. Their high quality has created a good impression abroad. Also, in recent seasons they have been more frequently used in the CBC's own broadcasting schedules at home, which is a good sign. Indeed, some of the works appear now to be slowly finding a position among standard repertoire in normal recorded-programme scheduling, which is a very desirable state of affairs, certainly.[2]

A word may be added on an important by-product of recordings, namely record reviewing. Some Canadian national magazines, and a number of newspapers as well, carry regular columns of comment on new records. It is perhaps in line with what has been said about the business itself that reviews of its products should so often duplicate the writings of American and British reviewers already widely read here. This seems regrettable, especially when most records nowadays tend anyway to be overly commented upon—and so often according to non-musical criteria. Far from wanting to know whether the record "brings the symphony orchestra into your living room" (as seriously proposed in one recent advertisement), many music-lovers would welcome sound musical evaluation in record reviews, and more reviewing space devoted to the smaller local enterprises which are now so full of promise.

Recording techniques are nowadays very highly developed, and record collecting seems to be increasing rapidly in popularity, in Canada no less than elsewhere. This country's musical achievement— the talents of her many fine performers and the writings of her composers—may become really known and appreciated most widely through records. Vision and a sense of responsibility are certainly called for both in those who manufacture the records and those who guide and inform us by commenting on them in the public press.*

[2]See "An Ambassador for Music," by Patricia Fitzgerald, in *TSO News*, vol. V, no. 3, Feb., 1953; also "A Booming Two-Way Trade in Music," in *CBC Times* (Eastern ed.), vol. III, no. 44, May 20–26, 1951.

*The writer wishes to acknowledge his debt to Mr. Edward Manning and Mr. Helmut Kallmann of the CBC, from whom he has received valuable assistance.

FILM MUSIC

Louis Applebaum

I am only a novice at this art of film music and some of my more practised colleagues assure me that when I have had all their experience my youthful exuberance will disappear, and I shall look upon film composing not, as an art but as a business. At present I still feel a morning blush which has not yet paled into the light of common day. I still believe that the film contains potentialities for the combination of all the arts such as Wagner never dreamt of.

R. Vaughan Williams, "Composing for the Films"

Most successful film-producing countries of the world have built their reputations on the basis of full-length, usually costly and lavish "entertainment" movies—the kind a theatre-goer in Toronto or Tokyo, Rangoon or Chicago, expects to see as he sits down in his neighbourhood movie-house. Canada has achieved respect throughout the world not on the basis of feature films, but as an outstanding producer of documentaries. Though we are here concerned with music in Canadian films, a brief review of the development of the documentary in this country might not be out of place.

In England during the late twenties, John Grierson, inspired by the isolated efforts of a few geniuses like Robert Flaherty, Joris Ivens, and the Russians Eisenstein, Pudovkin and Dovzhenko, and fresh from a stint in the United States where, under a Rockefeller grant, he was investigating mass information media, promoted and organized a film unit for the Empire Marketing Board. He gathered about him a group of bright, literate, energetic and talented youngsters who eventually produced films that are still classics of their kind. *Drifters, Song of Ceylon, Night Mail, Coalface* are all titles that are revered by documentary's disciples even as *Birth of a Nation, The Informer* or *Henry V* are cherished by most film-goers. From the beginning, the composer was in the scheme of things, working with the others to achieve an art (if you wish) out of the creative efforts of several minds and talents. This is at once the weakness and the challenge of motion pictures as an artistic medium. Even opera bends more freely to the will of the composer than does film to any one person—be he writer, producer, director, designer, cameraman or composer. Film is the result of the integrated artistic contributions of all these.

The "documentary movement" grew quickly in Great Britain. Within the government and under private sponsorship, many units, successors to Grierson's humble but vibrant group, came into being and flourished. In other countries, too, government departments, large corporations and utility services felt the urge and need to create informational and public service films. In the United States those exciting days produced such films as *The River, The Fight for Life, The Plough that Broke the Plains, Power and the Land* and dozens of others. The very titles speak of living, colourful and vital issues about which all should be concerned. These were the days before the war when slum clearance, maternity death rates, rural electrification and irrigation were the stuff newspaper editorials were made of. The film-makers took these subjects up and the power of the medium made of them leaders, spokesmen, fighters, reformers with perception and taste.

As with the English documentary, so in the United States it was not the experienced composer for feature films who was invited to contribute to these valiant and ardent film documents; almost without exception it was the inexperienced native composer, struggling on the lower rungs of success in the concert world, who was welcomed into the exciting world of the documentary film-makers. In England it was Benjamin Britten and Walter Leigh; in the United States it was Aaron Copland, Virgil Thomson, Roy Harris, Mark Blitzstein, Douglas Moore and Gail Kubick.

Canada had somehow managed to be practically unaffected by this flurry. Though not entirely inactive, Canadians were almost so. In 1921 the government had created the Canadian Government Motion Picture Bureau, whose function it was to produce and distribute films and photographs for various government departments. Limited largely by a restrictive budget, the Bureau remained small and relatively ineffective. In 1936, Ross McLean, working on the staff of the Canadian High Commissioner in London, was moved and impressed by the effect and power of the film as an educational and inspirational medium. Largely as a result of his urging, Grierson was invited to Canada to examine the Bureau and advise the government on its use of film.

As a result of his report, the National Film Act was passed in 1939; out of this grew the National Film Board. Grierson became the first Film Commissioner in 1941 and Ross McLean, his Deputy. Starting virtually from scratch, they built for the Canadian government, in a miraculously short time, an organization that could and did turn out several hundred films a year. Under the pressure of war much governmental red tape could be cut. The producers were for the most part youngsters fresh from courses in Canadian universities. Under the guidance of a few older hands from England such as Stuart Legg and Stanley Hawes, they quickly learned to handle film, issues and people. Soon their products were achieving recognition throughout the world. Not all of the films were good, naturally, but they accomplished an important job.

Music played its part in these films. It might be said that under the stimulus of war, the Canadian government had inadvertently become a major sponsor of new music. The National Film Board hired composers almost from the beginning and has always maintained at least three composers on its staff. In addition, scores have been composed for NFB films by many other Canadians on a free-lance basis. The staff composers, in addition to this writer, have been Maurice Blackburn, Phyllis Gummer, Robert Fleming and Eldon Rathburn. All have found in their work not only an opportunity to contribute to a vital national effort, but a means of reaching a tremendous audience. The need to write quickly and copiously (twenty to thirty scores a year is an average); the chance to have all their output played and recorded immediately; the opportunity to produce, mature and produce again, to experiment with the orchestra and with recording techniques, to learn by experience how to make the abstraction that is music apply to the specific of film, to make music functional—all these have provided a schooling of great value. In a land where musical composition is a relatively new art, this cannot but affect our nation's musical future.

The other composers who have been called on by the Film Board have complied mainly because they are eager to acquaint themselves with the problems of composing for film. John Weinzweig, Godfrey Ridout, Oscar Morawetz, Barbara Pentland, Morris Surdin, Howard Cable, Morris Davis and Neil Chotem are some of these. A special contribution has been made by Lucio Agostini. As Music Director of Associated Screen News, he was one of the very few experienced film composers in Canada when the Board struggled into being. Agostini's collaboration with Stuart Legg in the early forties resulted in many penetrating films in the series "The World in Action" and "Canada Carries On." The success of these films played a big part in establishing the reputation of the Board.

Just what is involved in this medium? What is the challenge that confronts the novice film composer? The mechanics are relatively simple and usually provide little trouble for him. With few exceptions, the composer of a background score begins his major task after the film is all but finished. A conscientious producer may have consulted the composer during some of the earlier stages of the film, but for the most part the music is one of the last items in its history. Thus the composer can be shown a "fine cut" (a final assembly) of the film's visual material; if there is dialogue, he can hear that also. After the initial screening, the producer and composer discuss at length the music's role in the context of the film. "Cueing" or "spotting" of music is a vital consideration; its entry or disappearance is a strong dramatic factor. A film composer should know where to be discreet and where to indulge in musical flamboyance, how to underline and support dramatic or emotional values without intruding on the spoken word, how to make a unit of diverse items and how to indicate time lapse. The orchestra's personnel is also considered at this early stage. Since most documentaries in Canada are made on a limited budget, an early decision must be made on the instrumentation of whatever small orchestra would best serve the film's need.

Now the strip of film can be measured. There is a precise mathematical ratio between film footage and time, so that a measurement of so many feet of film means so many seconds of time. The whole film, broken down into sequences, is therefore carefully measured; note is taken not only of the changes of scene but also of important details within scenes—explosions and other sound effects, entrances and exits, beginnings and ends of dialogue or narration. On the basis of these measurements, the composer writes his music to fit precisely.

He orchestrates his music, the parts are copied and he is ready for the recording session. This should take place in a properly equipped and acoustically correct recording studio. From the beginning the National Film Board has operated from a converted saw-mill in Ottawa, premises thoroughly unsuitable for film production. Because of this, recording is done in radio stations, unused halls and churches —in fact any auditorium of proper size and acceptable acoustic properties. Instead of permanently installed recording and projection equipment, portable units have to be used.

In most cases, the Canadian film composer is also the conductor for the recording. This arrangement has advantages and drawbacks, but Canadian producers cannot yet afford the elaborate "Music Depart-

ment" of the larger studios of Hollywood or London (with its hier-
archy of directors, conductors, orchestrators, editors and advisers),
and it works out reasonably well. The scores are carefully marked
with timings to guide the conductor, who follows a stop-watch or
footage counter. Off in a corner or in another room sits the recordist
with his expensive and delicate paraphernalia. Over the heads of the
orchestra hangs a complex of microphones. When a proper studio is
used, there is a screen in front of the conductor on which the film is
projected. On a prearranged cue, everything starts to operate; the
film is run on the screen, the recording equipment rolls, the counters
tick off the seconds and the orchestra plays.

Unlike a concert performance, a recording session does not offer the
hearer a continuous, ordered performance of a work. The music may
be broken up into small sections lasting from a few seconds to several
minutes. These can be recorded in any order that serves the conductor's needs. The orchestra may be scattered about the room at the
discretion of the recordist and the demands of his microphones. In
the few minutes a conductor can allot to the rehearsal and performance of any one sequence, he must solve all the normal problems of
balance, phrasing, dynamics and so on, and at the same time must
see that his tempi coincide precisely with the timings on his score. At
38⅔ seconds from the beginning he must be at exactly the place indicated in the score. A variance of even a fraction of a second can
create much difficulty, if not disaster, in the relationship of the music
to the film.

The recording cameras run at the prescribed ninety feet per minute
and record the sounds, which the microphones have translated from
sound waves into electrical impulses, on a strip of "sound track."
These long strips of film are subsequently delivered to the composer
or to a music editor in a "cutting room." Here he has equipment which
can play the sound track by itself or in synchronization with the
picture strip. All the prepared points of coincidence between music
and picture should then emerge as planned and the best "takes" of
the separate little pieces can be assembled into a proper music track.
Independently the dialogue, narration and sound effect reels have
been built and all are now ready to be blended.

In the "mixing room," each of these tracks is placed on its own film
phonograph. A well-equipped studio may have a dozen or more of
these machines, all of which are carefully interlocked to start and continue to run in absolute synchronization. The sound from each phono-

graph is fed into an elaborate console which has volume and equaliza-
tion controls for each track. The "mixer"—an engineer who should be
equipped with a sensitive ear as well as knowledge of electronics—
carefully controls the volume and tone of the sounds emanating from
each track and blends them into a pleasing effect. This resultant
sound, a judicious mixture of music, word and noise, is then recorded
again on a sound camera; it is this sound strip, printed beside the
picture, which is run off in a theatre or home projector, and which
adds an aural dimension to the two-dimensional visuals.

In Canada, especially at the Film Board, the approach of the composer has been one of creation rather than imitation. Possibly because
he was young and eager to try new ways, the Canadian film composer
has evolved many interesting and unusual techniques and attitudes.
Realizing immediately that he was not writing music for concert
performance, he could put his training and talent into the service of
the new medium without inhibition and without a feeling of sacrifice.

Although, to some degree, a film composer cannot help using some
types of concert music which he adapts to the functional needs of
film (or radio or television), this country has provided an environment that encourages experimentation. Thus Norman McLaren has
been stimulated to perfect his methods of creating music "syn-
thetically." McLaren has developed several means by which he can
either draw or photograph pictures of sound waves directly on to the
sound track strip so that what emerges is a musical composition which
no performer has played, which has not been recorded, and which can
be duplicated in no other way. McLaren has himself composed many
pieces for his own use—little works of wit and ingenuousness. Maurice
Blackburn has collaborated with him on several films in which the
sound track has in whole or in part been created in this way. For one
of these, A Phantasy, Blackburn wrote a very charming and effective
piece for saxophone quartet and synthetic sound. All of the saxophone
parts were played by one player, Bert Niosi, and by means of multiple
recording were synchronized with the synthetic track into a homo-
geneous quintet. In another film, a small group of players was directed
to improvise freely within certain time limitations and according to a
prescribed harmonic pattern: a kind of long-hair jam session for flute,
oboe, clarinet and cello. The results were trimmed, edited and re-
arranged in the cutting room to provide another ingenious sound track
for McLaren's improvisations in visual design and movement.

In 1951 the Festival of Britain invited McLaren to contribute to the
programme of the Telecinema a three-dimensional animated film—

probably the first ever made. In this new theatre, built for the Festival, stereoscopic films would, for the first time, be shown in England. For the first time, too, this theatre was equipped to play stereophonic sound tracks. This writer was able to collaborate with McLaren in what was probably the first original score for stereophonic performance. With the advent of Cinerama and Cinemascope, much work will undoubtedly be done in the future on music with a multiple-direction source. For the composer a wonderful new device has been created. He can now write directional as well as melodic counterpoint, can play off one orchestral ensemble from the front against another from the rear and can have a melody dance about the room against an accompaniment from the centre.

With their moviolas, synchronizers, splicers, dubbers, microphones and equalizers, cutting and mixing rooms have been a source of inspiration. The ability to play musical sounds at varying speeds, forwards and backwards, to superimpose one on top of another, to create new timbres and effects by clipping the attack points of notes or trimming their decay times—all this has led to the creation of unusual and sometimes very effective musical scores. In many of the film scores by Fleming, Rathburn, Blackburn and this writer, these devices have been proved practical as a composer's tool. The current interest in *musique concrète* has been foreshadowed for many years by the Canadian film composer's use and mastery of the art of "building" a musical score out of little bricks of recorded sound which he manipulates at his discretion.

The Canadian documentary film, in its role of interpreting Canada to Canadians and to other countries, is often concerned with peoples of many nations. The composer thus becomes involved with many different kinds of folk-music. One week he may be called on to study and write in the vein of the Chinese or Greek; next he may be utilizing Canadian Eskimo, Indian or French folk materials; for another film he may try to recreate the Legong of Southeast Asia. The composer is thus often impelled to seek for and invent new orchestral colours and to make much out of the small orchestral combinations at his disposal. It is not unusual, therefore, to find at a film recording session that a pianist is asked to play directly on the strings of a piano with a screw-driver instead of using the keyboard in the conventional way; that an ensemble of four or five bass and contra-bass clarinets is used; that a harpsichord is combined with alto flute; that a post-horn is required to play a be-bop melody or that a percussionist is asked to play a solo of bangs and crashes on his miscellany of instruments for use in conjunction with other passages of music. The ingenuity and imagination of the composer are here not restricted by the conventions of the concert hall.

On the other hand, the normal musical life of our nation has its place in the Canadian film. The National Film Board, especially, has taken note of outstanding and interesting musical activity throughout the country and has duly recorded it on film. One of its early successes was a film, called *A City Sings*, about the enormous annual music festival in Winnipeg. In 1945 two concerts on film were given by the Toronto Symphony Orchestra, conducted by Sir Ernest MacMillan. Eugene Kash's highly successful Ottawa children's concerts have been translated into an informative film for young folk, which contains some fine music by Eldon Rathburn. The excitement of Canada's first Ballet Festival has been recorded on film as have been the activity, hard work and glamour connected with the Royal Conservatory's Opera School. The peculiar life and talents of the Dominion Carillon-eur have been filmed in *The Man in the Peace Tower*, while the famous organ-builders, Casavant Frères, have been observed in their shops at St. Hyacinthe, Quebec, in the film *Music in the Wind*. Some of our popular performers, Oscar Peterson, Giselle MacKenzie, Neil Chotem, Evelyn Gould, Alan Mills, the Leslie Bell Singers, the Commodores, and many others, have been seen in Canadian films. In 1952 the works of two Canadian composers were featured on film. A movement of Harry Somers' Suite for Harp and Orchestra was conducted by Paul Scherman, with Marie Iosch as soloist, in the film *Rehearsal*. The other film in this series was based on the Winnipeg Ballet Company's performance of Robert Fleming's colourful ballet *Shadow on the Prairie*.

Films of Canada's cultural life have made much use of music. Many French and other Canadian folk-songs have been the basis for clever animated films. The Gregorian chant of the Benedictine monks enriches the film *Monastery*. Canadian painters and their works have been eulogized and analysed in a continuing and valuable series of films, many of which contain especially effective music scores by Blackburn, Weinzweig and others. Thus tribute has been paid to Tom Thomson, F. H. Varley, Arthur Lismer and Emily Carr, the painters of Quebec and the primitive painters of Charlevoix, folk artists and sculptors. The record in respect to the Canadian composer is not so bright, but there is hope that means can be found to honour our music creators and their work.

Of the twenty or so private film producers operating across Canada, only two can be said to employ composers on anything like a regular basis. One is Associated Screen News, in Montreal, for which Lucio Agostini acts as Music Director, succeeding Howard Fogg who served until 1942. This company's "Canadian Cameo" series, with music by Agostini, deserves special mention. The other, perhaps more active musically, is Crawley Films, Ottawa, which has since 1949 employed the valuable talents of William McCauley. For the rest of the producers, an active music department is possibly too heavy a financial burden. When they can afford to use "live" music instead of music culled from sound track libraries that are available on both disc and film, they usually employ neighbourhood composers with a little film experience. Lawrence Wilson, while resident in Vancouver, was occasionally asked by a west-coast producer to score a film.

For many years there has been, almost annually, an attempt on the part of one Canadian producer or another to embark on a programme of feature film production. The most ambitious was that of Quebec Productions which made *Whispering City* (*La Fortresse*). The score for this film was composed by Morris Davis, and featured in the film was the Quebec Concerto by André Mathieu, played by Neil Chotem. This company has since made a success of less costly films directed exclusively at the French-speaking market. For *Un Homme et son péché*, Hector Gratton was employed as composer; *Le Curé du village* has a score by Davis. Joseph Kosma, a successful French film composer, was brought here to write the music for *Son Copain*. Rudolph Goehr came from New York to compose for *Père Chopin*, produced by Renaissance Films. Maurice Blackburn's music for the stage production of *Tit-Coq* was used by Davis in his score for the film version. Blackburn also contributed a score to Renaissance Films' *Le Gros Bill* and Oscar Morawetz composed a long score for *Forbidden Journey*, made by the now defunct Selkirk Productions. Allan McIver, Germaine Janelle, Neil Chotem and Arthur Morrow have had occasional employment as composers for Canadian feature films and this writer has had the opportunity to work on several major films produced by Hollywood and New York companies. There is, however, not enough activity in Canada in the feature-film field to enable a composer to make a vocation of his occasional association with full-length films.

An important feature-length film produced by NFB is *Royal Journey*, an account of the tour of Canada made by the Queen (then Princess

Elizabeth) in 1951. Because of the need to release the film almost immediately on the completion of the tour, the services of six composers were used, each composing separate sequences which were finally integrated in a hectic recording session played by a band in Toronto. The fifty-odd minutes of music were prepared in a very few days.

If most of the preceding pages have been devoted to the National Film Board, it is because in the realm of film music most of the activity is centred there. The Film Board produces about one hundred films a year involving Canadian musicians, Crawley about a dozen, and in 1953, all of the other producers in the country, together, perhaps another dozen. The Canadian government, through its two agencies, the CBC and the NFB, is the largest employer of musicians in the country and also the nation's most active sponsor of creative music. It is to be hoped that when the government realizes that it has unconsciously assumed the role of music patron, it will take that role consciously and seriously, and initiate a comprehensive and efficient system for the regular support and encouragement of the creative arts. In the meantime, the film companies of Canada offer composers the opportunity to investigate and participate in the motion picture as a creative art.

CHURCH MUSIC I

Jules Martel o.m.i.

Quoniam Rex omnis terrae Deus: psallite sapienter.
For God is the King of all the earth: sing ye praises with understanding.

Psalm 47:7

At present there is in Canada what one might call a marked activity in the field of sacred music. We live at a time when, in this respect, a notable reform is taking place in the Catholic world. The nature and causes of this reform call for some explanation.

In spite of strong and frequent protests on the part of ecclesiastical authorities, serious abuses have over the years crept into the music of the Church. This has been especially the case since the sixteenth century and perhaps most of all in the nineteenth. Music of a secular style, suitable for concerts and operas but unfitting for the liturgy, found its way into Catholic churches. These abuses were excused on the false principle that in music whatever pleases is good. Such a principle cannot be justified on any grounds, ethical or aesthetic, but in church music especially one must consider whether "whatever pleases" befits the Sovereign Majesty of God and the worship offered to Him.

In the Roman Catholic churches of Canada today the trend is definitely towards a more consistent following of the principles enunciated in the *Motu Proprio* of Saint Pius X. This momentous document, issued in 1903, enunciates principles covering the music to be considered liturgical for use in the Latin (Western) rite of the Catholic Church and makes it a serious duty of those who are responsible for its selection and interpretation to eradicate all abuses. The following are the main principles on which the Holy Father bases the reform he ordered:

177

1. *The function of sacred music:*

Being a complementary part of the solemn liturgy, sacred music participates in the general scope of the liturgy which is the glory of God and the sanctification of the faithful. Its principal office is to clothe with suitable melody the liturgical text proposed for the understanding of the faithful; its proper aim, therefore, is to add greater efficacy to the text, in order that through it the faithful may be more easily moved and better disposed to receive the fruits of grace belonging to the celebration of the most holy mysteries. The music is merely a part of the liturgy and its humble handmaid: it must never assume the main role and present itself under a form even remotely akin to concert music.

2. *The qualities of good church music:*

(*a*) It should be holy; it must inspire true piety and not distract the congregation from prayer "and must therefore exclude the profane not only in itself but in the manner in which it is presented."

(*b*) It should be a true art, composed and performed according to the rules of musical art.

(*c*) It should be universal, i.e., acceptable to all.

3. *The different kinds of sacred music:*

(*a*) These qualities are to be found in the highest degree in Gregorian chant. The more closely a composition for church use approaches in its movement, inspiration and savour the Gregorian form, the more sacred and liturgical it becomes; the more out of harmony it is with that supreme model, the less worthy it is for the temple.

(*b*) These qualities are also possessed, to a high degree, by classic polyphony. It agrees admirably with Gregorian chant, the supreme model of all sacred music, and hence it has been found worthy of a place side by side with the Gregorian chant in the solemn functions of the Church.

(*c*) Modern music is also admitted in church, provided (according to Saint Pius X himself) it has been approved by the proper authority. The modern repertoire worthy of recommendation is, however, rather limited; too many modern composers either lack inspiration or write "sacred music" in a style suitable for concerts rather than for the liturgy.

4. *The use of the organ:*

The *Motu Proprio*, confirmed by a later instruction, *Divini Cultus*, issued by Pius XI, approves of the organ. This is the only instrument accepted *ex officio* by the Church; it may be used as an accompaniment to the chant as well as in preludes, interludes and the like. These must not only be governed by the special nature of the instrument but have the qualities proper to sacred music as above enumerated.

5. *The singers:*

The *Motu Proprio* approves of men, women and children joining in congregational singing but the male choir is regarded as the ideal liturgical or sanctuary choir. Boy singers are to be used for the high parts. A great number of boys' and men's choirs are now developing throughout Canada—such choirs as were and are found in the ancient basilicas, cathedrals and monasteries of Europe.

Having in mind the principles set forth above—principles which serve as a basis for judging sacred music—the reader will be in a better position to appreciate the scope of the activities this music has stirred up in Canada. I shall endeavour to give as clear a picture as possible of these activities on the strength of the information I have been able to obtain.*

THE TEACHING OF CHURCH MUSIC

Fine schools of church music are found in the three leading French-speaking universities: l'Université Laval, Quebec City, l'Université de Montréal and l'Université d'Ottawa. In each of these, the curriculum comprises solfeggio and musical dictation, classical vocal polyphony, choral conducting, accompaniment of Gregorian chant, history of music, harmony and counterpoint and the special course compiled by the monks of St. Benoît-du-Lac. L'Université de Montréal gives additional courses in fugue, orchestration, composition and extemporization on the organ. Many students come from distant parts of Canada and the United States to attend these schools.

L'Abbaye Bénédictine de St. Benoît-du-Lac (Abbey of the Benedictine Monks at St. Benoît-du-Lac) in the southern part of the province of Quebec is a notable centre of Gregorian culture; to a great extent it sets the tone for Canada in everything related to theoretical studies in Gregorian chant and to the practical interpretation of liturgical cantilena. In addition to the three universities named above, many other institutions have adopted its curriculum. Several choir-

*It is thanks to the good offices of Monsignor J. E. Ronan, Director of the Schola Cantorum of Toronto, that I have secured information regarding the English-speaking dioceses and the Ukrainians. I should like to thank Monsignor Ronan most cordially for the invaluable service which he has rendered.

masters of Benedictine abbeys in the United States were trained at St. Benoît-du-Lac. The Abbey has issued a treatise on Gregorian rhythm as well as a number of recordings; these have exercised a wide influence abroad. Among the institutions which follow the Benedictine teachings in their respective localities are: L'Apostolat Liturgique, Montreal; L'Institut Grégorien de Sherbrooke, P.Q.; L'Ecole Vincent d'Indy, Outremont, P.Q.; L'Ecole Normale de Musique, Westmount, P.Q. and two scholae cantorum—La Maîtrise de Québec at the Archbishop's Palace, where children are taught from the third to the final year of the elementary course, and the Cathedral Schola Cantorum of Toronto, which teaches children from the third year of the elementary to the second year of the high school course.

True scholae cantorum are institutions where children selected for their general talents and for their particular gift in music follow regular school courses with special emphasis on music and liturgy. Vocal, instrumental and theoretical music is given a prominent place in their curricula. One of the main objects is to ensure excellent rendering of liturgical chant. This is, of course, the ideal method of training church musicians. Scholae cantorum flourished in Europe until the eighteenth century and from them came the greatest composers of church music such as Josquin des Prés, Palestrina, Lassus and Victoria.

It is surprising that a greater effort has not been made to establish more of these institutions in Canada; there should be one in each of our large cities. However, several valiant endeavours have been made and it is not from lack of individual devotion and initiative that more notable results have not been achieved. Among others, Rev. Father Alfred Bernier, s.j., who died recently in Montreal, gave of his best to this end.

One must not minimize sincere efforts. It is more difficult to maintain even a mediocre choir in unfavourable circumstances than to carry out successfully a large and brilliant undertaking if given adequate facilities. Many a small parish choir is to be commended for its attempts, despite adverse conditions, to realize the finest ideals of church music. Nevertheless it is encouraging when our leading church authorities lend their fullest support, as has His Eminence Cardinal McGuigan to the Schola Cantorum in Toronto. This school, founded in 1936 and directed by Monsignor Ronan, is now attended by 185 boys, some coming from points as distant as Halifax, Winnipeg and James Bay. Its purpose is to train choristers, future organists and choirmasters; it is attended by both boarders and day-boys, chiefly the latter. The curriculum has been outlined above. Much of the musical work follows the standards of the Royal Conservatory of Music and many boys take the examinations of that institution. A large number of graduates have taken their place as church organists and choirmasters in the city and beyond.

Summer courses of one to four weeks' duration, several of which attract students from far and wide, and the curriculum of which is spread over two to five years, are given annually at: Regina (Rev. J. Molloy, Director); Toronto—Cathedral Schola Cantorum; Ottawa—Ecole de Musique de l'Université d'Ottawa; Montreal—l'Apostolat Liturgique and Ecole Normale de Musique, Westmount; St. Benoît-du-Lac—Abbey of the Benedictine monks; Quebec City—Ecole de Musique de l'Université Laval; St. Joseph, N.B.—l'Université Saint-Joseph; London—Sisters of St. Ursula, Brescia Hall; Halifax—St. Mary's University (Rev. J. Mills); St. John's, Newfoundland—Cathedral School (Mr. Rainer Reis). Regina and Saskatoon have combined to organize summer schools, Gregorian societies and two choir festivals yearly.

In certain dioceses a series of theoretical and practical courses of approximately sixty hours each year is given to parochial choirs. These choirs are grouped by zones and one parish in each diocese is selected as a centre where a visiting professor gives instruction. This method of teaching, which produces excellent results, is being carried out in the dioceses of Quebec, Three Rivers, Sherbrooke, St. Hyacinthe, Joliette and others.

Generally speaking, admirable work is done in the various educational institutions. The singing of liturgical services is prepared with great care in seminaries, religious institutes for both men and women, and also, though sometimes with less complete means of instruction, at secondary institutions. At certain seminaries and institutes the singing of the services is of a remarkably high calibre artistically and provides a practical lesson to the faithful who occasionally attend them. It is of course outstanding in the Abbey of St. Benoît-du-Lac and is also very fine in the major seminaries of Quebec, Montreal, Sherbrooke, Three Rivers, St. Hyacinthe and Ottawa, St. Augustine's and St. Basil's Seminaries, Toronto; St. Joseph's Seminary, Edmonton; Holy Heart Seminary, Halifax; St. Peter's Seminary, London, as well as the scholasticates of various religious institutes for men and a great number of religious institutes for women. In many such institutes the more talented are given facilities for the serious study of music and excellent organists and choirmasters may be found among their graduates.

For special training in ecclesiastical music many teachers have travelled far and wide to attend church music schools and summer courses provided in ecclesiastical institutions. A fair number have attended the Pontifical High School in Rome and the Gregorian Institute in Paris. Others have studied the English tradition of choir training.

It must be admitted, however, that by no means all of our organists and choirmasters are proficient. This is in most cases owing to the indifference and lack of musical understanding shown by too many of our educators. Music, regarded as unimportant, is given either no place or a very small place in the curriculum of some of our schools; students wishing to study music must do so outside regular hours. In elementary schools, where this evil is perhaps chiefly apparent, the lack of competent teachers is often given as an excuse for not teaching singing. This lack is only too evident but would not be so if greater efforts were made to train them.

CONGREGATIONAL SINGING

It is clearly the wish of the Church to encourage singing in the vernacular at private devotions and extra-liturgical functions, both of which form a great part of the Catholic life. Across our country in every diocese will be found vast gatherings at outdoor devotions—Rosary and Holy Name Rallies, etc.—with great congregations singing both in their own language and in Latin. Many dioceses report that Canadian children have developed a new enthusiasm for hymn singing, stimulated by their school training. Reference has been made to some of the hymn collections used in Canada.

In certain parts of the country many of our "New" Canadians of varied racial origin offer us a good example of the devotional power of vernacular hymns. But congregational singing in the vernacular is anything but new in this country. Its original inhabitants—the North American Indians—took readily, from their first contact with the white man, to the music of the Church, as the seventeenth-century *Jesuit Relations* testify. Today the tradition is still maintained by many Indian tribes who sing in their own language the liturgical melodies of the Mass.

UKRAINIAN CATHOLIC CHOIRS

The *Motu Proprio* regulates the liturgical music of the Latin rite only. We must not overlook the beautiful liturgical music of the Ukrainian Catholics who, in company with a number of Slovaks and Hungarians, follow the Oriental rite, each group having its own special characteristics. Across Canada we hear good choirs of this Byzantine rite, most of whom sing in the old Slavonic language proper to their liturgy. These liturgical chants are so traditional and standardized that the faithful may enter such a church in any part of the country and directly join in the chant. Very remarkable is the almost constant congregational singing; the people respond in full harmony to the chant of the celebrant, thus creating a beautiful and devotional atmosphere for the grace and splendour of the liturgical ceremony. Both men and women join in the singing of the choir, which is used for special occasions and chants proper to certain feasts, and of the congregation. The congregation may also be heard singing in the vernacular at extraliturgical functions. In common with the Greek and Russian Churches, these Ukrainians dispense with an organ and the music is choral throughout.

PUBLICATIONS

The list of works on church music issued in French-speaking Canada is a very extensive one. Laval and Ottawa Universities have taken a prominent part in their publication, some of the authors being Rev. Father Fernand Biron, Rev. Father Jules Martel and Rev. Father Conrad Latour. Important contributions have been made by Dr. Eugène Lapierre, whose *Traité sommaire d'accompagnement grégorienne* has been issued also in an English edition published in Toledo, Ohio, by the Gregorian Institute of America. Among periodicals, *La Musique d'Eglise*, edited by Rev. Father Lefebvre, ceased publication in 1927 but *La Revue Saint Grégoire* still appears monthly (address: P.O. Box 772, Quebec City). Other reviews, such as *Musique et Musiciens* (La Bonne Chanson, St. Hyacinthe, P.Q.), *Séminaire* (Séminaire de Saint-Sulpice, Montreal) and *La Revue de l'Université d'Ottawa* include occasional articles on church music. Collections of hymns include *Manuel de chants sacrés* edited by Rev. Father Destroimaisons, La Pocatière, P.Q.; *Recueil de cantiques* by Father Conrad Latour (Université d'Ottawa); *Cantiques choisis* by Rev. Father C.-E. Gadbois (La Bonne Chanson, St. Hyacinthe). Monsignor J. E. Ronan has published three books of *Jubilee Hymns*. Dom Georges Mercure, o.s.b., of the Abbey of St. Benoît-du-Lac is the author of *Rythmique grégorienne* to which reference has already been made; it is published by the monks of the Abbey, who have also issued five albums of recorded plain-song.

COMPOSERS

It has been exceedingly difficult—in fact wellnigh impossible—to gather much information on the church music of Canadian composers. This is owing to the fact that, in view of the very limited demand, it is almost never published. The valuable catalogue of Canadian composers compiled by Helmut Kallmann and issued by the Canadian Broadcasting Corporation lists many sacred compositions to which one would wish to have access. The writer would greatly like to have in his possession one liturgical work by each of thirty-five or so composers whose names appear on this list, works with which the composer himself is satisfied, but conditions must alter before this will be possible.

ORGANISTS

The ideal church organist is a phenomenon among musicians. He renders works full of difficulty and written on a score of three or four staves. He completely controls an instrument which, among all others, is the most noble as well as the most intricate. He is the ideal accompanist, knowing how to accompany Gregorian cantilena according to the principles of this exquisite art, always helping and never submerging the choir. During liturgical services, he makes it his duty never to be in the limelight himself, however easy this might be; sometimes his friends and admirers wish him to be less reticent. He knows he is there to serve the liturgy, to raise the minds and hearts of the people towards God. No nobler role falls to the lot of any musician. In underlining the liturgical chant when the choir is silent, his own presence almost forgotten, he reaches his greatest height.

Is such an ideal unattainable? Not quite: we have a goodly number of organists in Canada, trained by some of the finest contemporary masters, who closely approach it. But among the host of those who "play the organ" it must be admitted that many lack thorough musical training, an idealistic approach or the unremitting industry that the profession demands. The excuse most frequently offered is that "the clergy and the faithful are not sufficiently interested in good music." Unfortunately this excuse is often valid but the organist should never forget that his duty is partly that of a teacher: he plays an extremely important part in the re-education of both clergy and congregation with regard to liturgico-musical taste. To perform this duty conscientiously he must give more than he receives.

Although one might list a fair number of organists in Canadian churches who combine technical skill with the idealistic approach, we must refrain; such a list, even if extensive, has its dangers and worthy names might be omitted.

PARISH CHOIRS AND CHOIRMASTERS

Here again one is tempted to select bodies which, throughout the length and breadth of the country, give notable service to their respective parishes and some of which are known far beyond their own communities. Without making such invidious distinctions one can say that great numbers of our churches are served with musical skill and devotional fervour. In all our parishes, Gregorian melodies are sung in liturgical services throughout the year. Choirmasters are generally anxious to have them rendered as well as the means at their disposal will permit. When the essential choral components are available, a great number give the preference to classical polyphony rather than to more modern compositions.

Many choirs and choirmasters might well voice the same complaint as do the organists, namely that their work, even though accomplished according to the spirit of the liturgy, meets with indifference and carping criticism. In perhaps no human organization is success harder to ensure than in a church choir. It is increasingly difficult to secure recruits: music comes to us too easily through mechanical reproduction nowadays and too many shrink from making efforts without hope of financial reward. There is too much music on the air and too little in our hearts and minds. We must not of course put the blame for this on modern inventions but on our own deficiencies: lack of training and especially of idealism. Choirmasters and choristers would surely study and rehearse more intensively if spurred on by an ideal and convinced of the great educational value of learning liturgical chant.

It is deplorable that Gregorian chant is so often rendered without reverence, without artistic conscientiousness and without its true type of rhythm. Even the purest masterpiece will not be admired if it is distorted in performance. Neither Gregorian music nor classical polyphony can be rendered haphazardly. Both have certain subtle characteristics not found in modern music. Singers who render them must study and master these characteristics. However, as has been said, a marked improvement can be noted in many quarters and a list of first-rate Canadian church choirs and choirmasters would reach considerable proportions.

Leaders of boy choirs win our special admiration, one might even say veneration. Their onerous task, often hampered by the indifference of others, calls for the kind of wonderful "folly" that few but artists and saints display. But how poor a world ours would be without such idealistic "fools"! Whether because of this divine folly or of more favourable circumstances, several groups have achieved remarkable success and all are striving to make up for the scarcity of real scholae cantorum. No less than 109 boy choirs in Canada are listed with the *manécanteries* affiliated to those of Paris; these are distributed from Newfoundland to Vancouver Island and there are doubtless many others for which figures are not available.

Although, as has been said, efforts to stimulate an interest in massed singing have, in some parts of Canada, met with success, in others they have not. Complete success would involve laying a broader foundation through the preparation of liturgical chant in Catholic Youth groups and their attendance as groups at parochial services. Above all it would involve compulsory teaching of singing in primary and secondary schools by competent teachers, i.e., those who hold diplomas in this subject. Such teaching should, of course, be given according to a well-defined and set programme on the lines of the curricula followed in almost all other countries. Excellent results have been attained elsewhere: why not in Canada?

SPECIAL CHOIRS

By "special" choirs we mean those which, outside liturgical services, sometimes render sacred music in concert halls or over the radio:

1. The choir of the monks at St. Benoît-du-Lac, under Dom E.-B. Lemieux, o.s.b., which, besides being a living lesson in the singing of Gregorian chant for numerous visitors at the institution, has often been heard over the French network of the CBC.

2. The Schola Cantorum du Grand Séminaire de Montréal (directed by Rev. Father Clément Morin, p.s.s.) which has, over a period of twenty years, been frequently heard in concert halls and over the radio.

3. The Palestrina Choir of Ottawa (directed by Rev. Father Martel, o.m.i.) which was founded in 1947 and specializes in the interpretation

of classical vocal polyphony. It has been heard in twenty-seven concerts in Ottawa and Montreal as well as in fifteen broadcasts over the French network of the CBC, one of which was relayed to Europe and South America.

4. The choir of the Schola Cantorum, Toronto, under Monsignor J. E. Ronan, is heard regularly over the Toronto radio station CBL and in two periods yearly of Trans-Canada religious broadcasts.

5. The choir of Notre Dame d'Acadie (young women, directed by Sister Marie-Lucienne) which renders beautifully Gregorian chant and classical polyphony. This choir, located in Moncton, is the counterpart of the choir of l'Université Saint-Joseph described below; it has twice (in 1952 and 1954) won the Lincoln Trophy as the finest choir to be heard in the competition festivals of Canada.

6. The choir of l'Université Saint-Joseph, New Brunswick, which is composed of young men; founded and until recently directed by Rev. Father Léandre Brault and now directed by Rev. Father Soucie, it encourages liturgical music through concerts and broadcasts. Competing at musical festivals during recent years, it won the Lincoln Trophy in 1950 and an Eisteddfod Trophy in North Wales in 1951. Some tributes by adjudicators may be quoted: "The general blend and balance are exceptional for a choir of this nature and they have the spirit of the music completely" (Sir Ernest MacMillan at the New Brunswick Festival, 1949). "We are here as adjudicators from different countries of the world and are unanimously agreed that the most authentic Palestrina was sung by the St. Joseph University Choir. . . . In 'Alouette' we have found that folk tradition and high art have met each other in perfect balance" (Board of Adjudicators, North Wales, 1951, in awarding the International Folklore Trophy).

In our Canadian churches can be found music ranging from the excellent to the meretricious. The excellent proves our capacity for reaching great heights. It also proves that we could soon hear in our churches only good liturgical music properly rendered, provided everyone concerned—clergy, organists, choirmasters, choristers and the faithful—became more completely conscious of their responsibilities towards liturgical music and the dignity of divine worship. It is claimed that there is a notable awakening: I would like to believe this and certainly desire it with all my heart. May it grow *sempre accelerando e crescendo*! May God grant me the grace to play my full part in such an awakening!

CHURCH MUSIC II

Charles Peaker

Be filled with the Spirit; speaking to yourselves in psalms and hymns and spiritual songs, singing and making melody in your heart to the Lord.

Ephesians 5: 18, 19

That our Canadian churches give heed to at least part of Saint Paul's admonition is evidenced by the sheer amount of music to be heard in them week by week. How far our singers are "filled with the Spirit" can only be known in Heaven, and it would take a committee of experts some time to discover what artistic standards they achieve on earth. Be that as it may, there is one respect in which it can be said that church music in Canada thrives. Were some devoted statistician to compute what is spent annually on service music, he would find that there is no more consistent patron of music and musicians than the Church. A mundane speculation perhaps, but a significant one since it shows that the ministers and the councils of the Church are fully awake to the value and the uplifting power of music.

In Canada the Roman Catholic Church can claim the greatest number of adherents; French-speaking Canada is overwhelmingly Catholic. Next in numerical strength is the United Church, followed by the Church of England in Canada, the Presbyterian and Baptist Churches, the Greek Catholics, the Lutherans, Jews and Christian Scientists. I cannot discuss in this small space the music of other bodies, but I must acknowledge the Salvation Army, whose fine bands so often make music without the "walls of Zion."

Fundamental differences between one body and another naturally affect the nature of the music they use, but there is, with rare exceptions, one splendid common denominator, to wit, a choral tradition which inspires thousands of volunteer singers to trudge to and from church in all weathers for services and rehearsals. How this loyalty to the choir-loft became so well established, I do not know, but it may well be stronger here than in the lands from which it derived. It is more rarely found in the United States.

188

What do these choirs sing at church services? Looking over some hundreds of service lists from churches of different denominations I find a preponderance of English anthems, and, in Anglican churches, settings of the liturgy. The Elizabethans are represented chiefly by short works of Tye, Tallis, Batten, Wilbye, Weelkes, Gibbons and Ford; more rarely by the great William Byrd, although his motets "O God whom our offences have displeased," "Jesu, Lamb of God," and, at Eastertide, "Haec Dies" (in English) appear from time to time. Of later English composers Purcell, Croft, Greene, Attwood, Crotch and S. S. Wesley are frequently found but I am bound to admit that the complacent strains of Stainer, Barnby, Maunder and other Victorians are still the staple diet in some of our churches. Here too, we shall find well-worn copies of Gounod's music in the choir library.

Coming to present-day composers—men who followed in the wake of great ones like Parry and Stanford—the names of Harwood, Ireland, Charles Wood, Walford Davies, Geoffrey and Martin Shaw, Herbert Howells, Ley, Marchant, Bairstow, Bullock and Thorpe Davie recur constantly. Stanford is represented by noble anthems such as "How beauteous are their feet" and "The Lord is my Shepherd" and especially the Morning and Evening Service in B flat. Since the Coronation of the late King George VI in 1937 we frequently sing Parry's "I was glad" on festive occasions; his "Jerusalem" is in most of our hymnbooks, and the *a cappella* "My soul there is a country" is sometimes performed. Among Canadian composers, Healey Willan is naturally first and foremost; of his accompanied anthems (some of which antedate his coming to Canada) those chiefly used are "I looked and behold a white cloud" (Harvest), "In the Name of our God," "A Prayer of Rejoicing" (Saint Cecilia's Day, 1953) and "O Strength and Stay." His heavenly unaccompanied setting of Longfellow's "How they so softly rest" is often sung on Armistice Sunday. Over twenty unaccompanied motets of his appear on our lists, among them the deservedly popular "Hodie Christus natus est." Latterly, his anthem "O Lord our Governour," written for and sung at the Coronation of Queen Elizabeth II, has been sung by many choirs. The Coronation has resulted in a general interest in the music performed on that occasion, particularly Redford's "Rejoice in the Lord" and Vaughan Williams' "O taste and see."

Among German composers Handel is easily the best represented, but there has been a steady increase in the use of Bach. The most popular cantatas would seem to be "Sleepers, wake," "God's time is the best" and "Christ lay in bonds of death," but others are found, as well as parts of the *Christmas Oratorio* and the two *Passions*. The music of Mendelssohn, Brahms, Haydn and Schubert is also drawn upon, roughly in that order, two choruses of Spohr still survive, and one occasionally hears Beethoven's "Hallelujah" from *The Mount of Olives*.

Russian composers appear very frequently, with Tschaikowsky in the lead; one movement from Dvorak's *Stabat Mater* is heard regularly at Communion services. From sixteenth-century Italy and Spain we hear a little Palestrina and less Vittoria; of the later Italians, one work each by Pergolesi and Zingarelli complete this rather meagre list. We sing a few of the better American works, but too many of our choir-masters, when they look southwards, seem to prefer the sentimental ditties of yesterday. Here in Canada, besides Willan, such composers as W. H. Anderson, Gerald Bales, Hugh Bancroft, Alanson Brown, William France, Eugene Hill, Walter MacNutt, Frederick Silvester, John Weatherseed, Alfred Whitehead, Drummond Wolff and others have made fine contributions to our choir libraries. (The reader is referred also to the chapter on Composition, above.)

If it were not for the churches, most of the music I have listed would be rarely if ever performed. Similarly, it is through the churches that the great literature of the organ, past and present, is familiar to us. What a loss we would suffer, were the organ works of Bach never heard in their original form! There are thousands of fine organs, big and little, all across the continent and a few are found in concert halls and academic institutions. We have had some good builders, and latterly excellent work has been done by young and progressive firms, but, since Joseph Casavant built his first organ in 1837 at St. Hya-cinthe, Quebec, the firm of Casavant Frères has been pre-eminent. Their instruments are to be found also in the United States and else-where. The firm owes much to the intelligent guidance for many years of Mr. Stephen Stoot, who is known far and wide for his discernment in tonal matters. We have imported a few instruments from England, and there is an increasing tendency on the part of "Baroque" players to introduce American instruments of that design. Of late years many of our smaller churches have installed electronic organs of one sort or another, where space precluded the use of a pipe-organ. Improvements have been made in these instruments, some of which were atrocious at first, but many of us feel that they are, even at their best, a substitute for the genuine organ.

What of the organ-playing? I am afraid that, in spite of a number of well-equipped musicians, we are strangely backward as compared with the United States, where there are many brilliant virtuosi, and where excellent conservatories and colleges turn out a host of good students of church and organ music. In Canada there are summer schools in church and organ music for all denominations at the Royal Conservatory of Music in Toronto, the London School of Church Music in London, Ont., Mount Allison University in Sackville, N.B., and a Congress for Lutheran musicians in Waterloo, Ont. There may be others which have not come to my attention. On the whole, however, our schools seem to treat church music in general, and organ-playing in particular, as the Cinderella of the art. And yet churches are continually looking for well-qualified men to whom they will pay liberal salaries. I have examined a great number of church leaflets, and few of them list the voluntaries. I am afraid this means that the organist "improvises" and how many can? Again, with a few honourable exceptions, organ recitals here are poorly attended, and hearing some of them, one cannot wonder at it. After all, organ-playing is the one corner of the musical vineyard where rhythm retires while the performer plays dominoes with the stops or turns pages. Were we to practise half as much as pianists and violinists, these melancholy conditions might be reversed. I should add that Canada is one of the few places where, despite illustrious examples to the contrary, some music committees still believe that no woman can play the organ or lead a choir.

The examinations for Fellowship and Associateship of the Canadian College of Organists, founded in 1909 by the late Dr. Albert Ham, set standards similar to those of the Royal College of Organists in Great Britain. Unfortunately few of our students sit for these examinations and the musical influence of the College is far from what it should be. On the other hand, the College, which has eighteen centres from Halifax to Vancouver, does offer its members admirable opportunities to exchange views, discuss mutual problems and enjoy friendly intercourse. At its annual conventions, held in the late summer, capital recitals are given by members and visitors, and discussions, rehearsals and lectures are conducted by leading members of the profession. More than three hundred people attended the convention of 1954 in Toronto; these included about sixty visitors from the United States, some of whom came from as far away as Florida and Texas. The College has no headquarters of its own as yet, but has inaugurated a fund to provide a permanent building. In 1953 the College presented Coventry with £10,000 as a contribution to the organ that will some day be built in the new cathedral.

THE UNITED CHURCH OF CANADA

In 1925 a majority of the Presbyterians joined forces with the Methodists and the Congregationalists to form the United Church of Canada. Five years later, the *United Church Hymnary* was compiled by the Committee on Church Worship and Ritual, whose secretary was the eminent hymnologist, Dr. Alexander MacMillan. Dr. MacMillan, on whom fell the chief burden of editing the new book, was careful to retain the best musical traditions of all three communions. In addition to hymns of all ages and many metrical psalms from the Scottish and Genevan Psalters, space was found for a number of psalms and canticles set to Anglican chants. Congregational singing is vitally important in Protestant churches and his book (later adopted by the Baptist Church) has done much to establish a better standard in their worship.

Nowadays, many United Churches are being built with chancels and a divided choir; the pulpit no longer dominates everything from the centre and the worshippers are not blinded by a terrific display of gilded organ pipes across the back. Some good specimens of the old style have been converted and wear their new accoutrements rather self-consciously. Yet, while some of the concern with chancels and crosses, cassocks and surplices may be a superficial fashion, there has accompanied it a real interest in a more ordered and dignified service. Here the Anglican and the ancient Scottish prayer-books have had their effect, and—what is very germane to this chapter— the music has improved. The solos are of a better quality and there are perhaps not so many of them since the singer has become less conspicuous. Some use is made of Anglican chants, better hymns are sung and the service tends to become more liturgical in character.

In the United States, one service each Sunday is the rule, but in Canadian churches of most denominations we have two, morning and evening, and I know some where the morning service is held twice to accommodate the large congregations. Almost everywhere, however, the evening worship is a problem. In downtown districts this service can be very trying to a musician. Dignity gives place to sensationalism, the regular hymns to those of the gospel type, and the minister to a visiting evangelist who publicly contemplates his own sinful past with a sort of desperate joy. In contrast to this, some shrewd men nowadays are remembering Pope's lines, "And some to church repair, not for the doctrine, but the music there," and are pruning the sermon in favour of music. Then Handel strides in with the grand stories of the Old Testament, often prefaced by an intelligent outline from the pulpit. I know one United Church where the preacher, a splendid speaker, reviews once a month some current book, and the service is really choral Evensong and very well done too. In some churches a junior choir assists in the evening worship, and at Christmas presents very fine carol services in candle-lit surroundings. At other times I have heard them augment the senior choir in Bach cantatas.

THE CHURCH OF ENGLAND IN CANADA

The Church of England in Canada consists of twenty-eight dioceses. That of Toronto covers 10,000 square miles and comprises 130 parishes. This is small compared to the diocese of Athabasca with its 200,000 square miles, or the diocese of the Arctic (inspiring name!) whose area is 2,225,000 square miles of which 1,020,303 are water. Here, there is no synod; the Bishop (amphibious, I presume) is "lord of all he surveys." When I add that the diocese of Nova Scotia is separated by 3,052 air-miles from that of British Columbia it must be apparent that festivals such as the "Three Choirs" in England (Gloucester, Hereford and Worcester), could not be held here. It is not uncommon, however, for the churches in a particular deanery to unite for a special service, such as Ascensiontide, when some organist of accepted attainments directs the joint effort. A number of Anglican churches are affiliated with the Royal School of Church Music, doubtless to their advantage, but it would be a fine thing if there were some central body established here to deal particularly with problems which are peculiarly Canadian. A really good choir could be formed which would broadcast regularly across the Dominion and set a standard for all, however remote the parish. The Tallis Choir of Toronto, led by Mr. John Cozens, has made a practice of visiting smaller communities (by invitation), there to sing the service according to the principles of the R.S.C.M.

The new Diocese of Toronto Choir School, established as the result of a substantial bequest by the late Rev. R. W. B. Pugh, held its first sessions at Trinity College School, Port Hope, Ontario, in the summer of 1954. The enrolment was limited to fifty boys and twelve choirmasters. The Director was Dr. Healey Willan, who had the valuable co-operation of Francis Jackson of York Minster, John Hooper of the Royal School of Church Music, and Eric Lewis of St. Simon's Church, Toronto. Mr. John Bradley was the Secretary. The school made a splendid start, and it will be interesting to watch its development in future years. There are no full-time choir schools that I know of, and not many all male choirs, but what there are are usually of a very good standard indeed. The choir of St. George's Cathedral, Kingston, directed by Mr. George Maybee was accorded the unusual distinction of singing the services in Westminster Abbey during August, 1954.

In many Anglican churches one finds a mixed choir with a paid quartette and perhaps a score of boys. Ferial Responses, English settings from Walmisley to Sumsion, the Oxford Psalter, the Nicholson Psalter, the Parish Psalter Noted or even the Old Cathedral Psalter, and a good hymn-book (which would be even better with less Sullivan, Stainer, Barnby and Dykes)—these are the materials. I have mentioned seasonal cantatas, and it only remains to add that on Good Friday in many churches the *St. Matthew Passion* will be sung, though rarely in its entirety. One may also hear Brahms' German Requiem or the Requiem Masses of Mozart and Fauré.

At present plain-song is not used to any great extent except in certain churches where the Anglo-Catholic tradition prevails. A classic example and one that sets a standard for many others throughout the country is the Church of St. Mary Magdalene in Toronto, where Dr. Healey Willan has been organist since 1921. Psalms, canticles, office hymns, the Gloria and the Credo are all sung to plain-chant. The Propers of the Mass, as found in the English Hymnal, are sung to their own authentic music in an edition prepared by Dr. Willan himself. The plain-song is sung by a small choir of men in the chancel, and a mixed choir of about sixteen voices in the West Gallery sings *a cappella* the Kyrie, Sanctus, Benedictus and Agnus Dei together with *faux bourdons* and motets. Music of the sixteenth and seventeenth centuries (particularly the Tudor school) is largely drawn upon for the music of the Mass and for the motets. Dr. Willan has written no less than eleven short settings of the Mass in English as well as those motets I have mentioned elsewhere. Recitals of liturgical music are given both within and without the walls of the church as well as in broadcasts; in short, Dr. Willan has here realized an ideal by his skill and devotion, which has helped us all, whatever our own circumstances and practices.

THE PRESBYTERIAN CHURCH IN CANADA

In 1925 a number of Presbyterians, unwilling to follow their brethren into union with the Methodists and the Congregationalists, elected to continue as the "Presbyterian Church in Canada." Their music has much in common with that of the United Church, and naturally their hymnal owes a good deal to the early Scottish and Genevan Psalters. In other respects many Presbyterian churches have strayed far from the stern Calvinism of John Knox. In one fine old church in Toronto, the choir has performed, season by season, many Bach cantatas and a prodigious number of Handel's oratorios, sometimes with orchestral as well as organ accompaniment. In order to make this possible the church has cheerfully added a subsidy to the offering, the singers have given their services, and the organist (until recently Gerald Bales) has done a fantastic amount of scoring and copying. In Ottawa another Presbyterian church has a fine list of cathedral anthems to its credit and has instituted annual performances of Bach's *St. Matthew Passion*. The organist is Carman Milligan. In this church one may hear a Scottish metrical tune to one psalm and an Anglican chant to another. At the other extreme one still finds in Canada old-time Highland congregations with a double pulpit; here there will be no organ; the Precentor, according to the traditional practice of the Scottish "Wee Frees," gives out the psalm tunes line by line.

OTHER DENOMINATIONS

The Baptist churches show a similar diversity of practice; no ecclesiastical authority dictates either the liturgical or the musical procedure of individual congregations. Architecturally many of their modern buildings are hardly distinguishable from those of the Anglican church, and where there is a progressive pastor and a good organist the service will be fairly elaborate. The choir enters with a processional hymn and makes its way to a beautiful chancel there to sing an introit and an anthem, chant the Lord's Prayer, and the Gloria Patri after the psalm, and lead the congregation in good hymns. The only weak item in the service seems to be the solo, but it will sometimes be an appropriate aria from oratorio. Go to another Baptist church (and indeed to many of the smaller non-Anglican churches in downtown districts) and you may hear very poor music indeed and no proper decorum in the proceedings. Here, we are sometimes told, the music must have a "message," and there are found many highly successful publishers to meet the need, with cheap rubbish. Dr. George P. Gilmour, the President of McMaster (Baptist) University in Hamilton, Ontario, tells me that the University is now setting up a Faculty of Music which may give the Divinity students some sense of direction in these matters.

Compared to this looseness of church polity, the Lutherans are strongly unified. Hymnal, psalter, prayer-book and the music thereto are contained in one volume designed to furnish the proper order for every Sunday and feast day. The music of the liturgy is simple—and some of it not very impressive musically—but all join in the responses. The service as a whole is truly congregational. The hymns include a large number of German chorales; good Lutherans probably listen to Bach's chorale-preludes more intelligently than many of the rest of us do. The choir sings an introit and gradual at the morning service and leads the congregation in the antiphon, psalm and responsory at Matins and Vespers; the clergy generally intone their own part in the worship. In short, everything is designed to be in harmony with the Proper of the Day.

In many Canadian communities are found Greek and Russian Orthodox churches where clergy and choirs seem to be fully awake to their great responsibility of preserving and performing the music associated with the ancient liturgies of St. John Chrysostom and St. Basil the Great. Here, as in the Orthodox Jewish synagogues, there is no congregational song and no instrumental accompaniment. It is interesting to see how Russian composers such as Tschaikowsky, Archangelsky, Bortniansky, Rachmaninoff and others have not only illuminated the great moments of the Greek Orthodox service, but have also enriched the worship of other communions.

There is little to be said about the music of the Church of Christ Scientist in Canada. There is no choir, but only an organist and a solo singer. Congregational singing is very good, since everyone is provided with a hymnary with music.

JEWISH SYNAGOGUES

In the Orthodox synagogues, the music is severe and completely traditional; here the Cantor sings the ancient Hebrew chants. Music and order in the Reform Temples are much more ornate; professional singers and directors are engaged, and sometimes (as at Holy Blossom Synagogue in Toronto) there is an organ—a thing which would be anathema to orthodox Jews. In these temples, in addition to the traditional recitative of the Cantor, the choir presents music by contemporary composers such as Binder, Saminsky, Freed, Fromm, Weiner and the great Ernest Bloch, much of it cast in antiphonal form. This music is in accord with the true Hebrew ethos; it is music with its roots in the past, and it is displacing a wilderness of dreary commercial productions by men who, in the early days of the Reform Temple, turned their backs on their own rich racial heritage. Sulzer, Lewandowska, Naumbourg and Weintraub are pre-eminent in this restoration of synagogue music; indeed Sulzer has based much of his music on the old cantillatory melodies.

Church music is slowly achieving new and better standards in this young country of ours. We have many excellent musicians in our midst, *although we need many more*. There is one curious angle to the calling, and that is its dependence on the clergy. To use a metaphor, the parson is the Captain of the ship, and the organist the Chief Engineer, and the personal relations between the two should be based on mutual respect. In other words, having appointed a Chief, no wise skipper tries to tell him his business. This vital consideration, however, is in no way peculiar to Canada. Let us hope that clergy and musicians are together striving to realize the high ideal so well expressed by an organist, and the son of an organist, John Milton, who said:

> But let my due feet never fail
> To walk the studious Cloysters pale,
> And love the high embowed roof,
> With antick Pillars massy proof,
> And storied Windows richly dight,
> Casting a dimm religious light.
> There let the pealing Organ blow
> To the full voic'd Quire below,
> In service high, and Anthems cleer,
> As may with sweetnes, through mine ear,
> Dissolve me into extasies,
> And bring all Heav'n before mine eyes.

COMPETITION FESTIVALS

Richard W. Cooke

. . . in a COMPETITION *the persons strive to attain a common end, and may have the most friendly feeling towards each other; in* RIVALRY *there is rather the desire of one to supplant or get before another, and usually a certain hostility.*

Annandale's *Concise English Dictionary*

The keynote to the present growth and activity in music festivals in Canada is heard in the last words uttered to the writer by the late George Mathieson, affectionately known as the "Father of Canadian Music Festivals": "Carry on!" Behind these words lies a long history of tradition, experience and planning, most of which is closely integrated with the development of Canadian culture.[1]

Although such competitions in music did not see their beginning in Britain, the inspiration for the present form of competitive festivals, in common with so much of the artistic life of our country, came from the Motherland. The use of competition as a stimulus in the sphere of art is not of course new; it may be traced as far back as the Pythian Games of the sixth century B.C., which were primarily musical contests. The song contests of the Minnesingers at the Wartburg in the thirteenth century and of the Mastersingers in the sixteenth are pictured in Wagner's *Tannhäuser* and *Die Meistersinger* respectively. The Eisteddfod or meeting of the bards in Wales dates back at least to the Carmarthen Eisteddfod in 1451. It is recorded that Handel and Domenico Scarlatti competed together in Rome in the year 1708; also Bach and Marchand at Dresden in 1717. When in 1781 Mozart and Clementi competed in Vienna, the latter afterwards admitted he had learned a life's lesson in the "greater worth of solid musical structure as compared with showy brilliance." These instances supply some precedents for the competition festival of today.

Probably the Welsh Eisteddfodau were the first musical competitions in Great Britain. In the eighteenth century the love of choral

[1]The author wishes to express his sincere thanks to Mr. Reginald Hugo, President of the Federation of Canadian Music Festivals, for his kindly interest and advice. For further information the reader is referred to the annual *Digest Report* of the Federation.

song was exploited by rural publicans in the organization of competitions. Such announcements as this were typical:

TO ALL LOVERS OF MUSIC

At Mr. William Kirkham's at the sign of the Horse and Jockey on Warley Common near Brentwood, Essex, on Thursday, Whitsun Week, 1773, will be given gratis a Punch Bowl, etc. to be sung for by any company of Singers in this Country. Each Company to sing three part songs in two parts, and three catches in three parts, the catches to be sung out of Mr. Arnold's Catch Club Harmony. Singing to begin at 2, and to be decided by three proper judges of music, after which there will be a Concert of Vocal and Instrumental Music.

The first competitions in England on modern lines were possibly those organized in a few places where Welsh groups had settled. Here quite naturally the Welsh language was used; the English were not much concerned in them. In 1860 John Curwen held choir competitions at the Crystal Palace and Exeter Hall, London, and in 1882 his son, John Spencer Curwen, who had served as an adjudicator at Welsh Eisteddfodau, was inspired by his experiences to institute a competition at Stratford, near London.

It is, however, to Miss Mary Wakefield of Kendal, Westmorland, that we are chiefly indebted for the musical competition festival as we know it today. Miss Wakefield, a professional singer and a woman of means, organized competitions for vocal quartets at a village flower show. To quote the late Harry Plunket Greene: "All unaware of what she was doing for the country's music, she started the Country Festival. . . . She suggested to the neighbours around that it would be great fun for families, groups or villages to learn some part songs in the winter and come to compete with one another in a Tournament of Song sometime in the following year." In August, 1885, "the first contest took place in the covered tennis court at Sedgewick"—a humble beginning but one that spread quickly. "The lady of the manor in Cornwall, or the parson's wife in Kent, got the neighbours together and spread the news." Little festivals sprang up all over the country. From then on the competition festival has greatly widened in scope but in the picture of these quartets meeting at Sedgewick House and singing against each other "for fun" lies its true spirit. Perhaps the late Walford Davies has best expressed this spirit in the words "In Musical Festivals, the object is not to gain a prize, nor defeat a rival, but to pace one another on the road to excellence."

In the short space of sixty-nine years, hundreds of festivals have come into being in the British Isles and the British Federation of Musical Festivals now boasts 280 affiliated festivals which win each year the interest and attention of considerably more than a million competitors and listeners.

Canada can claim over ninety festivals in operation, representing every province except Quebec. Steps are now being taken to form a festival organization in the city of Montreal; this will in effect be a revival, for Montreal had a festival between 1937 and 1940. Although definite figures are not available, it is a conservative estimate that Canadian festivals attract over 30,000 entries each year. As each entry may include any number of competitors from a soloist to the personnel of a full choir or orchestra, the total number of individuals participating may run well over 300,000. Numbers in audiences are equally difficult to assess; in many instances the size is limited by the capacity of available halls. Even so, it is reckoned that approximately 750,000 people in Canada attend sessions each year.

In one important respect the development of the musical competition festival in Canada differs from that in the British Isles. Here the larger festivals came first, the smaller district festivals followed, and the evidence does not suggest that the movement owes its growth entirely to the idea's having been caught up from province to province. Rather does it appear that in many cases the seeds from which blossomed the movement in the western provinces were brought from the Mother Country by people born and bred in the atmosphere of the British festivals; the *fons et origo* is therefore Mary Wakefield. The provincial Festivals of the four western provinces have been the backbone of the movement since its inception in Canada.

In the year 1905 Saskatchewan and Alberta were detached from the vast Northwest Territories to form two separate provinces. At the ceremony celebrating their inauguration, the then Governor-General, Earl Grey, who was greatly interested in music and drama, expressed his intention of doing something practical to further the cause of these arts. Letters were dispatched to the provincial lieutenant-governors suggesting that groups interested be invited to take part in a Dominion-wide festival; at final competitions held annually one representative from each province would be eligible to compete for the "Earl Grey Trophy."[2] The Lieutenant-Governor of Alberta, His

[2]The Earl Grey Trophy, though for some time awarded in connection with drama festivals, is now presented annually to the best school chorus at the Manitoba Music Festival.

Honour George Hedley Vicars Bulyea, lent a receptive ear to the suggestion of establishing in Edmonton a music festival on the lines of those in Britain. With his encouragement Howard Stutchbury, a prominent singer and choirmaster, and Vernon Barford, organist and choirmaster of All Saints Cathedral, undertook the work of organization. Aided by a committee of organists, choirmasters and teachers, they drafted a syllabus providing for competitions in choral singing, vocal solos, duets, trios and quartets as well as instrumental classes and in May, 1908, the first music competition festival on the North American continent took place in Edmonton. Two adjudicators—Messrs. Matthews and Rhys Thomas—were brought from Winnipeg; there were a large number of entries and according to all accounts the standard of performance was very high. Financial difficulties were encountered but were overcome through the assistance of a sympathetic and far-seeing bank manager and the festival became permanently established. It is worthy of note that, beginning with 1908, the choir of All Saints Cathedral, Edmonton, under Vernon Barford (one of the founders and first president of the Alberta Festival) has competed in each year that the festival has been held in Edmonton—surely a record of faithfulness and regularity.

It was not long before musicians in other provinces, already familiar with the movement in Great Britain, began to organize festivals in their own localities. Saskatchewan established one of its own in 1909 and until well on into World War I, the two young provinces held festivals annually. Owing to a shortage of manpower, Saskatchewan was obliged to suspend operations during World War I but then resumed its activities. Alberta, however, managed to continue, and in the year 1916 instituted the system of holding the provincial festival alternately in the three centres of Edmonton, Calgary and Lethbridge; this is still in effect today. In the summer of 1918 Manitoba organized through the Men's Musical Club; it held its first festival in 1919. British Columbia followed, holding its first festival in Vancouver in 1923. From these main festivals have radiated in each western province a number of district festivals; there are now twelve operating in British Columbia, seven in Alberta, eighteen in Saskatchewan and seventeen in Manitoba.

In other provinces the development of the festival has been more recent. Toronto had a festival which functioned in 1923 and 1924; subsequently it lapsed until, in 1944, the Kiwanis Club, under the inspired leadership of Col. George W. Peacock of the Salvation Army (a former resident of Winnipeg), undertook its revival. A number of festivals had in the meantime come into existence in several of the smaller Ontario centres—notably Stratford, Niagara Falls, Fort Frances, and the twin cities of Fort William and Port Arthur. Encouraged by the success of the Toronto Festival, many other festivals followed in Ontario, a number of them organized through the efforts of the late J. S. Atkinson and the Canadian Bureau for the Advancement of Music; several are sponsored by local Kiwanis Clubs. There are today at least twenty-five festivals in operation throughout the province.

In the Maritime Provinces the festival movement has grown continuously in popularity since the middle 1930's, when the Halifax Festival was organized. Several other centres in Nova Scotia followed and in 1936 the first New Brunswick provincial festival was held at St. John. All the Maritime Provinces now boast a large number of provincial and local festivals, the latest being that of St. John's, Newfoundland, whose third annual festival took place in 1954.

Early in the history of festivals on the prairies it was found necessary for representatives to meet each year to exchange ideas and to plan their festivals consecutively so that the same adjudicators might be engaged to cover several of them. Through the efforts of the late George Mathieson of Winnipeg a "chain" of festivals was established; this made it possible to engage experienced adjudicators from Great Britain who, through many years of active participation in such work, had gained the necessary knowledge for this specialized branch of music.

In 1945 the annual meeting of representatives from the western provinces—then called the Conference of Festival Delegates—met in Winnipeg. Mr. W. B. Rothwell, an enthusiast in festival work at Stratford, Ontario, and newly appointed organizer of the Toronto Festival, attended as an observer. He invited the conference to meet in Toronto the following year. In 1946 the eastern festivals came into the picture for the first time and the festival "chain" expanded from a few prairie festivals to twelve across Canada. Now eighteen appear on the "chain" annually.

Originally the conferences were informal affairs, largely under the guidance of Mr. Mathieson who had been Secretary of the Manitoba Festival from its inception until 1943. He had no desire for power, but he had such an intense interest in festival matters, particularly as they affected children, that he dedicated his many talents wholeheartedly to the cause. This spirit, coupled with his natural gifts, gave him a position of leadership and ensured a continuity of service that made formal organization unnecessary at the time. It was not until 1949, when the conference was held at Niagara Falls, Ontario, that a national organization known as the Federation of Canadian Music Festivals was formed; this subsequently became incorporated. In recognition of his lifetime of service, Mr. Mathieson was made the first Honorary President; Mr. Reginald Hugo, also of Winnipeg, was elected President and still continues to direct the affairs of the organization. Along with this expansion has come a feeling of national responsibility on the part of those who manage festivals; the original necessity of arranging for adjudicators who operate from coast to coast has emphasized the fact that the festival movement has an important place in the cultural life of Canada. A distinct claim rests on all festival committees to maintain high standards of musical appreciation and performance.

The business of annual conferences now covers a wide field, the matter of adjudicators and their schedules being one of the main problems. This has become more complex with the growth of the "chain," which requires a minimum of four British adjudicators for a continuous period of almost five months. As a matter of economy the festival tour commences in eastern Canada late in January, is carried through to the west coast, then returns, finishing in the Maritimes in May, with a minimum of lost time. The "chain" festivals can thus use British adjudicators only when they are in their territory. There is a steady and insistent demand for the services of the British musicians; more could be used if they were available. Canadian festivals owe an incalculable debt to these adjudicators, who have for many years left their homes and professional responsibilities for long periods of time, in order to assist in the musical development of this country. In numerous instances they do so at considerable expense and inconvenience to themselves. It is evident that the true missionary zeal has been a motivating factor in their work. The advancement of standards of performance and appreciation is but one tribute to the excellence of their contribution: the fact that there are now a number of qualified Canadian adjudicators is due in large measure to association with their British colleagues. Canadian festivals point with pride to such visitors from overseas as H. Plunket Greene, Sir Granville Bantock, Herbert Fryer, Dr. T. Tertius Noble, Sir Hugh Roberton, Dr. J. Frederic Staton, Thomas F. Dunhill, Dr. Thomas Armstrong, George Dodds, Sir Percy C. Hull, Dr. Gordon Slater, Sir Steuart

Wilson, Maurice Jacobson, Max Pirani, J. Peebles Conn, Stanley Roper and a host of others, each of whom has left his mark on the Canadian musical canvas.

The balance of judging is done by Canadian musicians. Each year a large part of the work at the eighteen "chain" festivals, and all the adjudicating at other festivals outside the "chain," is handled by Canadians. For a number of reasons it is not possible to engage Canadian musicians exclusively. They cannot spare the necessary time; equally important is the fact that they cannot be employed in areas where they may have personal relations with competitors and teachers. Within these limitations, Canadian adjudicators are used extensively and it is a field of professional work to which they are welcomed.

The selection of British adjudicators is obviously left to a few, and the responsibility rests with representatives of the Federation in Great Britain. These are musicians who have adjudicated here and know Canadian conditions and requirements. The list has included names of several internationally known personalities such as the late Sir Hugh Roberton and H. Plunket Greene, as well as Dr. J. Frederic Staton, Maurice Jacobson, George Dodds and many others. At present Dr. Gordon Slater of Lincoln Cathedral and Alec Redshaw of Cleethorpes occupy the position of advisers. British representatives have always been pleased to serve the interests of Canadian festivals on a purely voluntary basis. Their burden is not light, for interviewing, screening and selecting suitable men call for much thought and effort throughout the year.

Apart from arranging the "chain," the Federation must deal with details of festival operation, arising largely from reports presented by various festivals. Items of national interest are also considered, such as the award of national trophies, standards of music teaching and supervision in schools and Departments of Education, choice and supply of music for test pieces and standards to be attained and maintained. Although not all festivals operating in Canada are affiliated with the Canadian Federation, a great number outside this organization seek advice and assistance in the conduct of their affairs and undoubtedly most festivals are influenced to some extent by the national organization.

Reference has been made to the award of national trophies. These are two in number. The Lincoln Trophy was the gift of the Lincoln (England) Musical Festival to the Manitoba Festival. The late George Mathieson, then Secretary of the Manitoba Festival, recommended that it be offered for national competition and consequently it is given annually to the best adult choir appearing on the "chain" of festivals. Those who have been fortunate enough to win the trophy are: 1949—The Bach Choir, Vancouver; 1950—Chorale de l'Université Saint-Joseph, St. Joseph, N.B.; 1951—New Liskeard Ladies Philharmonic Choir, New Liskeard, Ont.; 1952—Choir of the Collège Notre Dame d'Acadie, Moncton, N.B.; 1953—English Choral Singers, Halifax, tied with Metropolitan Church Choir, Toronto; 1954—Choir of the Collège Notre Dame d'Acadie, Moncton, N.B.

The second of these trophies is the George S. Mathieson Trophy, presented by the Men's Musical Club and Associates of Winnipeg. It was felt this was a suitable manner in which to commemorate Mr. Mathieson's abiding interest and inspired leadership in the cause of Canadian music festivals, and especially in the work of children. The trophy is awarded annually to the best children's or junior choir adjudicated by any member of the British team of adjudicators. The list of winners includes: 1952—Notre Dame Bon Conseil convent, Sudbury, Ont.; 1953—Riverdale Collegiate, Toronto; 1954—Daniel McIntyre Collegiate Institute Girls' Choir, Winnipeg, Man.

Festivals are for the most part self-supporting, the cost being met by entry fees and paid admissions to public sessions. While there is widespread support of the work of the festivals by civic governments, school boards, service clubs, newspapers, radio stations, private individuals and other agencies, this does not always include financial backing, and never in sufficient amount to preclude failure. Scholarships are an important feature at some festivals, but these are invariably donated, and such funds are not available for operating expenses. All work in connection with the running of festivals is voluntary, except that occasionally a business secretary is paid a small honorarium and a few units in one or two of the larger centres engage certain people for duties of a special nature.

In the early days in Great Britain there were superior people who—to quote the *Musical Times* of that period—"looked upon a competition as a low order of thing, to be classed with horse-racing, billiard matches and the like, and not to be thought of in connection with the fine arts." Fortunately the great majority of people in our time have a finer understanding of what the musical competition movement hopes to achieve. Her Majesty the Queen has been graciously pleased to grant her patronage to the British Federation of Music Festivals and some of the leading citizens of our Dominion, led by His Excellency the Governor-General, have bestowed on Canadian festivals a similar honour. The National Film Board has portrayed the work of Canadian festivals through what is acclaimed as one of its best efforts, *A City Sings*. This presents a graphic picture of the Manitoba Festival; it has been shown in practically all parts of the British Empire with most favourable reactions. Newspapers and national magazines frequently feature articles on Canadian musical festivals and the Canadian Broadcasting Corporation has on several occasions presented programmes of festival music, in Canada and abroad.

While it is true that the primary purpose of musical festivals is to develop sound musicianship among those of average natural ability, it is nevertheless a source of gratification that numerous professional artists who have gained international fame have at one time or another been competitors in musical festivals. The British Federation points with pride to Kathleen Ferrier, Denis Matthews, Norman Walker, Cyril Smith and many others going back to the days of John McCormack. Canada has its Nelson Sisters, Ross Pratt, Frederick Grinke, Betty-Jean Hagen, Freda Trepel—to mention but a few.

What then does the musical festival ideal mean to Canada and Canadians? It may be claimed that the music competition festival movement is probably the most potent musical factor in operation today, promoting the greatest advancement in musical intelligence among the largest number of people. The intensive and careful technical and interpretative study imposed on competitors, the opportunity afforded to both competitors and audience to hear different musical ideas of the same composition, the reasoned analyses and adjudications from the platform by fully qualified authorities—all these elements, sustained and fostered by the stimulus and interest of competition, ensure a great contribution to the cultural life of each community so favoured. The competition festival reaches all ages and nationalities, races and religions. It touches the rich and poor, talented and less gifted performers, teachers and audiences. It sets a high standard for all these, and in an age beset with many attacks on aesthetic values, it is inspiring to find so many responding to the challenge.

The festival movement also has brought forth from the genius of British composers, and to a less degree their Canadian counterparts, a wealth of new music which might never have seen the light of day except for the demand thus created. The use of madrigals and the like as test pieces has done much to revive and make familiar to tens of thousands of music-makers the riches of the great Elizabethans, whose works might otherwise have remained in the repertoire of only a few.

One of the most encouraging features at Canadian festivals is the manner in which competitors and audience enter into the true spirit of the festival. Close observers experience many thrills as they sense in the applause of the audience a discriminating response to the performances of competitors, which endorses in advance the subsequent decisions of the adjudicators. The audience has made great progress towards a fuller understanding of the language and meaning of good music. Competitors also seem to realize that their efforts are being taken seriously and intelligently, and that the audience, as well as the adjudicator, is to be trusted.

To those who have been privileged to play a part in shaping the destiny of the Canadian music festival movement and to watch the cumulative effect of this ever widening cultural enrichment, the future holds a prospect of still greater possibilities, though our anticipation is not unmixed with wonder at how much has grown from that tiny seed planted at Sedgewick House by Mary Wakefield.

EDITOR'S NOTE

In addition to competitions at festivals, many others of varying nature take place in Canada. At the Canadian National Exhibition held annually in Toronto extensive competitions in almost all types of music are held; classes for bands arouse exceptional interest. Welsh communities in several centres hold Eisteddfodau on the lines of those in Wales. Important competitions are also heard over the radio—notably the commercially sponsored "Singing Stars of Tomorrow" and "Nos Futures Etoiles"; these have a wide listening audience and have brought to light many of our most talented young singers who might otherwise have won only a local reputation. Their substantial money awards have been most helpful to young singers in facilitating further study. Leading educational institutions offer valuable scholarships, often on a competitive basis. Music Teachers' Associations in various provinces hold competitions for scholarships and prizes from time to time. In Vancouver competitions are held annually for scholarships in music and other arts offered by the MacMillan Fine Arts Clubs. Various competitions have been held in the field of composition for scholarships and prizes (usually of money) donated by institutions, corporations or individuals. Since 1937 the Composers, Authors and Publishers Association of Canada (formerly the Canadian Performing Right Society) has offered a scholarship in composition to be competed for annually. Several winners of past years have come to take an important place among Canadian composers.

POPULAR MUSIC

Leslie Bell

Sing—sing—Music was given,
To brighten the gay, and kindle the loving.

Thomas Moore

The term "popular music" is, to some extent, ambiguous since any music, be it by Bach, Bartok or Berlin, can be popular, depending upon the taste of the individual. This chapter accepts the common definition of the term and concerns itself with the music Canadians dance to, dine to and use as background for their everyday living. The endless "pop" tunes that are born and buried each month play a vital part in Canada's life and, despite their frequent lack of musical worth, offer a valuable index to her habits, customs and ways of thinking.

CANADIAN THINKING

Although Canada has retained some degree of individuality in her choice of popular music, one cannot ignore the influence exerted by other countries such as Great Britain and the United States. In the early years of this century, Canadians were particularly attracted to the songs of the British Isles and to the London music-hall type of entertainment. There is still evidence of this fact in the preferences shown by older Canadians today. In Ontario, for instance, a singer who wishes to appeal to older people must include in his repertoire a liberal number of Scottish and Irish ballads.

The same attitude, however, is not so apparent among Canadians born since 1920. The advent of the modern gramophone and of sound film, radio and television during the last thirty-five years has resulted in this country's being flooded with the popular songs of the United States. By and large, people in Canadian cities, where the bulk of the country's population is concentrated, accept these songs as their own, although with some degree of reservation. Canadians, for instance, are not as immediately attracted by novelty tunes and frivolous lyrics as are Americans and show a greater preference for pleasant melody.

Thus, although the songs appearing on Canada's weekly "Hit Parade" are substantially the same as the hit-tunes of the United States, they are not listed in the same order of popularity. It should be pointed out, too, that because of the relatively small negro population in this country, Canada has never shown quite the same enthusiasm for certain types of jazz as has her neighbour. In such Quebec cities as Montreal, American influence is not as great. The French Canadian combines with his interest in Broadway tunes a natural affection for the latest songs of Paris and for Latin American music.

It is in the rural areas of Canada that one finds a more truly independent national taste. Cowboy songs are extremely popular in the West and, curiously enough, in the Maritimes as well. The Maritimer apparently finds a kinship between his own folk-songs and western music. Singing cowboys are popular in all parts of rural Canada and such men as Wilf Carter, "Hank" Snow and "Lone Pine" enjoy an almost fanatical following. These men compose their own songs at an incredibly prolific rate and find a ready market for them, since Canadians seem to prefer them to the cowboy songs of the United States.

Equally successful are the writers and performers of square dance music. The Alberta Ranch Boys in the West, George Wade's Cornhuskers in Ontario and Don Messer's Islanders in Prince Edward Island have all won great acclaim. Cowboy songs and "old time" music outsell all other types in Canada and constitute important business for publishers and recording companies.

In certain parts of Canada, notably rural Quebec and Newfoundland, original authentic folk-songs are still the popular music of the people, although it must be confessed that these songs are losing ground against the onslaught of American radio. It is interesting, also, to speculate on what changes in Canadian taste may be effected by the large number of continental Europeans who are entering Canada under the present immigration policy.

COMPOSITION AND PROMOTION

Canada cannot boast of a very long list of successful popular song-writers. There have, it is true, been many well-known songs written by men born in Canada. George Johnson's "When You and I were Young, Maggie," Shelton Brooks's "Darktown Strutters' Ball," Geoffrey O'Hara's "K-K-K-Katy" and Gitz Rice's "Dear Old Pal of Mine" are all examples of famous songs composed by Canadians after they became residents of the United States. The newest of such men is Alex Kramer of Montreal who for several years was engaged there in radio work. In 1938 Kramer went to New York where he has become a prominent song composer with a great many successes to his credit.

Three resident Canadians, however, have won international recognition, each with one song. In 1919, the concert pianist, Ernest Seitz, collaborated with the Canadian-born actor Gene Lockhart to write "The World is Waiting for the Sunrise," one of the world's best-known light ballads. In 1939, Ruth Lowe of Toronto became famous for "I'll Never Smile Again" which, for a time, was one of the top favourites in the United States. In 1948 a slightly lesser success was achieved by Elizabeth Clarke, a Vancouver nurse, with "Bluebird on Your Windowsill."

It is only in times of national crisis that the Canadian song-writer appears to come into his own. The early part of World War I is a case in point. National feeling ran high at that time and there was a demand for truly Canadian patriotic songs which the United States, a neutral country until 1917, was unable to supply. Such songs as "We'll Never Let the Old Flag Fall," "Good Luck to the Boys of the Allies" and "When Your Boy Comes Back to You," all written by Canadians, enjoyed great popularity in this country although they were comparatively unknown elsewhere. During World War II a similar enthusiasm resulted in the success of Ernest Dainty's "Carry On."

In Quebec, the French Canadian composer is able to realize a certain success by writing songs for his own people in the Parisian style. Thus R. Beaudry, Leo Le Sieur, Enrique Miro and others are well known locally. Recently the songs of Felix Leclerc of Montreal have achieved public recognition in France.

The small number of great Canadian song successes is not the result of lack of effort. People in the entertainment field, such as this writer, receive as many as a dozen unsolicited manuscripts a week written by amateur Canadian composers who have been dazzled by the success stories of Broadway. Few of these people understand the economic conditions which make Canadian song publication difficult. Today, the success of a popular song is not nearly so dependent upon its musical worth as upon the promotion campaign organized to make it familiar. Such campaigns, however, are expensive and in most cases cost more than the revenue a publisher can hope to win from Canada's small population. Consequently, either the composer or his publisher must seek the help of the American market by selling his song to a New

York house. All the songs listed above were made popular by American promotion.

Most of the promotion carried on by Canadian publishers today is on behalf of American songs for which they hold the Canadian rights. At the same time, many of them have invested money in Canadian compositions in the hope that a growing country will eventually provide a market for its composers. Before the advent of radio, Canadian promotion was carried on by direct contact. Such well-known companies as Gordon V. Thompson employed singers who appeared on theatre stages, at public gatherings or at the Canadian National Exhibition to present new songs. Today, the "song plugger" has been replaced by the radio "disc jockey" who combines broadcasts of popular recordings with informal chatter. Canadian disc jockies command huge audiences and such people as Elwood Glover, Byng Whitteker and Dick MacDougal have become important personalities. Their influence on popular taste is considerable and it is on them that the Canadian song-writer pins his hope.

VOCAL ARTISTS

In the early days of the century, the popular vocalist was generally one who sang, played the piano and entertained in other ways with monologues and impersonations. Older Canadians still remember the names of Jimmie Fax, Will J. White and Jules Brazil. These men did not work in night clubs or on vaudeville circuits but found casual employment at what were known simply as "concerts."

World War I saw the beginning of organized entertainment for troops. Out of this came one of Canada's most famous popular units, an all-male show called "The Dumbells." "The Dumbells" were originally organized by Captain Plunkett to entertain Canadian soldiers in France. Upon their return to Canada in 1919, they toured the country successfully for almost a decade and several singers in the group, notably Al Plunkett, Ross Hamilton and "Red" Newman, enjoyed a national reputation.

Almost all the vocalists mentioned up to this point provided entertainment of the English music-hall type. This tradition was carried on by the well-known singers Al and Bob Harvey until about 1930. When the Harvey brothers left for England, however, the tradition gradually died out. Vocalists now turned to radio and imitated the sophisticated singing styles of New York and Hollywood. Today, the vocal stars of American radio and television all have their counterparts in Canada.

There are so many Canadian singers using the American style that one can only pick names at random. Art Hallman, Norma Locke, Fred Hill and Billy O'Connor are but a few of them. Canada, of course, has always had her reliable army of popular baritones and "Irish" tenors from Frank Oldfield and Harry Binns in the old days to James Shields and George Murray today.

During the last few years, modern popular music has found expression through a new kind of choral singing which involves the use of special arangements, vowel sound effects and so on. This form of choralism has been introduced to Canadian audiences by the Leslie Bell Singers of Toronto and by the Don Wright Chorus of London, Ontario, and has been imitated in various parts of the country sometimes to the dismay of more orthodox-minded choirmasters.

Small vocal units from the barbershop quartet to the swing group have had a great vogue in Canada. The Quatuor Alouette of Montreal and the Four Gentlemen of Toronto are well known across the country. Recently, two swing quartets, the Four Lads and the Crewcuts, both of Toronto, left for the United States where, at the time of writing, they are enjoying a phenomenal popularity.

INSTRUMENTAL ARTISTS

Prior to World War I dance orchestras in Canada were somewhat casually organized and music for dancing was supplied by well-known musicians (generally pianists) who contracted whatever players were needed for any individual occasion. Fred Fralick and Charles Bodley were two of the first to undertake this kind of work. Later on such men as Charlie Musgrave and Stanley St. John followed suit.

A variety of circumstances combined to bring about the establishment of permanent dance orchestras. During World War I, dancing became a national craze and the dance orchestra took on a new importance. In his Toronto theatre orchestras, Jack Arthur, an influential and versatile producer, introduced the idea of special instrumental arrangements to be identified with the particular group for which they were written. The use of special arrangements spread to the dance orchestras and as a result, the need arose for regular rehearsals by permanent ensembles.

An impetus to arranging was given by the advent of the radio orchestra. The first important Canadian arranger was Percy Faith (now living in the United States) who introduced many new, clever effects into his orchestral scoring. Equally brilliant was the work of Robert

Farnon who, since the last war, has become an important musical figure in England. By the time these men had left Canada, a whole school of Canadian popular arrangers had grown up. Today this school includes such men as Giuseppe and Lucio Agostini (father and son), Neil Chotem, Howard Cable and Morris Surdin, all of whom are kept extremely busy.

By the third decade of the century, the permanent dance orchestra had become a fixture in major Canadian hotels from coast to coast. Luigi Romanelli's group in Toronto and the orchestras of Jack Denny and Charles Dornberger in Montreal supplied "comfortable" dance music for Canada's well-to-do classes. Such orchestras were essentially commercial organizations. In contrast to them, Canada has her more serious-minded jazz groups who look upon their work as a form of art. Among the rather small number of jazz performers in this country are some exceptional musicians. Oscar Peterson of Montreal is considered by many to be the world's greatest living jazz pianist and such men as Bert Niosi, Bob Gimby and Calvin Jackson have important reputations.

Perhaps the most popular large dance orchestra in Canada is that of Mart Kenney from Vancouver. Through his recordings and tours, Kenney has made his Western Gentlemen popular from coast to coast. He now controls a large number of dance bands.

ECONOMIC FACTORS

The economic status of the Canadian musician working in the popular field has been affected chiefly by the growth of mechanical reproduction of music and by the proximity of this country to the United States. When talking motion pictures were introduced in the late twenties, hundreds of Canadian musicians were put out of work. Many of them found employment in radio stations but today their general complaint is that recorded programmes are taking this work away from them. This is true to some extent, although the situation is not as bad here as it is in the United States, since the Canadian Broadcasting Corporation has made a point of employing a certain number of musicians for "live" programmes.

Salaries and working conditions have been greatly improved by instrumental and vocal unions. The pitiful wages paid dance musicians forty years ago are no longer in evidence. At the same time, the unions admit that they have fallen far short of their goal of employment for all. The theatre organist is now practically a thing of the past; the café orchestra has given way to music on wire and the large dance band is all too often replaced by the cocktail trio or even by the juke box. This situation, of course, is not peculiar to Canada as the rest of the world knows.

Much has been written about the exodus of Canadian artists to the United States. It is true that musicians in the popular field are, by the very nature of their work, more commercially minded than others and more inclined to follow where fortune beckons. Thus Canada has given the United States Guy Lombardo, Deanna Durbin, Percy Faith and many others including the new television star Giselle Mac-Kenzie. To England she has lost Robert Farnon and the successful vocalists Edmund Hockridge and Russel Titus.

For a while this emigration gave rise to the assumption that Canada neither appreciated her native talent nor cared to support it. Fortunately this prejudiced thinking is now disappearing as Canadian musicians realize that there are growing opportunities for them at home, particularly in the larger centres from which radio and television programmes emanate. It is significant that during the last few years many artists (for example, Denny Vaughan, Morris Surdin and the late Jack Allison) have been attracted back to Canada from the United States and have found immediate employment here. It is also gratifying to note that some performers are winning recognition south of the border without the need of abandoning their homeland. Canada's beloved vocal and instrumental group, The Happy Gang, is frequently broadcast over American networks and the Leslie Bell Singers make regular scheduled tours to the United States every year.

THE POPULARIZING OF SERIOUS MUSIC

One of the healthiest musical developments in Canada during recent years has been the growing interest in serious music on the part of the general public. The former barriers between the so-called "highbrow" and "lowbrow" are vanishing, and judging from the reports of gramophone record salesmen, the modern Canadian citizen listens to Ellington and Mozart with equal relish.

There are several reasons for this increasing tolerance. The elaborate treatment of popular songs by modern arrangers has given these tunes a symphonic flavour and helped to prepare the layman for the sound of the legitimate symphony orchestra. Radio, of course, has played a great part in making good music available and familiar. Then, too, there have been the organized attempts of symphony orchestras to win the public by offering it programmes of more immediately attractive serious music. This approach, known as the "Pop" movement, probably traces its origin to the days when Jack Arthur at Toronto's Regent Theatre began introducing symphonic music during the intermissions between film showings. In the twenties, the Toronto Symphony Orchestra under Luigi von Kunits established the "five o'clock concerts" giving programmes of standard orchestral music but of only one hour's length; these became very popular with the public. They were later followed by summer symphony programmes under Reginald Stewart. Today, Toronto has two "Pop" series: the summer concerts of the Toronto Philharmonic Orchestra and the winter concerts on Friday evenings of the Toronto Symphony Orchestra.

Almost every Canadian orchestra includes a regular "Pop" series in its activities: the Montreal Chalet concerts are given amidst delightful surroundings; in Vancouver, the B.C. Electric Company offers symphony programmes in Stanley Park, and so on. Indeed, Canadian artists of all types seek to win the general public by meeting it halfway. An interesting example is the Solway String Quartet (see also the chapter on chamber music) which offers programmes combining legitimate chamber music with special arrangements of familiar tunes.

Certain kinds of popular music have had to be omitted from this discussion. Some, for example folk-music, have been dealt with elsewhere in this book. Under the present chapter heading might conceivably have been included Canada's national and patriotic songs as well as the great number of choral works written for school and amateur glee clubs. The degree to which such music can be labelled popular or serious, however, is a matter of opinion.

If the writer of this chapter has placed considerable emphasis upon the role of the United States in the story of Canadian popular music, it is not because of any lack of faith in Canada's talent or in Canada's potential for the future. One can only tell the truth. The truth is that in the past Canada has been greatly dependent upon the United States, but in the future the situation will certainly be different. Each day brings more evidence that the change is on its way.

MUSICAL ORGANIZATIONS

(This list, though far from complete, may be helpful to those seeking further information on various aspects of music in Canada.)

Acadia University, Wolfville, N.S.
Edwin A. Collins, Mus.B.(Cantab), F.R.C.O.,
Dean, School of Music

Maritime Conservatory of Music
301 Spring Garden Road, Halifax, N.S.
Ifan Williams, F.R.A.M., Director

University of King's College, Halifax, N.S.
Maitland Farmer, Mus.Bac., F.R.C.O.,
Professor of Music

Mount Allison University, Sackville, N.B.
Conservatory of Music
Howard Brown, B.A., Mus.B., Director

Université d'Ottawa
Rev. Jules Martel, O.M.I.,
Director, School of Music

Université Laval, Québec, P.Q.
Abbé Onésime Pouliot, B.A.,
Director, School of Music

Université de Montréal
Jean Papineau-Couture,
Secretary, Faculty of Music

McGill University and
McGill Conservatorium of Music, Montreal, P.Q.
Douglas Clarke, M.A., Mus.Bac.,
Dean and Director, Faculty of Music

Conservatoire de Musique et d'Art Dramatique
1700 rue St. Dénis, Montréal, P.Q.
Wilfrid Pelletier, C.M.G., Mus.Doc.,
Directeur

Queen's University, Kingston, Ont.
Graham George, Mus. Doc.,
Associate Professor of Music

University of Toronto
Royal Conservatory of Music of Toronto
135 College Street, Toronto 5, Ont.
Boyd Neel, Dean

Hamilton Conservatory of Music
James Street South, Hamilton, Ont.
Lorne Betts, Principal

University of Western Ontario, London, Ont.
Western Ontario Conservatory of Music
Harvey Robb, Principal

Brandon College, Brandon, Man.
Lorne Watson, B.A., L.T.C.M.,
Director of Music

University of Manitoba, Winnipeg, Man.
Ronald W. Gibson, Mus.B.,
Director of Music

University of Saskatchewan, Saskatoon, Sask.
Murray Adaskin, Professor of Music

University of Alberta, Edmonton, Alta.
Richard Stephen Eaton, Mus.B.,
Assoc. Professor of Music
also Banff School of Fine Arts
Donald Cameron, M.Sc., Director

Mount Royal College, Calgary, Alta.
Conservatory of Music
Harold Ramsay, L.Mus., Director

University of British Columbia, Vancouver, B.C.
Harry Adaskin, Professor
Department of Music

217

FEDERAL GOVERNMENT ORGANIZATIONS

Canadian Broadcasting Corporation
Director of Music, Geoffrey Waddington,
354 Jarvis Street, Toronto, Ont.

National Film Board
Commissioner, Dr. A. W. Trueman,
Sussex Street, Ottawa, Ont.

ASSOCIATIONS, FEDERATIONS, ETC.

American Federation of Musicians of
U.S.A. and Canada
Executive Officer for Canada,
Walter M. Murdoch,
279 Yonge Street, Toronto 1, Ont.
(Instrumentalists from abroad who wish
to settle in Canada are strongly
advised to secure information regarding the rules of the Federation.)

B M I (Canada) Limited
Assistant General Manager, W. H. Moon
229 Yonge Street, Toronto, Ont.

Canada Foundation
Director, Walter Herbert
56 Sparks Street, Ottawa 4, Ont.

Canadian Arts Council
Secretary, Louise Barette
3936 Parc Lafontaine, Montreal, P.Q.

Canadian Bandmasters Association
Secretary, A. L. Robertson
R.R. 2, Kilworthy, Ont.

Canadian Bureau for the Advancement
of Music
c/o Canadian National Exhibition, Toronto, Ont.
Director, Richard Edmunds

Canadian College of Organists
135 College Street, Toronto, Ont.

Canadian Federation of Music Teachers
President, Dan A. Cameron,
Regina Conservatory, Regina, Sask.;

Secretary-Treasurer, Yolande Hodges,
2064 Rae St., Regina, Sask.;
Editor, CFMTA Bulletin, Russell E.
Standing,
593 Spruce St., Winnipeg 10, Man.;
Also affiliated provincial federations in:
British Columbia, Alberta, Saskatchewan, Manitoba, Ontario, Quebec, and Nova Scotia.

Canadian League of Composers
President, John Weinzweig, M.M.,
135 College St., Toronto, Ont.

Canadian Music Council (affiliated with
Canadian Arts Council)
Secretary, John Cozens,
183 Avondale Avenue, Willowdale, Ont.

Canadian Music Publishers Association
Secretary, G. H. Stanford,
c/o Board of Trade, King Edward
Hotel, Toronto, Ont.

Composers, Authors and Publishers Association of Canada (CAPAC)
General Manager, W. S. Low,
182 St. George Street, Toronto, Ont.

Federation of Canadian Music Festivals
6 Old Law Courts Building, Winnipeg,
Man.
Secretary, R. W. Cooke

Les Jeunesses Musicales du Canada
Gilles Lefebvre, President,
1200 Bleury Street, Montreal, P.Q.

Otter Lake Music Centre and Festivals
Box 195, Outremont, Montreal 18, P.Q.

CONCERT AGENTS

Celebrity Concerts (Canada) Limited
270 Edmonton St., Winnipeg, Man.
President and Managing Director, A. G.
  Gee

Concert and Placement Bureau
Royal Conservatory of Music of Toronto
135 College Street, Toronto 5, Ont.

Concert Associations of Canada
4 Lonsdale Road, Toronto 7, Ont.
(Formed in 1951 for the purpose of
  providing engagements for Canadian artists.)

International Artists
Walter Homburger,
73 Adelaide St. W., Toronto, Ont.

Nicolas Koudriavtzeff
711 Castle Building, Montreal, P.Q.

Orfeo Agency for Fine Artists
1231 St. Catherine St. W., Montreal,
  P.Q.
Monni Adams, Representative

Overture Concerts
Artists and Concert Management
878 Hornby Street, Vancouver 1, B.C.

Harry Warlow
29 Colborne St., Toronto, Ont.

MUSIC CLUBS

These are too numerous to list in full
  and in many cases holders of office
  change frequently. Among the
  most representative are:

Community Arts Council of Vancouver
Secretary, Mrs. B. Howard,
581 Granville St., Vancouver, B.C.

The Duet Club (Hamilton, Ont.)
Mrs. Harold Beddoe,
35 Montgomery Drive, Ancaster, Ont.

Ladies Morning Musical Club of Montreal
1445 Crescent Street, Montreal

Men's Musical Club of Winnipeg
Secretary, R. W. Cooke,
6 Old Law Courts Building, Winnipeg,
  Man.

Ottawa Women's Musical Club
Mrs. H. O. McCurry,
66 Robert Street, Ottawa, Ont.

Sir Ernest MacMillan Fine Arts Clubs
Secretary, Kay Rollinson,
980 Denman St., Vancouver, B.C.;
Co-ordinator, Marjorie Agnew,
1306 Bidwell St., Vancouver, B.C.

Women's Musical Club of Toronto
Secretary-Treasurer, Mrs. Watson Lang-
  lands,
210 Bayview Avenue, Toronto, Ont.

Women's Musical Club of Vancouver
Secretary, Mrs. Martin Brown,
2942 West 28th Avenue, Vancouver,
  B.C.

Women's Musical Club of Winipeg
Mrs. Lyman van Gliet,
57 Edmonton Street, Winnipeg, Man.

INDEX

on l.
grante.
No. an

Transa